Ba

Mary Whitehouse and t

Ben Thompson is one of Britain's most respected cultural critics. He currently contributes to the *FT*, *Mojo* and the *Sunday Telegraph*. As well as two critically acclaimed collections of rock journalism (*Seven Years of Plenty* and *Ways of Hearing*) and a landmark history of modern British comedy (*Sunshine on Putty*), he has also co-written memoirs with Vic Reeves (*Me Moir*), Phil Daniels (*Class Actor*), Mike Skinner (*The Story of the Streets*), Dizzee Rascal (as yet untitled), and others who prefer the collaborative nature of their bestselling autobiographical endeavours to remain a private matter.

Further praise for *Ban This Filth!*:

'[A] splendidly entertaining book . . . finds the morality campaigner comically wrong on many matters but impressively prescient about pornography and paedophile TV personalities.' Mark Lawson, *Guardian*

'Subversive . . . committed . . . Thompson's true achievement is that one doesn't close the book feeling Whitehouse is a crank to be banished from the past, but instead wondering why no one so high profile has appeared in her place.' Matt Thorne, *Catholic Herald*

'We think we know the story of her life . . . Ben Thompson now supplies the historical meat on the biographical skeleton.' Christopher Howse, *Daily Telegraph*

'The temptation to play Whitehouse's letters entirely for laughs must have been immense . . . Intelligently, however, Thompson realises   re . . . He rations – heroically, in the circumstances – both the lofty har-rumphing and childish sniggering, just occasionally flexing spec-ulation calculated to disturb Whitehouse's eternal rest.' Andrew Mueller, *New Humanist*

'A fascinating time capsule from an age gone by.' Craig Brown, *Mail on Sunday* Book of the Week

'Ben Thompson's witty and engaging commentary is admirably even-handed.' *Independent*

Ban This Filth!

Mary Whitehouse and the Battle to Keep Britain Innocent

edited by Ben Thompson

based on an idea by Jonny Trunk
   and Jo Wheeler

faber and faber

First published in 2012
by Faber and Faber Ltd
Bloomsbury House
74–77 Great Russell Street
London WC1B 3DA
This paperback edition first published in 2013

Typeset by Faber and Faber Ltd
Printed in England by CPI Group (UK) Ltd, Croydon, CR0 4YY

A CIP record for this book
is available from the British Library

ISBN 978–0–571–28151–0

FSC
www.fsc.org
MIX
Paper from
responsible sources
FSC® C101712

10 9 8 7 6 5 4 3 2 1

Contents

Foreword

Come with me to the University of Essex; round the endless ring road encircling Colchester ('Britain's oldest town'). Turn a sharp right along the lane into the green fields of the campus, past the sign that says 'access only beyond this point', and into the kind of underground parking area that seems specifically designed to host a dourly climactic shoot-out in *The Sweeney* – although the speed bumps are set just too high for a Ford Granada to get over in safety.

The university building is celebrated for being made from six different kinds of concrete, each of which seems to be engaged in a race to prove it can decay the fastest. Slowly keep on going up the gentle incline into the very furthest reaches of this unabashedly municipal space, and park in the final loading bay on the left. Here the obliging caretaker will kindly let you into the crisply temperature-controlled environment of the Albert Sloman Library Special Collections rooms.

As you turn the lights on and walk through the closely packed book-stacks full of unread volumes of German sociology and back copies of the *West Mercia Gazette*, the atmosphere is three parts Wernham Hogg (*The Office*'s fictional antiseptic workspace) to two parts Borgesian labyrinth. When you reach the final compartment at the far end, known as 'The Cage', there's an incongruous heavy-duty metal door to be opened. Beyond its thick steel grille lies the collection of three hundred large box files which constitute the Mary Whitehouse archive.

Preserved in this sarcophagus of respectable fears are nearly all of the thousands of letters this redoubtable campaigner sent, and most of the many thousands more she subsequently received (some of impassioned support, but others of vehement

opposition). The records of Whitehouse's National Viewers'
and Listeners' Association include endless newspaper clippings,
handbills, mail-outs, legal documents, monitoring forms, draft
speeches and completed book manuscripts, all tied up in carefully knotted pink ribbons.

Every now and then, as you open up these Pandora's box
files, an artefact of a rather less respectable nature will fall out;
perhaps a set of saucy miniature playing cards, or a seven-inch
vinyl copy of Alice Cooper's 'School's Out'. There are also an
inexplicably large number of photostatted printouts of the lyrics to the Anti-Nowhere League's 'So What', and a hardcore
porn handbill that was once posted through the letter box of an
eighty-six-year-old woman.

Bridging the gap between these two warring sides – filth and
anti-filth – are the poignant physical traces of the domestic
environment Mary's letters were written in. One half-finished
missive is scrawled on the back of a receipt for the anti-anxiety
medication Declinax, another decorates an oatmeal pancake
recipe from a fellow churchgoer who had recently recov-
ered from cancer. Then there's the yellowing invitation – long
ago pressed into service in defence of the nation's morals – to a
'Barbecue Cheese and Wine Party': 'Swimming, dancing, side-
shows . . . bar licence applied for, proceeds to Claverly Village
Hall rebuilding fund'.

Did they barbecue the cheese *and* the wine, I wonder? There's
no way of knowing, but hopefully this book will be the next-
best thing to actually going to that party. And whether the Britain that swims into bleary focus through the Mary Whitehouse
archive's evangelical Hipstamatic App looks more or less appealing than the one we currently inhabit will be very much in the
eye of the beholder.

Ben Thompson, September 2012

Women of Britain

CLEAN UP
TV
CAMPAIGN

1964

"CLEAN-UP TELEVISION CAMPAIGN"

This campaign was launched on January 27th, 1964, by Mrs. Norah Buckland, the wife of the Rector of Longton, Staffs., who is the Stoke representative on the Watch and Social Problems Committee and mother of three children, and by Mrs. Mary Whitehouse, whose husband, Mr. E. R. Whitehouse, is a company director. She also has three children and is a Senior Mistress in a large secondary modern school.

MRS. B. BUCKLAND, The Rectory, Longton, Staffs.

MRS. E. R. WHITEHOUSE, "Postman's Piece", The Wold, Claverley, Wolverhampton.

'Women of Britain' manifesto frontispiece

Introduction:
The Only Way Is Whitehouse

Anyone who grew up in the UK in the 1960s, 70s or 80s will have clear childhood memories of Mary Whitehouse. At once reassuring and slightly scary, she was both the butt of endless jokes and someone adults had good cause to take seriously: a stringent moralising voice in an age when those whose traditional function had been to deliver such improving messages – from politicians to churchmen – seemed reluctant to take on that role.

The launch of the Clean Up TV Campaign which she co-founded in early 1964 made this devoutly Christian Shropshire schoolteacher a media star overnight. Over the next three and a half decades, her name became a byword for affronted decency. A one-woman anti-permissiveness SWAT team, she was lampooned by comedians and rock stars, yet feared by liberal churchmen, playwrights, politicians and TV programme-makers alike.

The following crisp early-seventies exchange perfectly encapsulates one aspect of Mary Whitehouse's reputation.

Letter to Lord Hill of Luton, then chairman of the BBC

16 June, 1972

Dear Lord Hill,

I understand that the new Rolling Stone's record, 'Exile on Main Street' is being played on Radio 1.

This record uses four-letter words. Although they are somewhat blurred, there is no question about what they are meant to be.

I feel sure you will understand the concern felt about
this matter, for it is surely no function of the BBC
to transmit language which, as shown in a recent court
case, is still classed as obscene. The very fact that
this programme is transmitted primarily for young people
would, one would have thought, have demanded more, not
less, care about what is transmitted.

We would be grateful if you would look into this
matter.

Yours sincerely,

(Mrs) Mary Whitehouse

Reply from Lord Hill

20th June, 1972

Dear Mrs. Whitehouse,

Thank you for your letter of June 16th in which you
state that the tracks from the Rolling Stones record
'Exile on Main Street', played on Radio I use four-
letter words.

I have this morning listened with great care to the
tracks we have played on Radio I. I have listened to
them at a fast rate, at a medium rate, at a slow rate.
Though my hearing is excellent, I did not hear any
offending four-letter words whatever.

Could it be that, believing offending words to be
there and zealous to discover them, you imagined that
you heard what you did not hear?

Yours sincerely

Ally Luton

Mary Whitehouse's most readily mockable incarnation was
as an indefatigable seeker after offence where none need have
been taken – a tendency with which this valiant attempt to discern non-existent four-letter outrages would seem to fall neatly
into line (excepting the diplomatic veil Lord Hill draws over the

song title 'Turd on the Run'). And yet – as anyone who has read any of the various forensic retrospective accounts of the abyss of drug-fuelled degradation from which the album in question is now known to have crawled will be obliged to admit – in this case the superficial absurdity of the critique did not preclude the possibility that her hypersensitive moral smoke alarm had detected a real fire.

Nor does the *Exile on Main St.* episode turn out to be an isolated incidence of Mary Whitehouse missing the trees but seeing the wood. Sifting through the vast compendium of outrage that is her correspondence – from her exquisitely testy entanglements with successive generations of BBC top brass, to the often less eloquent but sometimes even more heartfelt expressions of shock and horror penned by her sofa-bound army of TV and radio vigilantes – a startling new perspective on Whitehouse's public life soon begins to reveal itself.

As divisive a figure as Mary Whitehouse undoubtedly was, in one respect the campaigning career of this famously prim and proper polemical powerhouse has been the subject of a rare degree of consensus. Friend and foe alike have generally agreed that her ultimate objective was to shore up the belief systems of the past in the face of a threatening and uncertain future.

Whitehouse herself had no patience with such backward-looking interpretations of her work. She always claimed that tomorrow belonged to her, and in the years since her death in 2001, this seemingly improbable contention has begun to appear increasingly well founded. Looked at from a twenty-first-century perspective, the amazing thing about Mary Whitehouse's instinctive reactionary postures is how many of them have now acquired a prophetic resonance.

Mary Whitehouse's certainty that blasphemy was an idea whose time was not yet up has certainly proved more well founded than the conviction of such urbane legal adversaries as Sir John Mortimer and Geoffrey Robertson that religious censorship was a doomed anachronism. From the skilfully orchestrated *Daily Mail* brouhaha over the Ross/Brand 'Sachsgate' affair, to the 'top-down' naming-and-shaming strategies latterly adopted by anti-tax-avoidance campaigners, the lessons of her formidably strategic campaigning skills have been absorbed – often unconsciously – on all sides of the political spectrum.

One contemporary observer called Mary Whitehouse 'The Little Canute exhorting the waves of moral turpitude to retreat', but could she also have been the harbinger – if not quite the agent – of a change in the tide of history? One thing's for certain: she was not the last of a dying breed. From feminist anti-porn campaigns to UK Uncut, and the Taliban to Mumsnet, Mary Whitehouse's monuments are all around us.

The origins of the Whitehouse campaigning odyssey are very much in the public domain – not least via the adroit myth-making of her sequence of meticulously updated autobiographies. Born in the West Midlands in 1910, she qualified as an art teacher and went on to become senior mistress at a Shropshire secondary school.

It was here, in the early 1960s, that she found herself called upon to teach sex education. On discovering just how far the expectations of a rapidly modernising British establishment had already diverged from her evangelical Christian prescription of 'chastity before marriage and fidelity within it', she began to formulate the stance of perpetual moral outrage that would sustain her through almost four decades as a major public figure.

The avowedly domestic nature of her initial concerns should not now be allowed – as Mary Whitehouse cleverly encouraged it to at the time – to distract from the fundamentally political nature of her campaigning. On a range of issues from the Black Panthers (whom she did not much like the look of) to water fluoridation (again, not in favour), and state provision of birth control (*Kondome, nein danke*) to torture in South Vietnam or South Africa (which she felt got far more attention than it should do given that these countries were our allies in the fight against Communism), she somehow managed to adopt a pretty much unbroken sequence of classically right-wing positions without ever being entirely pigeonholed as a party political animal.

Yet for all her innate conservatism (with both a small and a big C), Mary Whitehouse was fundamentally an anti-estab lishment figure. At the heart of her Joan of Arc-style mission was her determination to stop what she regarded as nothing less than a conspiracy on the part of a secular left-wing Oxbridge elite to remake Britain in its own godless image.

The more contemptuously Britain's cultural gatekeepers shrugged her off, the more determinedly she came back at them. As these two tetchy responses from (then BBC director of pro- grammes – his later days as Darwinist poster-boy and nature's TV emissary still some way off) David Attenborough and then Postmaster General Anthony Wedgwood Benn clearly indicate, Mary Whitehouse didn't just write to them, she got on their last nerve.

Reply from David Attenborough

6th December, 1971

Dear Mrs. Whitehouse,

Thank you for your letter.

I suspect that there is little profit to be gained in setting down in a letter arguments justifying a particular sequence in a play. You have made your own view clear on this particular example and I do not believe that anything I may say would change it.

May I thank you, nonetheless, for having put down your
points so clearly. You may be sure that they will be
taken seriously.
  Yours sincerely,
  David Attenborough

Reply from private secretary to the Postmaster General

6th May, 1965

Dear Mrs. Whitehouse,
  The Postmaster General has asked me to thank you
for your telegram in which you told him about the
constitution of the Viewers' and Listeners' Association,
and asked him to meet the committee to discuss the aims
and purposes of the Association.
  Mr. Benn has asked me to say that, as I am sure you
would expect, he is already well aware of the views you
have publicly expressed in connection with the 'Clean up
television campaign'. But if the aims and objects of your
new Association are materially different from those of
the campaign, he would of course be interested to know in
what way. Perhaps however the best course then would be
for you to let him have the information in writing.
  Yours sincerely,
  Private Secretary

  For the new liberal establishment whose assumptions she
questioned with unflinching certainty, Mary Whitehouse was a
folk-devil every bit as alarming as the 'subversives' and 'perverts' her followers imagined were now running the nation's
major institutions. Partly as a result of his wartime experiences
(he was present at the liberation of Auschwitz), BBC director
general Sir Hugh Greene – her first, and in some ways most
formidable adversary – thought her activities 'dangerous to the
whole quality of life in this country' and effectively banned her
from the network.

The clear contradiction between the professed goals and the actual methods of those who sought to silence Mary Whitehouse in the name of free speech – Johnny Speight was not just 'having a laugh' when he scripted the episode of *Till Death Us Do Part* in which Alf Garnett's son-in-law Mike burned one of her books to cries of 'Unclean, unclean' – is just the first of a series of fascinating paradoxes that her correspondence illuminates. The personal struggles – family health traumas, emotional frailties and ideological contradictions – which lay behind Mary Whitehouse's artfully constructed aura of unshakeable conviction are another intriguing line of enquiry.

Perhaps the biggest mystery that this book will attempt to clear up is the following one. How did someone with very little campaigning experience – who fully entered public life at the relatively advanced age of fifty-three, as just one of a number of concerned citizens pledged to 'Clean Up TV' – end up moulding a mass movement in her own image with a ferocious energy and ruthlessness reminiscent of that which (although it would be fair to assume that this is not a comparison Mary herself would have enjoyed) Lenin brought to Bolshevism?

Mary Whitehouse's organisational odyssey fell into three distinct phases. The first was the start of the Clean Up TV Campaign, and the subsequent formation of the National Viewers' and Listeners' Association (NVALA, pronounced 'National Vala', in the manner of a slightly dubious assemblage of Scandinavian patriots, rather than 'Nvala', like a fictional African chief). The central theme here was her epic battle of wills with Sir Hugh Greene – who would actually congratulate programme-makers for eliciting 'another letter from Mary Whitehouse' in the face of vehement protests against such landmark broadcasts as *Till Death Us Do Part*, *That Was The Week That Was* and *The Wednesday Play*.

Buoyed by the partial success of Greene's resignation in 1968 (in which she would subsequently be revealed to have had, if not a hand, at the very least a fingertip), but frustrated by her inability to impose her will on Harold Wilson's Labour government, Mary Whitehouse began to define a new role for herself as (in the phrase of regular courtroom sparring partner Geoffrey Robertson) 'Director of Private Prosecutions'. The *Gay News* blasphemy trial of 1977 and the *Romans in Britain* obscenity case of three years later were only the best-known of numerous legal landmarks left behind by NVALA's move into the courts.

The third and final stage of Mary Whitehouse's campaigning career saw her moving closer than ever before to actual political power – exercising real influence on a series of different pieces of government and private members' legislation during the Thatcher era – but at the same time going back almost to square one. The vindication embodied in the setting up of her long-sought-after Broadcasting Standards Commission (later incorporated into Ofcom) was small compensation for the advent of Channel 4 (a new, partly public-funded national TV station, even more hell-bent on corrupting the nation's morals than the BBC of Sir Hugh Greene had been), never mind the imminent moral apocalypse of satellite TV and the internet.

Rather than be bound by this rigid chronological structure, the chapters to come will trail the tireless tip-tap of Mary Whitehouse's typewriter through a sequence of evolving relationships with Britain's key cultural and political institutions. Few if any positions of authority in domestic public life escaped the reach of her epistolary interventions. From the press to the BBC, through the Houses of Parliament, the courts and the Church, via the music, film and publishing industries, she left her mark on everyone, from porn barons to the Archbishop of Canterbury.

To say that posterity has not upheld all of her forty years' worth of complaints would be putting it mildly. Sometimes – often, even – Mary Whitehouse's objections to TV comedy shows, news broadcasts and pop lyrics can now (as they often did at the time) seem ludicrously po-faced. But in endeavouring to establish the true nature of her legacy, it is important to focus on the things that Mary Whitehouse got wrong as much as the things she got right, and not just because – as in the following cosmic overreaction to an innocent hand gesture made by a regional TV news icon (whose name she misspells), and his sweetly regretful response – some of these misjudgements are very entertaining in themselves.

Letter to BBC Nationwide *presenter Michael Barratt*

1st October, 1971

Dear Mr. Barrett,
  Because of the excellence of many of your programmes I am sorry that you saw fit to give the 'V' sign following your interview with Mr. Harvey Smith. It gave great offence.
  You will perhaps have noticed that within the last week a man has been found guilty of using obscene gestures of precisely this kind. For you to make such a gesture at any time would have been offensive to the great majority of your viewers. For you to do it during 'family viewing time' is surely to go against even the most basic of the BBC's obligations to the public.
  On the other hand, I would like to thank you, most sincerely, for the excellent coverage last night of the 'Jesus People'. It was most moving, and one was particularly grateful that the item was allowed to stand on its own without comment of any kind.
  Yours sincerely,
  (Mrs) Mary Whitehouse
  Copy to Lord Hill

Michael Barratt's reply

5th October, 1971

Dear Mrs. Whitehouse,

  Thank you for your letter. I am most concerned that you
should consider my 'V' Sign on 'Nationwide' the other
night offensive. That's the last thing it was meant to be.
  My intention, as a mildly amusing way of saying
'Goodnight' was to give the Churchillian Victory Sign.
There was some discussion among my colleagues afterwards
about whether I'd 'got it right', or whether the palm
of my hand was facing in the wrong direction. But I
certainly did not raise my fingers in the manner that has
come to be regarded as obscene. Nevertheless, of course,
if I gave offence, however unwittingly, I am sorry.
  I note, by the way, that you write of my 'interview
with Mr. Harvey Smith'. I did not interview Mr. Smith
and this makes me wonder whether you personally did
not see the programme and are passing on a member's
complaint. I like to think that if you had been
watching, you might not have been offended and I might
have retained your kindly regard!
  Yours sincerely,
  Michael Barratt
  c.c. Lord Hill

In seeking to get her message across to a nation that prides
itself on its sense of humour to an almost self-destructive extent,
Mary Whitehouse's inability to get the joke was both her Achil-
les heel and her secret weapon. Perhaps Britain's determination
to see the funny side sometimes blinded it to the possibility that
some of the dangers she strove so hard to protect us from were
more real than we liked to imagine.

That possibility is underlined by the way in which some complaints which might have seemed ludicrously old-fashioned
twenty years ago have now taken on a macabre new relevance.

Consider, for instance, this letter from a disgruntled *Crackerjack* viewer.

Letter to Michael Aspel from a concerned viewer

18th February, 1973

Dear Michael Aspel,
  On Friday 16th February, I happened to be at home,
when my children aged 11 and 9 years asked if they could
watch 'Crackerjack'. Having regarded this as a decent
programme I readily consented. I was disappointed at the
rather untalented group who appeared but took little
notice as I was reading, until my wife asked if I was
listening to the words, whereupon I was horrified. As far
as I can remember they were singing:-

  Do you want to touch?
  Do you want to touch me there?
  Where?
  There?
  Do you wan to run your fingers through my hair
  Every little boy
  Needs a little joy
  Do you want to touch me there?

If the words are not suggestive, perhaps you could
explain them to me. I do not think it a figment of the
imagination either that innuendoes were contained in the
actions also.
  As both a father and a Probation Officer I am becoming
increasingly concerned that a good deal of pop music
is used to subtly communicate sex and drugs to young
people. I certainly believe that an excellent programme
like 'Crackerjack' should never be guilty of committing
this kind of error.

As the US TV producers who decided to feature the song in a
2011 episode of *Glee* found to their considerable chagrin, Gary

Glitter's 'Do You Wanna Touch Me?' now carries the kind of baggage no one wants left on their doorstep. But just as some of NVALA's most seemingly innocuous bugbears ultimately turned out to have a twist in the tail, it's equally true that much of what Mary and her followers saw as 'the propaganda of disbelief, doubt and dirt' ended up as the mulch from which the most treasured musical and televisual memories of later generations were to grow.

From *Doctor Who* ('Teatime brutality for tots') to Dennis Potter – whose mother sued Whitehouse and the BBC for libel and won (it's a long story and it's all in chapter 7) – and the Beatles – whose *Magical Mystery Tour* escaped her bowdlerising intervention by the skin of its psychedelic teeth – to the Rolling Stones, the list of Mary Whitehouse's targets will look to many nostalgic readers like a roll of honour. If she had got her way, our artistic heritage would have been immeasurably impoverished, yet isn't it worth considering how much less fun the second half of the twentieth century would have been without her?

Clean T.V. Campaign

A MEETING

will be held in

St. John's Church Hall

BAKER STREET, POTTERS BAR

on

FRIDAY, APRIL 17th

at 8 p.m.

for the purpose of hearing

MRS. E. R. WHITEHOUSE

who is a joint organiser of this nation-wide movement

**Further details from Mrs. K. Andrews,
30 Borough Way, Potters Bar**

Ted Ditchburn Ltd., 7 Southgate Road, Potters Bar

Poster for early Clean Up TV Campaign meeting, with Mary still identified by her husband's initials

1. Becoming Mary

When Philip Larkin drily imagined sexual intercourse beginning in 1963 – 'Between the end of the *Chatterley* ban / And the
Beatles' first LP' – he made no mention of the possibility that this
process of erotic awakening might be reversible. But the 'Annus
Mirabilis' commemorated in Larkin's famous poem also saw the
emergence of a figure who would do everything in her considerable power to restore Britain's rapidly crumbling inhibitions.

The first public political controversy in which Mary Whitehouse became involved followed a speech by the Education
Ministry's chief medical officer Dr Peter Henderson in which
he had seemed to condone pre-marital sex. At a Westminster
conference of Moral Re-Armament – the evangelical Christian
movement of which she had long been a member – she spoke
out in condemnation not only of Henderson but also his boss,
the education minister Sir Edward Boyle, who when bearded in
his Whitehall den by a two-person deputation of Mary and her
husband Ernest had expressed unease about possible reactions
from the teaching profession were he to start laying down the
law in matters of morality.

The *Daily Express* of 5 December 1963 reported her comments anonymously – as those of 'a woman teacher' – and gave
Sir Edward the opportunity to query her account of this meeting. 'It is difficult to remember the exact words one uses on
these occasions,' he dissembled grandly, 'but I do not recollect
saying to her that I could not speak on Christian standards
and that if I did I would offend the majority of teachers in
this country. What I did tell her was what I said in the House

of Commons – that I was against imposing conformity where there were genuine differences of view.'

To the casual reader of half a century later, this early piece of national newspaper exposure for Mary Whitehouse's campaigning activities does not have the look of an unalloyed triumph. Nonetheless, in an early instance of the 'carrot and stick' strategy which she would adopt so successfully in dealing with the media over the decades to come, she still wrote to the editor of the *Daily Express* to thank his newspaper for its responsible reporting of her comments, an initiative that left its object purring like a well-fed tomcat.

Reply from the editor of the Daily Express

13th December, 1963

Dear Mrs. Whitehouse,

  Thank you for your letter of December 8. It is most kind of you to express appreciation of the manner in which your speech at the Moral Re-armament Conference was handled in the Daily Express.

  Very often readers write to newspapers only when they feel they have a grievance, so that a letter such as yours gives an editor considerable pleasure and satisfaction. I am greatly obliged.

  Yours sincerely,

  Robert Edwards

There were other, less propitious, tonal foreshadowings of Mary's future engagement with Britain's political and media hierarchies. The personal terms in which Whitehouse and other more intemperate allies had attacked the perceived dereliction of duty by a civil servant who was (by the terms of his employment) in no position to answer back were the subject of adverse comment in Hansard. And Henderson's boss, Sir Edward Boyle, had earlier rebuffed her with the first of many telling left/right combinations of the word 'travesty' and a quotation from John Stuart Mill's *On Liberty* to which she would find herself subject in the decades to come.

Reply from the Minister of Education

27 August, 1963

Dear Mrs. Whitehouse,

Thank you for your letter on the subject of Dr. Henderson's address to the seminar on health education.

I enclose a copy of the relevant passage from this address from which you will see that it really is a travesty of Dr. Henderson's views to suggest — as some have done — that he was 'advocating promiscuity'. His object was, rather, to consider the positions of charity and chastity in the hierarchy of moral values, bearing in mind both the words of the New Testament and our continuing concern with 'the mental and moral improvement of the coming generations'.

Whether or not one agrees with Dr. Henderson's views, I am sure it would be wrong for me as Minister to appear to 'lay down the law' authoritatively on a difficult moral issue with regard to which equally good and honest men, both inside and outside the Christian churches, genuinely differ.

Furthermore, while I do of course recognise the genuine difficulties which face many teachers who are asked — or feel it their duty to give — moral guidance, I cannot believe that the right way to resolve these difficulties lies in the direction of placing limitations on public discussion and controversy. As Mill said in his essay 'On Liberty', 'Complete liberty of contradicting and disproving our opinion is the very condition which justifies us in assuming its truth for purposes of action . . . Strange it is that men should admit the validity of the arguments for free discussion, but object to their being "pushed to an extreme"; not

seeing that, unless the reasons are good for an extreme
case, they are not good for any case.'

  These words are surely as true to-day as when they
were first written a little over one hundred years ago.
I think it is true of many young people nowadays — this
is something that I have often been told, for example,
by principals of teacher training colleges — that they
are very responsive to discussions on moral questions
provided that these are presented in terms of real
situations. And I am sure they can be brought to realise
that a close personal relationship can be either the most
life-enhancing and joyous, or alternatively the most
destructive, thing on earth. But I don't believe we serve
their interests best by trying to conceal from them that
there are some moral issues on which intelligent and
sincere men are not all agreed, so that they must make
up their own minds and (as one modern writer has put it)
carry the cross of being human for themselves.

  I do of course respect your sincerity in this matter,
and the importance of the points which you raise. But
I think the right approach to young people, after they
have left school, does raise difficult issues, and I
can't find it in my heart to condemn Dr. Henderson for
wishing to focus the minds of his audience upon them.

  Yours Sincerely,
  Sir Edward Boyle

  After receiving a letter from Dr Henderson himself explaining
the personal distress the vehemence of her attacks had caused
him and especially his wife, Mary pondered her next step.
Should she initiate a meeting with the embattled public servant,
or restrict herself to writing a letter of apology for personalising
the issue? As she agonised over the most appropriate course of
action to take, she was advised by one of her friends in Moral
Re-Armament that, in this instance and perhaps in others, the
end justified the means.

Letter from MRA contact

25th September, 1963

Dear Mary,

Many thanks for your letter. I hope you have an excellent time with the Bishop and equally that the date with the Regional Controller went well.

My chief desire with the other man is to keep him faced with the challenge that he must face. I personally think you would be wiser to reply to his letter in writing, but you will know whether you wish to do so. It needs to have a certain directness.

If I were writing, I should say that naturally you endorse his views, which are the views of all sane and patriotic people, about the priority importance of sound family life. This is the foundation of democracy and the rightful heritage of a Christian nation.

But his letter still leaves the central question unanswered. He is reported as having said that there is justification for young men and young women who contemplate marriage to sleep together as if they were married. If people have written to him in violent terms, I do not justify them in doing so, but it may also be because they feel the urgency of maintaining the sanctity of the marriage bond, and because they see the danger of unmarried sexual union.

Surely the simplest way would have been to come out with a clear word to the nation that he had been misinterpreted and that he is against intercourse between unmarried people in any circumstances on the ground that it reduces the sanctity of marriage and may lead to all kinds of other difficulties which it would be easy to enumerate. A clear word from him to this effect would have silenced the press overnight, and would actually have spared his wife the pain to which he refers.

Could he not, even now, make such a statement with complete clarity, since you have to ask him to believe

that his earlier word, whether it represents his full
opinion or not, has in fact made the task of many
teachers harder and has left a very clear impression in
the public mind.

You may or may not want to write him in this way,
but I do feel we need to guard against any softness
or sentimentality over the way his letter to you was
worded. No one wants to cause him or his wife trouble.
But from the beginning it has lain in his hands to free
himself from all embarrassment.

The question I ask is, why does he not do it?

With best wishes to Ernest and you,

Yours ever,

In an early demonstration of the capacity for independent
thought and action which would serve her well, Mary Whitehouse had already penned the following response to Henderson's poignant missive.

Reply to Dr Henderson

11th September, 1963

Dear Dr. Henderson,

I am writing to you because I feel I owe you an
apology.

After the publication of your remarks about pre-
marital intercourse between engaged couples I felt
very angry & full of bitterness towards you because I
believed that you had under cut all that which, over
the last two years, we have battled so hard to establish
in the school in which I teach. While still believing
this to be true, I am sure that to have such personal
feelings is quite wrong and I'm sorry.

Perhaps you spoke as you did not realizing that it is
possible for young people — indeed for all of us — to
find a fully satisfying life without sexual intercourse,
if that is that right and necessary way for us.

We have in our school, a course in sex instruction
which goes way beyond just teaching children the 'facts
of life', I am enclosing a copy of a report we were
asked to make on this. You will no doubt understand why
I feel that your remarks would make it infinitely harder
for people to make clear cut decisions on what is right
& what is wrong.

It would mean so much to us all, Dr. Henderson, if
men who carry your degree of responsibility would
really speak out in a way which would strengthen the
determination of young people to live clean & straight
— I am sure you could yet say something for which the
whole country would be grateful.

With best wishes.

Yours sincerely,

Mary Whitehouse

(Mrs Ernest Whitehouse)

The extent to which the Clean Up TV Campaign could be
seen as a front organisation for the MRA was a topic of heated
debate. Not only for critics like the MP recorded in Hansard as
suggesting that the ethical malaise Whitehouse and co. claimed
to have detected might be 'not so much a moral problem, more
a moral re-armament problem', but also for Mary Whitehouse
and her MRA contacts themselves.

The friends and advisers in the MRA with whom she maintained long-term correspondences would often warn her against
the consequences of allowing her public persona to become too
publicly associated with them. Mary and co-founder Mrs Norah
Buckland were both members, so the mystery of how the Clean
Up TV infrastructure managed to spring up as if from nowhere
is at least partly solved by the clear overlap between the two
organisations. However, the speed with which Whitehouse's
campaign generated its own momentum ultimately suited everyone's interests.

The gravity of the MRA's image problem is most easily explained with reference to the visit by the American Lutheran pastor Frank Buchman – founder of its immediate forerunner, the Oxford Group – to the 1936 Berlin Olympics and his subsequent portrayal of the Nazis as a valuable bulwark against Communism. In itself this totalitarian flirtation was probably no more (or less) inherently inexcusable than those of George Bernard Shaw or David Bowie, but Buchman's movement's subsequent identification with the policy of appeasement ensured that, as far as the MRA was concerned, the fascist mud stuck.

In terms of the propensity of the MRA's name to conjure up sinister associations, the clearest twenty-first-century analogy would probably be with Scientology. The revelation that someone was involved in it wouldn't quite cut them off from respectable society, but it wasn't something a person wishing to establish a profile as a trustworthy public figure would shout from the rooftops either. And while she obviously didn't share the scepticism with which society at large regarded her point of spiritual departure, Mary Whitehouse was prudent enough to be discreet about it.

Anyone still in doubt as to the wisdom of this approach is advised to read the second, third and fourth paragraphs of this further letter on the Henderson issue (from a second MRA mentor) out loud in the voice of Austin Powers' devious nemesis Dr. Evil.

Reply from another MRA mentor

22 Sept, 1963

Dear Mary,

  Those are interesting letters. I am sorry his wife has been in difficulty with all the press, but he still does not move an inch nearer recognising the harm his utterance did and we must not allow any desire to change him to blur the clarity of that line. Had he really wanted to spare his wife this trouble, all he needed to do was to issue a short statement to the press, which every newspaper in the land would have printed, saying that he had been wrong in his earlier statement, and that he wished to withdraw it. That would have silenced the press instantly.

They used to say, 'If everyone strokes the cat up the wrong way, the simplest answer is to turn the cat round.'

I am grateful, wholeheartedly grateful, for your initiative in these days. Be vigilant that we are not fooled by the feelings and even the flattery of bad men. You may be on the right wicket with this man, and he may change. All I would say is, I see no sign of it, and it is just possible that your letter of apology has taken the heat off him at the moment when it ought to have been kept on.

Do not let your feelings be hurt by what I say, but weigh it as a mature and God-led person. I regret the stupidity of people who have written what he calls 'filthy' or 'tortured' letters to him. I also regret the tragic misdirection of hundreds of thousands of young people which came from him and his official position, and which he firmly reiterates without an inch of repentance in his letter to you. Some of the 'torture' in the people who wrote may be God's moral fervour and fire trying to penetrate the hard skin of a man who certainly played Satan's game, wittingly or unwittingly, in a big way.

I have written thus frankly because we are dealing with great matters and I know in my own work on national issues of this kind I need a wider wisdom than my own. Would there have been value in consulting one or two of us before writing your earlier letter?

Ever your old friend,

P.S. He says he said simply that family solidarity is the most important thing in life: that is certainly not the thing he said by which the world remembers him.

It is not this book's place to delve too deeply into Mary White-house's private life, but the vexed question of her relationship with the Moral Re-Armament movement was one area where the personal and the public did definitely cross over. Not only was it through the MRA – or more precisely its earlier guise as the Oxford Group – that she first met her husband Ernest, but this controversial and vaguely cultish organisation had already been the vehicle for the religious awakening that followed on from her falling in love with a married man while working as a teacher in Wolverhampton in her early twenties.

Although Mary Whitehouse always insisted that this relation-ship remained platonic, its intensity clearly prepared the way for the whole-heartedness of her commitment to the cause of Moral Re-Armament. She even referred to it as harnessing 'The same energy that was going out to him – this ability to care'.

Mary Whitehouse's puritanical postures could sometimes make her look detached from the real world ('I'm not at all ashamed of being called puritanical', she told an interviewer on ATV's *Personally Speaking* in 1971, 'The Puritans were people with a very happy family life, who laughed and danced'). Yet her rigid ethical stances were often founded in the most intense personal experiences – from the break-up of her parents' mar-riage, to the loss of twins who died at birth after she had refused the medical abortion doctors had recommended ('Though my babies did not live,' she wrote later, 'I've never regretted the decision we made').

The strong views she held on the right and wrong way to approach sex education in schools were no exception. The fol-lowing draft of an article Mary Whitehouse wrote for a special-ist educational magazine in the autumn of 1963 finds both her rhetorical armoury and chosen ideological battlefield already clearly defined. For any readers who might find its thousand-plus words a little heavy-going, she helpfully boiled down the essential message of the piece into two catchy slogans – 'Girls know why they wear tight woollies' and 'We're so afraid of being called "square" that we've no established shape left at all!' I also like the way its strangely soporific undertow lulls the reader into a kind of trance so the line about the moral laxity of contemporary TV drama being part of 'a deliberate plan to so soften up the characters of men and women that they will become "useable" and traitors' passes by more or less unnoticed.

'Tomorrow May Be Too Late', credited to 'A Senior Mistress'

Parents and teachers everywhere in the country are deeply concerned about the kind of society into which their children are growing up and by which they are so constantly and deeply affected.

How can we give them some kind of roots? How can we give them what it takes to face the onslaught of dirty, materialistic atheism which attacks them on every side? One small part of the answer to this comes through the right kind of sex education.

The place for this is in the home – the incidental instruction which is given and accepted, out of maturity on the one side and trust on the other. But how many of us, to our sorrow, have found ourselves unable through one reason or another to give our children the help they need. This is where the school must step in, and it was in an attempt to fill this gap that we, in our large, mixed secondary modern school, decided on a series of talks and discussions. Very early on a fourteen-year-old boy wrote this: 'Will you please stop the girls teasing and tantalising the boys into deep sexual relationships?' After this we quickly realised that if we were going to help them on this level – and we could not do less to be effective – we had to do some hard thinking, and honest thinking at that.

How do you help girls not to tease and tantalise? How do you help boys to assess the girls' behaviour for what it is and be firm enough to withstand it? How do you help them to understand the pressures to which they are subjected through press, television and advertising? How do you help them to be so objective about their own motives in their relationship with the opposite sex that they can then act in a responsible

manner? How do you, indeed, help them to <u>want</u> to live straight
and clean and find this a joyous thing to do in a community
where all the pull is the other way?

Sex education is an enormous challenge to parents and
teachers. It isn't something which can be done in 'a lesson'
or group of lessons. The starting point must be acceptance of
the truth contained in the Albemarle report: 'One cannot, in
fact, indict the young for the growth of delinquency (here
read sexual promiscuity) without first indicting the older
generation.' The responsibility lies fairly and squarely on
our shoulders. We have no right to expect from our children
standards of behaviour and attitudes of responsibility which
we are not prepared to accept ourselves. Unless we act on this
we shall be humbugs and the children will see us as such —
setting one standard for ourselves and another for them. Added
to which we need to be honest about the kind of people we
ourselves are. We cannot help other people to sexual maturity
if we are immature. Unless we become increasingly aware of
ourselves — our tendency to demand, our urge to be central,
of how we play off one against another for our own ends, of
the anxiety which grows alongside love as we seek to find
roots and security in people, we do not have the beginning of
wisdom or understand the nature of real love, and will not be
able to lead others to find these things, no matter how many
'principles' and 'facts of life' we may give them.

We realised, too, that just as in a home teaching about
sex cannot be separated from the atmosphere, relationships,
attitudes and priorities within, neither can it within a school.
If the need for 'discipline' is properly balanced with the need
for 'self expression', if reading matter is assessed for its
effects on character as well as on its power to stimulate the
imagination, if morning assemblies are used to the utmost to
set the values for the rest of the day, if children can be led
to see that their personal decisions are not private matters
but have an effect not only on them, but on their school, their
home and beyond, then we set the background against which
specific sex instruction can be given wisely.

There are many things in the accepted fabric of children's
life today which need to be dealt with in a forthright way —
pop records for one. 'My love can't wait' says the pop song.
'Tomorrow may be too late' says another. Children accept many

of these words on their face value, but nevertheless they are being constantly brainwashed with the pornographic ideas which lie behind many of them. And we should not be afraid to fight out these issues with the children — so many of us have abdicated our responsibilities because we shy at the cost of drawing a battle line! We're so afraid of being called 'square' that we've no established shape left at all!

Children are not fools and there's nothing gained by talking down to them. They get mad if we switch off in the middle of a sexy play out of our own prejudice, but if we give them the facts — that many of these plays and much of what appears in the press are parts of a deliberate plan to so soften up the characters of men and women that they will become 'useable' and traitors — at least to what they truly believe in — then they respond to being treated as responsible adults and will decide for themselves what to watch or read. And then we may well get more and more of these teenage 'Watch Committees' who have set themselves up to wipe out what we, to our shame, have not only nurtured but grovelled in.

I'm sure this business of giving the children the chance to be responsible is most important. Girls know why they wear tight woollies — and why other people wear them too! They'll admit, at least to themselves, who they are trying to attract with their make up and hair styles. They respond with extraordinary honesty and objectiveness to this kind of challenge and they'll go on to think out with you how to be attractive without being cheap, how to be a woman without being loose and then, constructively, how to use their energies creatively in their own immediate circumstances and beyond.

If the parents are brought into the school to take part in their children's sex instruction, as they are in our school, a bond is forged which goes far to withstand the pressures brought to bear on the family.

Young people need a battle to fight in every age — continents are explored, the depths of the ocean are plumbed and space is conquered. The fight left for our young people is the fight of the spirit.

The authoritatively generic mantle which Mary Whitehouse donned as the writer of the above article ('A senior mistress'!)

was not her first brush with an occupation-related byline. It was very much an article of faith of the Clean Up TV Campaign that the organisation was the mouthpiece of 'ordinary housewives', but at least one of its founders had considerably more experience in dealing with the corrupt machinery of the national news media than she was initially willing to let on.

Long before the Clean Up TV Campaign made her a public figure, Mary Whitehouse was identifying herself as 'Contributor to BBC, *The Sunday Times*, and *Good Housekeeping*'. The Whitehouse archive box file devoted to her earlier writings reveals that far from being an innocent in the ways of the media – an anguished and articulate everywoman who emerged fully formed from a Christian chrysalis – Mary Whitehouse had actually been honing her persona as a campaigner for the purity of home and hearth for more than a decade.

The fascinating thing about her pre-1964 media profile was that it was entirely anonymous (or pseudonymous, depending on her mood). Ten years before her unnamed cameo in the *Daily Express* as 'a woman teacher', Mary Whitehouse had proved the answer to the prayers of BBC researchers struggling to locate a suitably loyal yet faceless subject to herald Queen Elizabeth II's accession to the throne with her 'A Housewife's Thoughts on the Eve of the Coronation', which went out live as the last item on *Woman's Hour* on the afternoon before the big day.

Nor was this Mary Whitehouse's first experience of the perils and benefits of media exposure. Whitehouse's 1971 autobiography *Who Does She Think She Is?* (the second and probably the pithiest of her numerous volumes of memoirs, as befits its publisher New English Library – also home to Richard Allen's *Skinhead* books) recounts her involvement in a charitable collection of food and clothing parcels for the relief of the civilian population of Germany in the immediate aftermath of the Second World War.

Having 'begged' the *Wolverhampton Express and Star* to cover a meeting at the local public library attended by 'two or three dozen people', she looked anxiously through the small news items in her local paper, but to no avail. 'Suddenly my eye was drawn to a banner headline across the width of the paper – "Mother pleads for Europe's suffering children". I was horrified! And quite over-whelmed, for I suffered from the not uncommon dislike of "see-ing my name in the papers" – and to have it "splashed" like this. There seemed something almost indecent about the notoriety, and it was several days before I ventured outside.'

Subsequently forced to acknowledge that 'the publicity brought in a great deal of support', Mary Whitehouse would eventual-ly get over her reticence about seeing her name in the papers. But not before she had explored a number of different branding options, for example in the presentation of this dramatic Bible-infused family reminiscence (which by the fact that the carefully typed manuscript in the archive is not accompanied – as others are – by a press clipping of its public incarnation, we can reason-ably assume to be published here for the first time), which was written under her maiden name.

'Another Exodus' – A true story of a little boy, told by his mother, Mary Hutcheson

It had been going on for a long time now. Not every day, but frequently during the long, hot summer, the little face would half bury itself in the crumpled sheet, till only the solemn gaze beneath the tousled head still showed. They were lovely eyes, their darkness startling against the golden hair. He clutched the sheet, and I knew what was coming. I'd heard the words so many times — 'Something to tell you mummy, but I can't, it's too bad.'

I was afraid. There seemed no end to the sickness and restless nights. I knew that something was eating away his heart; something was locked tight within him, and fear was standing tall. His whole world bound by fear, my whole world bound by

fear, Love seemed powerless to break in. I had wheedled and
cajoled, bullied and promised no punishment. It was all useless,
and he stayed in bondage. Bondage? In a strange, irrelevant
way I found myself thinking of pyramids and plagues. Yes, of
course, children in bondage, Egypt had been full of them. But
that had been thousands of years ago, and they weren't my kind
of child . . . What to do? and what to say?

I thought again of the other children. What did they do? How
did they get free? Grudgingly the answer came — because they
listened to God, and obeyed what he heard. How silly to think
of my child and his little problem alongside Moses, Pharaoh,
and the people of Israel. But fighting for his peace of mind,
I clung piously to the hope. Perhaps I could listen too.

The brown eyes searched and pleaded.

It came to me from nowhere, that memory of a lovely, rosy
apple, at the top of the sack, and of how, in a moment, it was
buried in my pocket. I felt the hot stinging guilt flush over
me again, the longing to put it back unseen. But I couldn't,
and I fled home, held onto my shame for thirty years, till I
told it, now, to my son. His eyes opened wide, and the sheet
came off his face as he raised himself on one elbow, 'Grown
ups, too, mummy?' he asked, and then out it poured. 'Garden
. . . gooseberries . . . all of them . . . but a man came out
of the house as we ran away, and he'd got a camera in his hand
. . . and I'd little red trousers on . . . and he sent the
photo to the police. Yes he did, mummy . . . you were in the
garden when I came home, and I tell you, mummy, and I felt like
a thief. You see burglars take things from inside, and thieves
take things from outside. Do you think the policeman has still
got the photo, mummy?'

The storm was over, and I held him close. The little heart
emptied, but how to heal it strong, and pure? How to make this
something which would give growth, and strength, and future
riches? Was it within my power to lead him out of bondage,
and into a promised land? I might ask Him how to go about it.
Quietly we sat and listened.

'Mummy, I'd like to take the lady some gooseberries back,
tell her I'm sorry.' 'So you shall, my son, we'll go together.'

And so we did. He never forgot, and when the summer came,
we passed the fields with our bag of fruit. Standing before
the strange doorway, my heart reached out to the smallness of

```
him. This meant so much, and we needn't have feared, for their
hearts reached out to us, and once all was done, he turned and
ran. A heap of soft sand caught him as he flung himself down and
rolled over, 'That's better, mummy' he cried, 'That's better'.
```

Is it just me, or does this story operate at a level of psycho-sexual intensity which might have made Angela Carter blush?

Mary Whitehouse's fetishisation of the domestic sphere is very much bound up with the authority she derives from her pre-eminent place within this private realm. But it's also interesting that the picture of family life she paints is far from the untroubled landscape of so many authoritarian imaginings.

The sanctity of the home is constantly imperilled – beset by doubts, physical and mental challenges and external threats (the latter best encapsulated in one of Mary Whitehouse's most apocalyptic fusions of the personal and the political, a 1955 article for *The Weekly Scotsman* – reprinted in the magazine of the Townswomen's Guilds – called 'The Scientists . . . The Bomb . . . and The Housewife'). We could imagine it as a fairy-tale damsel in distress, or perhaps a silent-movie heroine: chained to the railway tracks, with any number of potential bad guys (communists, homosexuals, liberal theologians, cast members of *That Was The Week That Was*) cackling demonically at the controls of an oncoming locomotive.

This overwhelming sense of jeopardy was very much to the fore in perhaps the strangest of all Mary Whitehouse's pre-celebrity publications. In late 1953 – presumably emboldened by the success of her *Woman's Hour* coronation broadcast – she submitted a piece, ultimately entitled 'Mothers & Sons', to the *Sunday Times*. The basic subject matter of this extended *cri de cœur* was how a mother could best protect herself from the anguish which must inevitably be generated by the possibility of inadvertently doing something that could lead to her child one day becoming homosexual.

Mary's willingness to be guided by the celebrated *Sunday Times* editor Henry Vincent 'Harry' Hodson in the matter of how best to present such delicate material showed her to be still some way short – in terms of confidence at least – of the ebullient public presence of the next decade.

Reply from the editor of the Sunday Times

20th November, 1953.
Dear Madam,
   Please forgive me for the delay in acknowledging your article entitled 'A Mother's Approach to Social Problems'. I was very much interested in your article, and would like to use it if a suitable occasion arose. I cannot be sure when this may be, and we have deliberately not pursued the subject further in the last couple of weeks.
   I think your pen-name, Mary Munroe, would be the best indication of authorship, but it would be interesting to know a little more about you without betraying your identity. Could you let me have any such information that you think might serve, such as your husband's occupation or profession, the kind of schools your sons go to, whether you also have any daughters and so on.
   Yours sincerely,
   H.V. Hodson (editor)

Further reply from the editor of the Sunday Times

3rd December, 1953.
Dear Mrs. Whitehouse,
   Very many thanks for your letter. We are now thinking of publishing the article without a name on it at all. There are arguments both for and against an admitted pseudonym as contrasted with simple anonymity, and we are now inclined to think that the arguments against are the stronger in this case.

I enclose a proof in case you may have any corrections
to make, though I hope not. I am also enclosing a draft
of the note that we intend to use by way of explanation
at the head of the article.

Yours sincerely,

H.V. Hodson (editor)

The nursery of social problems is in the home, and in the
relations of parents and children. This is true, as of
others, of that social problem, associated with inversion and
abnormality, which has lately aroused so much public anxiety.

In a self-searching and human article a mother of three
sons tells how she believes mothers can help to bring their
children's natural urges into right channels.

Her willingness to grapple in – at least relatively – straight-talking terms with 'that social problem, associated with inversion and abnormality' showcased Mary Whitehouse's sharp eye for a hot-button topic even at this early stage. And so extensive and impassioned was public response to her article that the *Sunday Times* reprinted it in a special pamphlet, alongside numerous readers' letters and a carefully worded (and, in retrospect, prophetic) rebuttal from Lord Wolfenden (chairman of the government committee whose landmark report published the following year would conclude that 'homosexual behaviour between consenting adults in private should no longer be a criminal offence').

For all the furore 'Mothers & Sons' caused, Harry Hodson pronounced himself less taken with – and thereby unable to publish – Mary Whitehouse's next submission, and the *Sunday Times* trail went cold as quickly as it had heated up. But her capacity to hold the attention of a national audience with an impassioned digest of traditionalist Christian teaching had been clearly demonstrated.

Ten years later, the sense of a gathering storm which is often to be found in those whose husbands read the Book of Daniel for pleasure was really starting to kick in. '1963 was, by any standards, an extraordinary year,' she recalled in *Who Does She Think She Is?*, 'the year of the Profumo scandal, "Honest to God" [a controversial theological broadside by John Robinson, the Anglican bishop of Woolwich], "kitchen sink" plays, late night satire . . . "Homosexuality", "prostitution," "intercourse" became the routine accompaniment of the evening meal and the topic of excited conversation in the cloakrooms and playgrounds.'

Intercourse the routine accompaniment of the evening meal? Something needed to be done about this, and Mary Whitehouse was the woman to do it.

The four-page brochure with which she launched the Clean Up TV Campaign – in tandem with the Staffordshire vicar's wife Norah Buckland – on 27 January 1964 set out the position they had been formalising together since the summer of 1963.

Extract from CUTV Campaign launch brochure

After the renewal of the B.B.C. Charter early this year it seemed clear that neither the Board of Governors nor Parliament intended to come to grips with a situation which had developed wherein a Public Service was propagating ideas entirely contrary to the philosophy on which our civilisation has been built; and the attitude of the B.B.C. to criticism on this point appears so insensitive as to approach contemptuous indifference.

Nothing seemed left but for the ordinary women of Britain to take matters into their own hands and to make it quite clear to the B.B.C. that we were prepared to fight for the right to bring up our children in the truths of the Christian faith, and to protect our homes from exhibitions of violence. We therefore drew up the following manifesto and issued it to the press:

THE MANIFESTO

1. We WOMEN OF BRITAIN believe in a Christian way of life.
2. We want it for the children we bear and the country we love.
3. We deplore present day attempts to belittle or destroy it, and in particular we object to the propaganda of disbelief, doubt and dirt that the B.B.C. pours into millions of homes through the television screen.
4. Crime, violence, illegitimacy and venereal disease are steadily increasing, yet the B.B.C. employs people whose ideas and advice pander to the lowest in human nature, and accompany this with a stream of suggestive and erotic plays which present promiscuity, infidelity and drinking as normal and inevitable.
5. We call upon the B.B.C. for a radical change of policy and demand programmes which build character instead of destroying it, which encourage and sustain faith in God and bring Him back to the heart of our family and national life.

As the placement of their names on the poster at the start of this chapter indicates, Mary Whitehouse initially played second fiddle to her co-founder. What these original documents also give us – when compared with the publicity material for the pivotal public meeting at Birmingham Town Hall on 5 May 1964, where Mrs Whitehouse is out and proud as 'Mary' – is the precise eighteen-day timeframe within which she stopped identifying herself in public via her husband's initials and started using her own name.

She didn't stop referring to herself as 'wife of a company director' (she wasn't Germaine Greer). But while sceptics might suggest that the former Mrs Ernest Whitehouse had found her own voice by attempting to censor or even silence those of others, the actual evolution of her public persona was – as should already have become clear – a far more complex and creative process than that.

BRITISH BROADCASTING CORPORATION

BROADCASTING HOUSE LONDON W1A 1AA

TELEPHONE 01-580 4468   CABLES: BROADCASTS LONDON PS4

TELEGRAMS: BROADCASTS LONDON TELEX   TELEX: 22182

Reference: JMJ/27   1st July, 1971

Dear Mrs. Whitehouse,

    Thank you for your letter of the 22nd June,
which has been passed to me for reply.

    I have pleasure in enclosing a selection of
photographs of Lord Reith for you to choose one for
publication in "The Viewer and Listener" next Autumn.

    I would be grateful if you would return the ones
not required.

    Many thanks,

                    Yours sincerely,

                    (Miss J. Marr-Johnson)
                    Photograph Librarian, Publicity

Mrs. M. Whitehouse,
National Viewers' and Listeners' Assoc.,
Triangle Farm House,
Far Forest,
Kidderminster,
Worcs.

Enc. 4 prints
GB

*The V. V. m—ind. for sending
he photog. of L.R. one of picture
I have kept, the other I return
with thanks.*

BBC reply to request for photograph of Lord Reith

2. Mary and the BBC

The defining relationship of Mary Whitehouse's campaigning career was with the BBC. But is 'relationship' really the right word here? Whether several decades' worth of interaction between one human being and the constantly shifting personnel of a national broadcasting network can safely shelter under the same linguistic umbrella as a holiday fling or a surprisingly enduring May-to-December romance is definitely a moot point.

That said, like all the best romantic comedies, this one started out in an atmosphere of clipped vituperation. If you were casting the infuriatingly arrogant and haughty BBC, it would have to be played by Cary Grant, George Clooney or – at the very least – Matthew McConaughey, while Mary Whitehouse would be one of those prim, virtuous heroines with a core of high-tensile steel – Daphne Zuniga in *The Sure Thing*, Sandra Bullock in just about anything, or even (at a pinch) Katherine Hepburn in *Bringing Up Baby* – whose indefatigable uptightness ultimately gets under the skin of the cocksure swain till he finally falls helplessly in love with her (or invites her to appear on *Songs of Praise* and lets her host a whole week of 'Thought for the Day', as happened in this case).

Such cinematic analogies might appear somewhat frivolous, but the key romantic-comedy motifs of seduction, betrayal, and the gradual erosion of resistance would crop up again and again as Mary's public persona as the voice of the BBC's lost Little England conscience became ever more sharply defined. As 'meet cutes' (the romcom technician's jargon for the protagonists' first encounter) go, the initial CUTV manifesto was definitely at the

running-over-your-puppy end of the spectrum, with the decision
to focus all the campaign's energies on the BBC explained in the
following forthright and philosophically cohesive terms.

Extract from CUTV manifesto

We are, of course, aware that there is also much wrong with
I.T.V., the theatre, the cinema, and the book trade. In fact
it looks as though an attack on the Christian character of our
country is being made throughout our culture. The Edinburgh
Drama Conference last summer, the growing flood of pornography
— both cheap and expensive — and the kitchen sink on the
London stage are some of the indications of it.

However it will be noted that our manifesto mentions the
B.B.C. exclusively. We decided to do this because the B.B.C.
is, after all, a public service and should be responsible to
the people for what it does in a way in which the others are
not. We have a right to say to the B.B.C. what we do and do
not want.

CUTV literature would often quote a translation of the Latin
words on the dedicatory plaque located (to this day) in the
foyer of the BBC's home at Broadcasting House. It reads: 'This
temple of the arts and muses is dedicated to Almighty God by
the first Governors of Broadcasting. It is their prayer that . . .
all things hostile to peace and purity be banished from this
house, and that the people, inclining their ear to whatsoever
things are beautiful, and honest and of good report may tread
the path of wisdom and righteousness.' If you had to sum up
exactly what it was that Mary Whitehouse was telling the BBC
she wanted, it was a board of governors who took that inscrip-
tion literally.

Even Mary's most diehard supporter would have to acknowledge her occasional penchant for exaggeration, but when
she described the early-sixties BBC response to criticism as
'approaching contemptuous indifference', she was, if anything,

understating her case. When it came down to dealing with complaints from outside its own antiquated and almost wilfully non-functional apparatus of regional advisory committees (a system accurately described by Whitehouse as 'feudal'), the BBC didn't so much approach contemptuous indifference as set down its picnic basket there and dine on a sumptuous feast of smoked salmon and chilled Sauvignon Blanc.

No one was in any doubt about the source of this imperious attitude – it came right from the very top. Far from being cowed by the kind of criticisms contained in the three hundred letters a week the Clean Up TV Campaign was receiving at its height, the BBC's director general Sir Hugh Carleton Greene – brother of the author Graham Greene – took them as confirmation that he was doing his job properly.

Greene's insistence that 'in matters of liberalising, the BBC should be one step ahead' probably had as significant an impact on the culture of post-war Britain as the contribution of any other single individual. The depth of his convictions – and of the ideological chasm between him and Mary Whitehouse – can only be properly understood in the context of his formative experiences of the previous decades.

As the *Daily Telegraph*'s chief correspondent in Berlin in the 1930s, he reported bravely on the Nazis' increasingly vice-like grip on the will of the German people until he was expelled from the country and moved on to Warsaw in time for the formal outbreak of hostilities in 1939. His distinguished contribution to the British war effort included spells as an RAF interrogator, a daring mission to Norway to head off a Nazi signal-jamming initiative, and being present at Auschwitz shortly after its liberation.

With this background, it's no wonder he took a dim view of any kind of authoritarian consensus. The creative upsurge that followed Greene's taking up the reins of the BBC in 1960 (the satire boom, the ground-breaking topical dramas of the

Wednesday Play strand masterminded by the Canadian former *Armchair Theatre* producer Sydney Newman) did certainly have an irreverent – even subversive – undertow. Yet as far as the director general of the BBC was concerned (and he had a point) these were the very freedoms for which the sacrifices of 1939–45 had been made.

Given moral rearmer-in-chief Frank Buchman's advocacy of appeasement, it was hardly surprising that Greene should have detected 'some pretty nasty people – real Nazi types' in the murky MRA mist that swirled around the foothills of the Clean Up TV Campaign's supposed moral high ground. Mary Whitehouse had – Greene wrote to his Hungarian mistress and later third wife Tatjana Sais (surely not the sort of connection his more outwardly respectable predecessor Lord Reith would have maintained) – 'chosen to pick on me as a sort of Anti-Christ engaged in a conspiracy to undermine the morals of the nation', and her decision to identify him as the man she held 'more responsible than any other for the moral decline of the nation' confirmed the accuracy of this assessment.

Whitehouse wouldn't even give Greene the credit his war record might seem to merit. Rather than acknowledging the part he'd played in defending British democracy against the Nazis, she preferred to portray his wartime experiences as a sinister grounding in the black arts of TV's potential as a 'propaganda medium'.

Decades after the collapse of the Soviet Bloc, the obsessive fear of Communism which held sway in the Whitehouse household is perhaps the hardest aspect of her mental make-up for twenty-first-century readers to encompass. The following quote from the American evangelist Billy Graham's 'Message to Broadcasters' – reprinted as a collect for the day at the head of at least one Clean Up TV Campaign newsletter – gives some idea of the extent to which she believed the Cold War was being fought on the home front of the nation's TV screens.

'You who control the mass media of the air', Graham thundered with his best McCarthyite trilby on, 'can influence a nation to think, to buy, or to do anything you want it to do. You can make people pro-communist, anti-communist. You can make men moral, immoral or amoral.' In this overloaded context, it is possible to at least understand the urgency – if not the substance – of Mary Whitehouse's conviction that the BBC had become 'a sounding board for those whose ideas undermine the basis of our Christian faith and our democratic way of life through drama and discussion'.

As 'a divorced man – unmarried and an unbeliever', Greene's unsuitability for the task of carrying the torch so decorously held by his less progressively minded forerunner Lord Reith was, Whitehouse believed, self-evident. It also made him the perfect bogeyman for those already predisposed to discern a left-wing secular conspiracy at the heart of the British establishment.

Whitehouse was no more likely to accept the extent of Greene's achievements in revitalising the BBC (which had been made to look hopelessly out of touch by the advent of ITV in the mid-fifties) than Greene was to accept even the slightest validity in any of her criticisms of the output he oversaw. The entrenched nature of these positions led both parties to behaviour that was unworthy of them.

Whitehouse's campaign of personal vilification against Greene took her into territory that was not really compatible with Christianity in any meaningful sense. Greene in turn (a particular irony this, given his sterling service in the fight against Hitler) cultivated a bunker mentality wherein the obvious contradiction inherent in censoring someone in the name of free speech could somehow no longer be discerned.

The acrimonious character of relations between the BBC and CUTV was established right from the start. Lurking within the Whitehouse archive is the following anonymous (though the

hand of Mary might fairly be suspected) account of media coverage of the movement's inaugural public moment (an event
which will be covered in greater detail in the next chapter). The
level of mutual suspicion that was already operational is encapsulated in the disapproving tone of the title.

The Behaviour of the BBC at the Birmingham Town Hall on 5 May 1964

Shortly before the Clean up T.V. meeting at the Birmingham
Town Hall on May 5th, the organisers were approached by a
member of the BBC T.V. camera team, who asked permission to
film the meeting from the inside. He was asked: 'Do you intend
to interrogate anyone inside the Town Hall?' His reply was an
emphatic 'No' given in the presence of five witnesses. With
this one stipulation permission was given.

 During the meeting a youth tried to create a disturbance.
Immediately the commentator (Roy Ronnie) was heard to give
instructions to the camera man to train his lights and camera
on the interrupter, thereby distracting the attention of
the audience from the speakers. One of the camera team was
heard to use the words 'blow it up', then the commentator
walked across the stage without permission and proceeded to
interrogate the interrupter in spite of the previous promise
about no interrogation.

 That night in the late T.V. news a totally false picture of
the meeting was given which conveyed to millions of people the
impression that the meeting had broken up in disorder. Actually
the interruption was a negligible incident and the meeting
proceeded as scheduled. The behaviour of the BBC camera team on
this occasion clearly demonstrated to the 2,000 people present
the very thing that has made their campaign necessary.

The meeting did actually suffer at least one other significant
disruption. David Turner – a writer whose recent TV play, *Trevor*,
had been subject to the kind of stringent vituperation which was
fast becoming the CUTV's stock-in-trade – approached the chair
with a written request to be allowed to defend his work. He

was denied this opportunity, but subsequently had his say in the only other way he knew how – by writing a not so much thinly as diaphanously veiled attack on Mary Whitehouse and her campaign.

The resulting TV series – charting the misguided attempts of a certain Mrs Smallgood to launch a 'Freedom from Sex' crusade in the fictional titular town of Swizzlewick – progressed through the writing and commissioning process to be ready for broadcast in just three months. This was presumably a measure of how well the concept had gone down at the very highest levels in the BBC. The popular and critical reception which the series received on its first broadcast in August 1964 was a good deal less favourable.

The BBC of this time subsequently became notorious for wiping the recordings of even the most acclaimed sectors of its output, so it is hardly surprising that no episodes of *Swizzlewick* are to be found (at least, not by me) in even the most esoteric realms of the internet (although apparently there are a couple languishing in the BBC archives). But it seems reasonable to assume that the first of many satirical ripostes to which Mrs Whitehouse's work would be subject over the years fell some way short of being the most distinguished (this last honour probably belongs to the classic *Goodies* episode featuring Beryl Reid as 'Mrs Desiree Carthorse', but more of that later).

As well as a leading character called Councillor Salt (the chairman of the Birmingham meeting who had refused Turner the right to speak was called Councillor Pepper), Swizzlewick's denizens also included a somewhat flaky individual called Ernest the Postman (Mary's husband was of course called Ernest, and the Whitehouse family had lived in a house called Postman's Piece). While these references were clumsy if relatively harmless, one otherwise mystifying plot development took inspiration (if that is the right word) from real life in a way that suggested outright malice.

Of the many traumatic incidents involving her or her family's health which Mary had allowed into the public domain, perhaps the saddest was the occasion when driving home at night on a country road in thick fog, Ernest had come round a corner to find a suicidal serviceman lying in the road. He was unable to stop in time, and although the subsequent inquest cleared him of any blame for the man's death, the psychological trauma led to him suffering what his wife described as 'a nervous collapse' some months later.

In *Quite Contrary* – the last of her six instalments of polemical autobiography – Mary recounts the scene in the Whitehouse household on the night the character of Ernest the Postman made his debut. The real-life Ernest – getting better by this time and hard at work in his study – had asked to be called at the first appearance of his on-screen simulacrum, which Mary was on the point of doing when she apprehended the way the story was going. Ernest the Postman had been taken ill, and had no option but to lie down on the sofa because he was 'suffering from guilt after having hit a dog with a football'. Mary was left frantically stalling to keep her husband away from the TV.

If her opponents wanted to fight dirty, Mary Whitehouse was not afraid to roll her sleeves up either. After she somehow got hold of a copy of the script of an upcoming episode of *Swizzlewick* and passed it on to the Conservative Postmaster General Reginald Bevins, a scene involving a corrupt councillor's interaction with a prostitute called Blousie was removed. With the local and national press in full cry – that cry being 'Where's Blousie?' – Turner disassociated himself from the show in protest at 'unethical cuts', and *Swizzlewick* was quietly shuffled off the screen.

Whitehouse took much satisfaction in the reported fury of Sir Hugh Greene at this turn of events, although she also identified it – fairly plausibly – as the beginning of an informal but fairly rigidly policed moratorium on her appearing on BBC TV or radio. The *Swizzlewick* farrago (or was it more of a brouhaha?) also set the pattern of future engagement – or non-engagement – between Mary and the BBC in one other important respect.

It is a guiding principle of the news media's operations that nothing delights one branch of that collective enterprise more than a story which reflects badly on another. Although this was long before the time when newspapers rigorously hostile to the BBC would be – coincidentally or otherwise – owned by proprietors of rival TV networks, there was always at the very least a healthy rivalry between print journalists and their more glamorous and higher-paid televisual counterparts.

Mary Whitehouse's ability to capitalise on this tension was one of the key weapons in her tactical armoury. The nervousness she had felt about seeing her name 'splashed' in the local paper way back in 1946 gave way to a steely determination to use the fourth estate as an informal fifth column in her lifelong struggle to bring the broadcast media to heel.

She was often moved in the pages of the CUTV newsletter to 'pay tribute to the very responsible and sympathetic attitude of the press, both local and national', in one matter or another. And Mary Whitehouse was no less loyal an adherent of the gospel of 'you scratch my back and I'll scratch yours' than of the ones that bore the names of Matthew, Mark, Luke, and John.

Whether this meant routinely releasing to the newspapers craftily – and often quite misleadingly – edited versions of one or both sides of correspondences in which she was engaged (a habit which particularly infuriated those BBC executives who did grant her censorious missives the honour of a personal reply), or putting out press releases 'announcing' the contents of letters she had not yet sent (ditto), the Whitehouse conscience seems to have been a surprisingly flexible friend in the matter of her interaction with the print media. And if the necessity arose to take a national newspaper to court for repeating a slanderous

suggestion made about her by one of the seditious fraternity of
late-night TV satirists, Mary's special relationship with the press
could easily be set on one side.

Statement read in the High Court of Justice, Queen's Bench Division, after Ned Sherrin libel case

MARY WHITEHOUSE (Married Woman) Plaintiff
  - and -
ASSOCIATED NEWS PAPERS LIMITED Defendants

The Plaintiff, who lives at The Wold, Claverly, Wolverhampton,
was until December 1964 a school—mistress, but in January,
1964, together with another woman, she founded a movement
known as 'The Women of Britain Clean-up T.V. Campaign' the
principal objects of which were and are to try to persuade
the B.B.C. and Independent Television Authority to reduce
the degree to which violence and sexual matters feature in
television programmes and to show programmes which tend to
build character rather than destroy it and which encourage
and sustain faith in God. The response to this movement was so
great that at a public meeting in October 1964 the Plaintiff
announced that she had decided to give up her long career as
a school-teacher in order to devote herself full-time to the
movement which she had founded.

In their issue of the 'Daily Mail' for November 6th 1964
the Defendants published a report of an interview with Mr.
Ned Sherrin, referring to the then forthcoming programme 'Not
So Much a Programme More a Way of Life' of which Mr. Sherrin
was the producer: in this report there appeared the following
quotation of words spoken by Mr. Sherrin at the interview,
which referred to the Plaintiff:

'I think we've dulled people's capacity for shock and surprise,
but there's always the lunatic fringe. I'm told one woman has
already given up her job so she can monitor the programme and
be ready to protest. What puzzles me is: what sort of job was
she doing that kept her busy at the hour of the night when
we're going to be on the air? I suppose she must have been on
the streets.'

The Plaintiff was not greatly concerned with the effect of
these words on anyone who knew her and who could at once
recognise that they could not have the slightest foundation
of truth in relation to her; but she was understandably very
much concerned about their possible effect on the thousands of
supporters of her movement who might be unaware that she was
a respectable schoolteacher and happily married woman with a
grown-up family.

The Defendants for their part in reporting these words
spoken by Mr. Sherrin had no intention of referring to the
Plaintiff whom they did not identify from Mr. Sherrin's
statement: indeed they did not realise that the words might
be taken seriously.

However as soon as the matter was drawn to their attention
they recognised that the words might well be taken seriously,
and as such were likely to be read as casting a serious slur
upon the Plaintiff's character for which there is not the
slightest foundation.

They have expressed their deep regret and attend by their
Counsel today to offer sincere apologies for the publication
of these words and in recognition of their gravity they
have agreed to pay the Plaintiff substantial damages and to
indemnify her against her legal costs.

The first of the numerous libel cases in which Mary Whitehouse would be involved (as either plaintiff or defendant) earned
her what was described – with modest pride – as 'a three figure
sum'. But if she thought this judgment would stem the tide of
ridicule coming her way from Hugh Greene's new model BBC –
with tacit, if not direct encouragement from the director general
himself – she was very much mistaken.

The presentation of the petition version of the CUTV Campaign's manifesto to Parliament in June 1965 – its six large parcels of signatures wrapped in patriotic red, white and blue ribbon
– did nothing to improve relations. The BBC chairman Lord
Normanbrook's terse response to Mary Whitehouse's subsequent
demand for a face-to-face meeting makes it fairly clear why.

Open letter from Mary Whitehouse to the BBC's chairman of governors

8th June, 1965

Dear Lord Normanbrook,

  As you will perhaps know a petition was presented
to the House of Commons on behalf of 366,355 men and
women of Britain on Thursday 3rd June. The signatories
included leaders of Church and State, Chief Constables,
medical men magistrates and teachers.

  It has been agreed, to approach you, for the second
time, and ask whether you, and the Governors of the
B.B.C. would receive a deputation representing these
people. We would value the opportunity of laying
before you the reasons for our concern about certain
aspects of B.B.C. policy, evidence as to the effects
of certain television attitudes and programmes, and
some suggestions as to the part we feel broadcasting
could play in strengthening family life, building the
character of our people and establishing a healthy
society.

  We trust that you will see your way clear to do so,
  Mary Whitehouse

Reply from Lord Normanbrook

21st June, 1965

Mrs Whitehouse,

  The B.B.C. follows, as a matter of first importance, any
proceedings in parliament which relate to the conduct of
broadcasting. The Board of governors have accordingly
taken note of the presentation by Mr James Dance of the
petition to which you refer in your letter of June 8th.
I should add the Board have also taken note of the views
expressed by Mr. Dance — in particular, of his comments
on the work of the Governors — in the recent debate
on broadcasting in the House of Commons, and of the

subsequent statement by the leader of the House about the
programme standards observed by the B.B.C.

I have studied the terms of the petition. I note that
the third and fourth clauses refer to the programme
output of the B.B.C. as an outpouring of 'propaganda
of disbelief, doubt and dirt', and to the staff of the
B.B.C. as 'people whose ideas and advice pander to the
lowest in human nature', and who are responsible for
'a stream of suggestive and erotic plays which present
promiscuity, infidelity and drinking as normal and
inevitable'. These charges would represent more than
adequate grounds for the resignation of each member if
the Board believed them to be true, or for the dismissal
of the Governors if it were generally accepted as true
by the public at large and by the Queen's advisers.

The Board do not accept them as true. They recognise
that in the substantial programme service offered by
the B.B.C. there are occasional errors of judgement,
but they do not believe that an impartial critic
would regard these as warranting the language of total
condemnation which is used in these clauses in your
Manifesto. The board are fortified in this belief by the
opinions expressed at meetings of the B.B.C.'s. General
Advisory Council, and of its other advisory bodies, and
in correspondence from Members of Parliament and from
the general public.

We welcome constructive criticisms and if you were
ready to make positive suggestions about programmes, we
should be happy to consider these. We are always anxious
to examine any sincere and constructive suggestion on its
merits. But until we have had some opportunity studying
specific suggestions about the kind of programmes which
your supporters would approve, I cannot see that we
could have a useful discussion, since, as I have said,
we cannot accept the validity of your criticisms in the
terms in which you have chose to express them.

Yours sincerely,

(signed) Normanbrook (Chairman)

As firmly as the above letter seemed to shut the door in her face, Mary Whitehouse somehow discerned a chink of light just big enough to squeeze a ladylike court shoe into. By the time of Lord Normanbrook's death in June 1967, the barrage of 'positive suggestions about programmes' he had received from the Whitehouse camp had played an important role in softening his attitude towards her, and far from being the end of her dream of an actual role in shaping the corporation's policy, the coming of Normanbrook's replacement – the Tory peer and former ITV chairman Lord Hill – would signal the beginning of the end of the Hugh Greene era of patrician disdain. That didn't mean the director general had to start answering her letters in person, though – even when not literally on the other side of the globe, they remained worlds apart.

Reply from director general's secretary

7th March, 1968

Dear Mrs. Whitehouse,
  In Sir Hugh Greene's absence in New Zealand I am
writing to thank you for your letter of 5th March with
which you enclosed a copy of a letter which will appear
in the next issue of your newsletter. Sir Hugh will see
these on his return to this country.
  Yours sincerely,
  Director-General's Secretary

In lieu of any more extensive acknowledgement from Sir Hugh Greene, Mary Whitehouse had already been reduced to the last refuge of the powerless – writing to the BBC's *Points of View*. It was a measure of the extent of her blacklisting by the organisation that executive clearance for the following letter to be read out was only given on the condition that its author should be identified as '*a* Mrs Whitehouse' rather than *the* Mary Whitehouse.

*Letter to Kenneth Robinson (Anne Robinson's spiritual –
though not actual – father) of BBC TV's* Points of View

8th August, 1967

Dear Mr. Robinson,
   After watching the story of the beheading of King
Charles in 'The Three Musketeers' last Sunday, one is
driven to ask whether 'realism' has become a god at the
B.B.C. Did the producer stop to think of the effect of
the dripping blood and swinging head on the countless
little, impressionable children, who would be watching
in the early evening?
   Yours sincerely,
   Mary Whitehouse

   A slightly more productive strategy was to cultivate relationships with the succession of up-and-coming BBC executives who
found themselves promoted to the role of Secretary (a seemingly
golf-club-inspired position whose duties consisted largely of
answering the letters Mary Whitehouse had originally addressed
to those higher up the chain of command). Kenneth Lamb –
whom she had once congratulated on a theological discussion
show in his earlier capacity as head of religious programming –
was harder to curry favour with in his new position. This early
response evinces an almost clinical determination not to give
Whitehouse credit for making a complaint which had actually
been deemed to be justified.

Reply from BBC Secretary

14th June, 1967

Dear Mrs. Whitehouse,
   Thank you for your letter of 9th June.
   We had already concluded that the programme to which
you refer was unsuitable for the time of evening at

which it was shown. The subject with which it dealt will
not recur in 'Z Cars'.
   As you will appreciate from what I have said, the BBC
intends to maintain its policy in respect of the 9 p.m.
'watershed'.
   Yours sincerely,
   (Kenneth Lamb)
   The Secretary

When it came to drawing people into debates they didn't really want to have, Mary Whitehouse had few equals. One of her
most tried and tested strategies was the tactical withdrawal, followed by an unexpected new foray, as in this masterly double
segue from an agreement to differ on a new Terry-Thomas show
through an absurdly overstated allegation of blasphemy on the
part of her arch-enemy Johnny Speight into an eye-catchingly
random attack on Allen Ginsberg.

Letter to BBC Secretary

5th July, 1967

Dear Mr. Lamb,
   Thank you for your letter of this morning. I accept
what you say about 'The Old Campaigner', but am amazed
to see that you do not consider 'To Lucifer — A Son'
blasphemous, especially as it contained the line 'Big
G's gone raving mad — he thinks he's Harold Wilson'.
This was the line which gave offence to so many,
otherwise I agree with you that most people found it
trivial and of no consequence.
   I am enclosing, for your interest a copy of a letter
which I have sent this morning to The Home Secretary. It
is certainly beyond my comprehension to understand how
or why the B.B.C. should play any part at all in turning
Allen Ginsberg into a public figure in this country. I
noticed that no Christian had been invited to take part

```
in the discussion of violence in which he played such a
large part.
  Yours sincerely,
  Mary Whitehouse
```

To call this a dance of seduction would be putting it a little too strongly, but Mary Whitehouse would occasionally send Kenneth Lamb a copy of NVALA's newsletter *The Viewer and Listener*, holding out a tantalising promise of future editions to come if he played his cards right. Lamb would respectfully rebuff this papery overture – courteously implying that as grateful as he was to accept the issue she had already sent, that was probably sufficient bounty to contend with for the moment. Yet even as he thought he was keeping Mary at arm's length, Lamb was being subtly beguiled, and before he knew it he was up to his neck in an ongoing discussion of the issues of the day, and receiving imperious smack-downs on a wide range of topics, including the amount of deference that should still be accorded to the Scouting movement.

'With reference to your remarks about our complaint over the treatment of the Boys Scouts,' Whitehouse replied tartly to Lamb's stout defence of some TV satirist or other's right to deride the legacy of Lord Baden-Powell, 'there are far too many "light hearted digs" at "well established and much respected institutions". This is why an increasing number of them are now less respected and established than they used to be.'

This Lamb-to-the-slaughter pattern was also followed with Kenneth's fellow incumbents as Secretary – the devoutly Catholic Charles Curran (an important contact for Mary to make, as he was later to succeed Greene as director general) and Colin Shaw. The latter's erudite and expansive responses to her letters are among my favourites in the whole BBC Secretarial canon.

Reply from the Secretary of the BBC

12th November, 1970

Dear Mrs. Whitehouse,

May I deal first with the question of nudity which
you raised? If I may recall a letter which I wrote to
you some weeks ago, I wrote that we believed audiences
did not object to the display of the naked human body
if it is done in a seemly way. I believe I read a
newspaper report subsequently in which you were quoted
as commenting that you did not see how it could be
done in a seemly way. I would only point out that the
use of the nude body has been a feature of art for a
great many years and suggest that no-one could describe
Michelangelo's 'David' as an unseemly work. If we were
to show, as indeed we have done, that work, would you
want to describe the showing as improper or out of touch
with the majority of people?

There is, of course, a great deal of difference
between the use of the nude body in a static work of
art and its use in plays. It is possible that you might
feel able to accept the former while rejecting the
latter. But perhaps you would consider whether it is a
difference in principle or only a difference in degree.
If you take the former view, then you could, I think,
reasonably maintain that in no circumstances should the
nude body be used in plays. If you say, as we do and as
we believe most people do, that the difference is one
of degree, then the problem becomes one of where a line
is drawn. That is, I think, the difference between us in
our approach to the Bergman and Potter plays.

I am not sure what you mean when you talk of Potter
and Bergman as members of the Henry Miller school of
'anti-law'. I can find no evidence for suggesting that
either of them is looking for an anarchistic society — a
concept which almost any reasonable person must regard
as self-defeating. It is the rules of society which are
being opened to question by them, rather than the need

for rules, which the phrase 'anti-law' suggests. Anthony
Trollope, you will remember, wrote a book called 'The Way
We Live Now' and that title really reflects the dilemmas
of the Bergmans and the Potters in their writing. It
also, I would suggest, reflects the dilemmas of a great
many people who are themselves uncertain of the way in
which their lives should be lived. They are aware of
solutions, political and religious, which are offered to
them, yet they continue to be perplexed. That perplexity
has provided the seeds of drama since time began.

You may feel that one solution is manifestly superior
to all the others. Yet it is not the business of the
BBC to propagate the acceptance of one solution to the
exclusion of all others. Our business is to provide a
forum for the discussion of different solutions. Out of
that one may emerge victorious, in which case we should
reflect its emergence. But we have no mandate to exclude
doubts and skepticism when they are expressed. Is that
not, in fact, what you are asking us to do?

Yours sincerely,

(Colin Shaw)

The Secretary

As befitted his (and, in this era at least, it was always 'his') all-
encompassing job title, the Secretary had to be all things to all correspondents (well, this one specifically). In his dealings with Mary
Whitehouse he had to act as a formal apologist for modernity,
delicately drawing a line between those aspects of contemporary
culture that 'reasonable people' (a vague social grouping which
it was tactful to imply she retained at least an outside chance
of being included in) were obliged to accept as no longer up for
debate and those – in the above letter's example, 'an anarchistic
society' – that they might still hold out some hope of resisting.

In doing this, it was always a good tactical move to make reference to Trollope. One of the other perks of the position was
that it was sometimes possible to have a little bit of restrained

fun at the expense of your epistolary tormentors, as seen in
Shaw's following Spaghetti Western-inspired riposte to a complaint about use of an illegitimate epithet.

Reply from the Secretary of the BBC

2nd July, 1971

Dear Mrs. Whitehouse,
   Lord Hill has asked me to thank you for your letter of
29th June, 1971.
   While sympathy is felt towards those who have
personally suffered the consequences of illegitimacy,
it is not thought that an outright ban on the use of the
word 'bastard' is practicable. Like many other words,
its force is undergoing change and you may have noticed
that there is currently advertised a feature film called
'A Town Called Bastard'. This film is being advertised
on the sides of London buses, some indication of the
way in which attitudes have changed. Nevertheless, the
word is one which is not used lightly in programmes, but
there are some occasions when it arises quite naturally
in a piece of dialogue, although sometimes without the
connotations which your correspondent draws attention to.
   I am passing your letter on to the Directors of
programmes in Radio and Television.
   Yours sincerely,
   (Colin Shaw)
   The Secretary

   By the time Colin Shaw was breaking the news that 'it is not
thought that an outright ban on the use of the word "bastard"
is practicable', Charles Curran had held the keys to the BBC
kingdom in his new role as director general for over two years.
While Mary Whitehouse was still some way from being fully
invited in from the cold, Curran's relatively decorous earlier
response to the following letter of protest from her husband at

least suggested a slight thaw in the climate. The cause of her husband's complaint – an unchivalrous suggestion by the maverick handlebar-moustachioed Tory MP Gerald Nabarro on the late-sixties equivalent of *Have I Got News For You* or *Mock the Week* – may be considered as an unfortunate throw-forward to the age of Frankie Boyle.

Letter from Ernest Whitehouse to the director general of the BBC

22nd July, 1969

Dear Sir,

In public life, it is expected that there will be much criticism as well as praise and no little name calling.

I think it is fair to say that those who partake, expect it and are willing to accept the hurts patiently, especially if they sincerely believe in what they are putting forward.

There are nevertheless, bounds to what is tolerable in this activity and I must draw your attention to remarks passed about Mrs. Whitehouse on Saturday Evening's T.V. 'Quiz of the week'.

The remarks by the panel and attributed to Lord Goodman were that she was 'a hypocritical old bitch'.

Such can only be classified as gratuitously scandalous, if not indeed defamatory of character: what is worse they were made against a person, not in a position to defend herself and mostly barred from T.V. anyway, by those exhibiting their verbal prowess to gain cheap laughs for money.

As the body entirely responsible for this piece of obloquy I must insist that a full apology and withdrawal of these remarks be included at the beginning of the next Broadcast of this programme.

Yours faithfully,

Ernest Whitehouse

cc. Lord Hill

Reply from Sir Charles Curran to Ernest Whitehouse

25th July, 1969

Dear Mr. Whitehouse,

Thank you for your letter. I have looked very closely into the circumstances in which the words you complain of were spoken during 'Quiz Of The Week'.

Sir Gerald Nabarro, on seeing the photograph, said: 'I think he (Lord Goodman) is looking very dubious about it all. I think Lord Goodman is thinking "you hypocritical old bitch". As you will appreciate, Sir Gerald's remarks were unscripted and the programme was live. There was no way, therefore, of the producer knowing that Sir Gerald would speak these lines.

We have since spoken to Sir Gerald about your complaint. He was at pains to point out that he is a member of NVALA, and that furthermore he supports whole-heartedly the attitude that NVALA has taken towards the proposed obscenity laws. You will recall that the photograph concerned was of Lord Goodman, as a member of the Working Party studying these laws, listening to Mrs. Whitehouse's comments. The offending words, therefore, could never represent his opinion of Mrs. Whitehouse. They were, however, as was made clear from the text, what Sir Gerald imagined Lord Goodman might be thinking.

Sir Gerald, therefore, felt that the only statement he could make was that he was sorry Mrs. Whitehouse should have felt aggrieved that he should have thought that Lord Goodman had this opinion of her.

Under these circumstances, it would seem to me that perhaps it would be better not to resuscitate on the screen the whole discussion, which would require the repetition of the offending words. I hope you will agree that this is the least undesirable course to take.

Perhaps I may just add an expression of my personal regret that this incident should have occurred.

Yours sincerely,

Charles Curran

Ernest graciously accepted Charles Curran's apology for the slur on his wife's good name. Of course his fervent wish in his letter of gracious acceptance that 'the B.B.C.'s broad avenues of satirical comment might not again be used for such expressions of gratuitous insult against her person' was not granted, but he probably never imagined that it would be.

No doubt Mary Whitehouse would have gladly swapped any notional moratorium on personal abuse for the face-to-face meeting which Curran (probably to his own surprise as much as hers) did ultimately end up succumbing to a couple of years later. By the time this landmark could be achieved, she'd have spent not far short of a decade at the helm of an organisation built not just in her own image, but also seemingly designed to mirror the BBC's paradoxical blend of representative autocracy . . . Ladies and gentlemen, it is time for us to dance the waltz of NVALA.

VIEWERS AND LISTENERS!

Do you REALISE

? that your licence makes you a
"SHAREHOLDER" in the B.B.C.?

? Have YOU a Vision for
Television + Radio + what
they could to to build a better world
for our children?

Then. Join

the * Viewers And Listeners.

Association

We Aim

    - --- -- ---
    -- --- ---
    -- --- ---

    - --- ---

We Need.

1. The positive thinking of all normal
   men + women - young and old.

2. MONEY to expand the Campaign
   + consolidate.

(↓
Detachable Enrolment form.
inc. request for donation

    * V.A.L to be i largest
    possible following

Handwritten notes for NVALA's constitution – author uncertain, but it's not
Mary's handwriting

3. From the Town Hall Meeting to NVALA

Every true cultural phenomenon has its 'I'm not just ready for my close-up, this *is* my close-up!' moment. The Stone Roses had Spike Island, the Sex Pistols had Bill Grundy, and for Mary Whitehouse it was the Birmingham Town Hall meeting of 5 May 1964. Many aspects of this occasion caught the public imagination – the clump of the heavy shoes of a group of supportive nuns stamping their feet to drown out the noise of less devout protesters, the uniformed schoolgirls proclaiming their disdain for the free and easy new morality – and it marked the point at which CUTV could begin to think of itself as a mass movement.

That historic night's two-thousand-strong packed house was by no means a foregone conclusion, though. As this impassioned appeal for a good turnout in a round-robin communication of a few months before makes clear, Kevin Costner's *Field of Dreams* mantra 'If you build it, they will come' was already in operation here.

CUTV newsletter, March 1964

Dear Friends,

  Birmingham City Councillor Pepper chaired a tremendously enthusiastic meeting in the Midland Hotel last Saturday. About 150 men and women from the Midlands as well as representatives from Cumberland, Sheffield, Derby and the South heard him declare: 'It is time the B.B.C. stopped sheltering behind the moral bankruptcy of modern playwrights.'

  Mrs. BUCKLAND said that the B.B.C. should take note again of its own dedication, and emphasised that the time had come for united, concerted, large scale action and appealed to all, individuals and organisations alike, to join with us at this time to make a mighty and sustained effort, which cannot be ignored.

Mrs. WHITEHOUSE spoke of the evil effects of certain shows on T.V. on young people and declared that parents had to be aware too of the dubious plays and books which are now being offered to school-children. She emphasised too the irresponsibility shown by the B.B.C. in putting on programmes which militate against what the Home Secretary and the Minister of Health are doing to fight crime, illegitimacy and V.D.

It was decided that there should be a mass meeting on <u>TUESDAY, MAY 5th at 8 p.m. in the BIRMINGHAM TOWN HALL</u>, at which Mrs. P. McLaughlin, M.P. and Mr. Barnett, Chief Constable of Lincoln, have agreed to speak. We know that the B.B.C. is watching our progress with great interest — what happens at this meeting may well decide the future of our country. Nothing less than a mass turn out, with an overflow if possible, will have any effect. A lady from Sheffield said after the meeting that she would bring a coach load. Can we all think in these terms of getting whole groups of men and women there, as well as our personal friends? We need hundreds of thousands of signatures for the Manifesto, too. One lady returned four sheets on which she had collected 134 signatures in 'bus queues and shops. She has also offered to pay to have the Manifesto printed in the local paper, with a space for signatures so that it can just be cut out and posted in.

Our next Planning Meeting will be in the <u>GRAND HOTEL, COLMORE ROW, BIRMINGHAM, at 3 p.m., MARCH 21st</u>. Please do come and bring your friends and all your ideas and experiences in spreading this campaign — we want to hear from you all. It has been suggested that one of the most effective ways to work is in local groups. Will anyone willing to take on the job of contacting the people in their area who have written in, please write and say so and then we can really start planning 'in depth'.

With all good wishes and much joy in the fight.

As the assertion 'what happens at this meeting may well decide the future of our country' makes clear, CUTV had never lacked a lively sense of its own significance. In its determination to counteract what Mary Whitehouse — in one of her most Hyacinth Bucket-like formulations – termed 'that voice of authority – the tele', her campaign was willing to call upon any source of legitimacy it could lay its hands on. This agenda for the Birmingham Town Hall 'mass meeting' shows how clearly its self-image as a democratic upsurge was channelled through pre-existing networks of social status.

Extract from agenda for Birmingham Town Hall meeting of 5 May 1964

MAIN SPEAKERS:	
Councillor Pepper, J.P.	
Mrs. Mary Whitehouse,	Senior Mistress of Secondary Modern School. Mother of 3 and co-initiator of campaign.
Mr. Ernest Whitehouse,	Businessman. Treasurer of campaign.
Mrs. Norah Buckland,	Mother of 3 and co-initiator of campaign.
Rev. Basil Buckland,	Rector of Longton, Stoke-on-Trent.
Mr. Patrick Hamilton,	Editor of 'The Layman'. Speaker on 'Lift up your hearts' programme of B.B.C.
Mrs. Patricia Duce,	Niece of Sir Ernest Shackleton. Wife of motor engineer.
POSSIBLE SPEAKERS:	
Mrs. Victor Crowther,	Wife of Warwickshire County Councillor. Will read the message to the Queen.
Mrs. Laird Will speak for Chester and the Wirral.	
Mrs. Hutcheson Messages from the Bishops of Chester	
Mrs. Spruce and Shrewsbury.	
Mrs. Williamson,	Representing the Catholic women of Liverpool.

Mrs. Miller,	Representing Wolverhampton.
Mrs. Price,	Dudley.
Mrs. Lawrence,	Representing Machynlleth.
Mrs. Thompson,	Representing Huddersfield.
Mrs. S. Collins,	Representing Stoke-on-Trent.
Mrs. Goodwin,	" " " "
Mrs. Spooner,	Representing Sheffield.
Miss Dobson,	Representing Stafford.
Mrs. Higgitt,	Harborne. Introducing a group of youth.
Miss R. Jones,	Schoolmistress. Swanshurst Park. Introducing five fifth-formers.

Delegations from:

London	Sheffield	Derby	Coventry
Glasgow	Liverpool	Stoke-on-Trent	Hagley
Cumberland	Chester	Bridgnorth	Malvern
Surrey	Manchester	Wolverhampton	Worcester
Potters Bar	Southport	Shrewsbury	Rugby
Bristol	Stafford	Nuneaton	Cheltenham
Machynlleth			

Messages of Support from:

Lady Parker of Waddington, Wife of Lord Chief Justice.
Miss Anna Neagle
Sir Adrian Boult
Air Chief Marshal Sir Theodore McEvoy, K.C.B.
Lieut. General Sir Francis Tukor
Mrs. Shephard Fiddler, Wife of City Architect, Birmingham.
Mr. J. Barnett, Chief Constable of Lincolnshire.
Leo Ormston, Founder of 'Youth Impact'
Roman Catholic Bishop of Shrewsbury
Anglican Bishop of Chester
International Council of Christian Churches

```
Branches of:-
Mothers' Union
Catholic Woman's Organisations
Women's Institute
Townswomen's Guild
Churches of all denominations, including the Salvation Army.
Youth Clubs
```

While the expression 'too many chiefs and not enough Indians' should never be used lightly (especially not in this context, as history fails to record if there were actually any Indians at this meeting), it would be fair to say that Mary Whitehouse was one of a number of CUTV's bigwigs-in-waiting with the potential or aspiration to supply leadership. The following extract from a speech by Mrs Patricia Duce – whose illustrious family connections would be made clear from the off for the benefit of anyone who had yet to notice them – is certainly not the work of a shrinking violet.

It is interesting to note that the pseudoscientific presentation of vast aggregations of subjective opinion – which would become very much a hallmark of Mary Whitehouse's contributions to public debate in the decades to come – was already CUTV best practice some time before Mary had assumed the mantle of supreme leadership. And readers struggling with Mrs Duce's rhetorical flourishes are given leave to skip to the end of her speech in order to find out where the title of this book came from.

Edited extract from TV Survey Report given to Birmingham Town Hall meeting

```
My uncle (Sir Ernest Shackleton) became famous because he was
a pioneer, because he was a brave man and because he epitomised
many people's idea of a Britain that was worthwhile, clean
and strong. What is more, he evoked these qualities in other
people; when he advertised for 50 men to go with him on one
of his Antarctic expeditions, promising only low pay, danger
```

and hardship, he had applications from 5,000 people.

I am convinced that we need today pioneers in another sphere, those brave men and women who are prepared to fight in today's conditions and on today's battle-lines to restore true greatness to Britain. No one questions that television is one of the most important influences that can work for or against such an aim.

Like a lot of other people I have been increasingly disturbed by the trend in BBC television. So when I heard of this campaign I was keen to take part. It was agreed that 15 of us should view systematically for 4 weeks from mid-March to mid-April during what are regarded as the peak hours, i.e. 6 to 11 o'clock each night.

In the event, we reported on 121 hours viewing time, covering 217 separate BBC programmes. We have taken the standpoint that any programme, whether a play or not, can be technically well produced or presented or acted; what we were looking for in this survey, however, was the overall impact on the viewer and whether this impact was in fact negative, destructive or offending against moral standards. For this reason we did not assess the news programmes, whether local or national (these numbered 50), although the comment was made more than once that certain interviews on the news were so conducted as to draw out discontent, and emphasise the negative.

This left 167 programmes which we have classified as being praiseworthy, neutral and objectionable, the latter meaning that the programme was marred by one or more of the following features:

Sexy innuendoes, suggestive clothing and behaviour.

Cruelty, sadism and unnecessary violence.

No regret for wrong-doing.

Blasphemy and the presentation of religion in a poor light.

Excessive drinking and foul language.

Undermining respect for law and order.

Unduly harrowing and depressing themes.

Certain composite programmes, though containing some good features, we had to classify as objectionable because they also included such items as a discussion on whether a relationship was homosexual or not; a review of a book which led to discussion on abortion, sterilization, etc., excerpts from a play which ridiculed the armed forces as well as having much bad language, etc.

In our assessment on the foregoing basis, we felt that 84 of the 167 programmes, i.e., 50% were praiseworthy, some being very good. 22% (36 programmes) we called neutral, i.e., not positively good but without objectionable features. This means that no less than 47 programmes, or 28% came under the heading of objectionable.

I would like to stress that these particular programmes with objectionable features were not only drama (which has come in for blame) but covered all kinds of programmes — features, documentaries, comedy shows, etc.

Some examples from this category which we called objectionable include a 'Monitor' programme shown on Easter Sunday which was considered wholly negative in its impact because of the way it dealt with the issue of capital punishment and because it brought out the worst side of a person's character.

On Palm Sunday in the programme 'Dig this Rhubarb' the comment was made that it was in order for Jesus Christ to wear a beard 'because He was after all not a gentleman'.

[Another] 'Monitor' featured sequences from the play 'Caligula' which we considered vile and sadistic. It was claimed during the programme itself, however, that this was 'good theatre' because it demonstrated 'complete freedom' — apparently meaning freedom from the restraining influence of any decent instinct.

Yet another programme in a series depicted a man going off the rails and losing his standards and self-respect. Not everyone may look upon this as entertainment.

Apart from this survey, I would like to mention certain other items which have come my way, either from letters and clippings sent from various parts of the country, or from my own observations. A number of instances of the ill-effects of TV have come in from teachers and medical men. One girl stated that having watched discussions on sex on the BBC quote 'The right time for me to have intercourse is when I am engaged' unquote. And this child felt she had made a moral decision. In another instance a group of 14 year old boys and girls had intercourse — the girls said they had decided to do this because they got the impression from the kind of TV coverage to the Christine Keeler case that this was the smart, easy, successful thing to do.

A doctor reports how his anti-smoking campaign with 1200 children was completely undercut because of the smoking habits

of their television heroes. 'If Dr. Kildare can do it, why
can't we?'
   Last week another doctor, speaking at the Royal Society of
Health Congress at Torquay, condemned films and television
plays based on sexual and homosexual behaviour and urged the
Government to ban this 'filth'.

Let us respectfully press Mrs Duce's pause button at this auspicious oratorical climax. While now may not be the time to
ponder the implications of viewing 'sexual' and 'homosexual'
behaviour as completely separate circles on a notional Venn dia-
gram, one more immediate question does present itself: why is
it that this book offers a digest of Mary Whitehouse's letters
rather than (the above being the exception that proves the rule
. . . don't worry, readers, she's history from here on in) Patricia
Duce's speeches? Apart from anything else, the tabloids could
have called her Il Duce.

An edited version of Whitehouse's address to the same excited
gathering will give us the beginnings of an answer. It is her willingness to think (in both the televisual and non-televisual senses
of the phrase) 'outside the box' that gives Mary her 'X-factor'.
To make further use of the degraded language of that staple
of twenty-first-century family viewing time which she (perhaps
mercifully) did not live long enough to be appalled by, Whitehouse is not interested in 'comfort zones'.

Thus she progresses with inexorable momentum (and sometimes logic) from a strategic decision to present the reckless
amorality of the BBC as inimical to the more responsible
endeavours of other arms of government (an assertion that
would form the template for her relations with Britain's political elite), to an apocalyptic vision of 'a nation gone soft at the
centre and ripe for fall and takeover', to a ringing – and self-
critical – demand for positive action from her audience. All in
all, it's a Little Englander's rewrite of John F. Kennedy's 'Ask

not what America can do for you, but what you can do for America'.

Extract from Mary Whitehouse's speech at the Town Hall meeting

Over and over again, since we started this campaign, by letter and by mouth, we have been asked — why concentrate on the BBC?

And this is the first question I would like to answer now. Our position as far as ITV is concerned is that there is very great need for change, and if my information is correct a play that was put on last Saturday night is an example of change that is needed. But the immediate object of this campaign is to restore the BBC to its real position of respected leadership of this country. We are NOT against the BBC, we are FOR the BBC.

We are for what the BBC has done in the past and can do again and needs to do in this country and in the world. It is a public service in a Christian country and as such should lead the people on and up not down and out. We have actually, at the moment a quite incredible situation in this country which I sometimes think could only happen in Britain. We have the Minister of Health deploring and writing to us about the shocking rise of V.D. and promiscuity. We have the Home Secretary sending out an SOS to every town and village in this land for suggestions as to how we can control the lawless young ones. And then we have the Minister of Education who accepts the Newsome Report in which he says in black & white 'the young must be given sexual guidance on the basis of chastity before marriage and fidelity within it'. Three government departments, and a fourth government responsibility which is constantly putting on programmes which aggravate the very problems which other departments are trying to deal with . . .

'What sort of people are they?' 'Why did they start it in the first place?' 'What are they aiming at?' These are some of the questions being asked about the Clean-up T.V. Campaign. The first one is not for us to answer, but on the other two there are things to he said.

This campaign was born out of frustration and concern. Frustration at the attitude of the B.B.C. to letters of complaint, and at the apparent unwillingness of anyone to accept responsibility for programmes which offended, not only against public taste, but against the best interests of the nation. Concern over programmes like for example, the one put out on July 14th last year, when Dr. Alex Comfort defined 'a chivalrous boy as one who takes contraceptives with him when he goes to meet his girl friend'.

Countless parents were deeply distressed over this. Medical men, trying to find an answer to growing promiscuity and the resultant venereal disease, were exasperated that such ideas should have been propagated into the homes of the land.

We find it difficult to understand that those who weald power at Broadcasting House do not take account of the lesson history teaches — that a nation going soft at the centre is ripe for fall and take over. This isn't a campaign against 'dirty' plays or 'for censorship', the issue at stake is far greater than either of these. The Bishop of Leicester, speaking at his Diocesan Conference earlier this year said this — 'Prominent articles in papers like 'The Listener' set out plainly the desire of many to turn our country into a humanist secular country in which the Christian religion, if it survives, will survive as the private fad of the few, rather than as the faith of the nation.'

Since the roots of our democratic way of life are set deep in our Christian faith it is worth considering the inevitable outcome of such intentions. Do we want a materialistic philosophy to control our country and have power over the minds of our children? We, in the campaign, and many others no doubt, have already made our choice and it is on this battlefield that we are fighting. Against such issues the public exploitation of minds and bodies in the name of 'realism' is indefensible and the stories that come in from magistrates, teachers and police, of young people whose virginity has become common coin because of what they 'see on the tele' have a tragic significance far beyond the personal one. That this is being realised, and realised with great anxiety, is evidence in the letters that have come to us.

Nevertheless it has to be said that we get the television — as well as the government — we deserve. Certainly, for ourselves we realise that we abdicated our wider responsibilities in the tired years after the war. Young enough to want the fun we'd missed, part of an affluent society coming to terms with so much, we failed to grasp at what was slipping unnoticed through our

comfortable fingers — our children's and our nation's future.
It is to do what we may to right this wrong that we have thrown
overboard our anonymity and come out to fight!

In the months after the Town Hall meeting, just as CUTV
was broadening the base of its popular support and becoming a
fully nationwide concern, the campaign was also becoming ever
more closely associated with the commanding personality of the
woman who was suddenly its de facto leader. As the following impassioned letter of support from nearby Sutton Coldfield
makes very clear, if this was now a crusade, there was no doubt
about the identity of its Richard the Lionheart. Luckily, Mary
Whitehouse's direct appeal to the *soi-disant* silent majority was
translating itself very effectively into the establishment of an
informal infrastructure.

Undated summer 1964 letter from CUTV supporter

Dear Mrs Whitehouse,
   I am very pleased to read in 'The Birmingham Post' of
the success of your campaign.
   I have been hoping and praying that we shall achieve
success.
   The women of Britain need to give their all to ensure
an end to this portrayal of them as a sex symbol. I
think that this is another 'battle of the sexes'. My
experience is that the men seem very reluctant to sign.
The women do so willingly.
   I think that you have received 10 signatures from
a friend of mine, Mrs Quarmby of Beacon Rd, Sutton
Coldfield. She also wrote to me and said that she had
written to the Postmaster General.
   I am sending the petitions out and asking them to
send them back to you, rather than to me. It will save
time. All Saints' Church is backing the campaign and I
have written to two other vicars enclosing a copy of

the Manifesto. I have sent the Manifestos all over the
place, to organisations, and private individuals. I have
also written to Monica Dickens and Godfrey Winn, asking
them to support our campaign.

I hope we win; I never felt so near fury as I did last
might, when I saw 'Viewpoint' and Doctor Comfort was
on, so was another Doctor, and when a viewer suggested
educating children concerning V.D, he said it was no use
using fear as a mean of making them refrain from doing
something. Well, all I can say, is why half educate them,
and tell them half of the story? In any case I cannot see
the need for all this sex education. I did not know the
facts of life at thirteen but the moment I was confronted
with a difficult situation, my natural instinct told me
what was right and wrong. In fact, the man said 'Well,
don't look at me as if I have raped you.' I found my
breath, and said 'Well isn't that what you want to do?'
He ended by saying that he respected me.

One of the people on that programme said 'The young
can now feel free and without constraint, if he may have
any, it is within themselves'.

I swear I will send him a postcard asking him if he
allows his children to have intercourse when they feel
like it. If he doesn't, how dare he preach it to us, and
if he does, he is little better than an animal.

I spent a sleepless might I was so annoyed, but I
really blessed your name, and thought to myself, 'Thank
God we have someone who is doing something.'

    Yours Sincerely,

By the latter stages of 1964, what had started as a collective cry of rage was coalescing into an organisation substantial
enough to demand an institutional framework of some kind. A
CUTV newsletter of November that year spoke of the need 'to
consider this matter very seriously', and – in financial terms at
least – the campaign's very success was threatening to exhaust
its limited resources.

Extract from CUTV newsletter, November 1964

People have been extremely generous and until recently your
gifts have covered expenses. However, owing to the ever-
increasing interest and activity, our costs are soaring, and
we feel you would like to know that we now face some heavy
bills for printing (for example, 55,000 copies of the manifesto
and 20,000 copies of the 'Women of Britain' leaflet have been
requested and sent out) and postage. Every newsletter costs
almost £50 now for envelopes and stamps alone.

In a 'personal footnote', Mary Whitehouse broke the significant news that she was giving up teaching to essentially embark
on a new career as a professional anti-Hugh Greene agitator.
Her work in the classroom, she insisted, could not hope 'to have
lasting results so long as the children's minds are exposed to
insidious attack through a certain kind of stage, T.V. screen and
book production'. On the upside, the large amount of extra time
at her disposal would give her 'opportunity to move about the
country and to give support to anything which you may wish to
organise' – an eventuality by which the slim prospect of Britain
returning to its proper state as 'a nation which is strong and
clean' could only be greatly advanced.

Mary Whitehouse's new-found availability as a platform
speaker was not going to do the job on its own, though. How
best to formalise her campaign into a new and enduring structure without losing the spontaneity and ecumenical character
that had got it so far so quickly? The field of overlapping charity and Church organisations into which the new body would
be stepping was already a crowded one, and CUTV's ability to
unite a broad range of religious and social constituencies behind
a single issue had been perhaps its greatest asset.

The cornucopia of different headed notepapers lurking within the Whitehouse archive offers a poignantly fading snapshot
of the diversity and vigour of British social networking in the

pre-internet era. The following is a selection of the different
representative bodies that reached out to the Clean Up TV
Campaign and later NVALA (and if the occasional potentially
fractious overlap reminds anyone of the timeless animosity
between the Judean People's Front and the People's Front of
Judea in Monty Python's *Life of Brian*, then hopefully Mary
Whitehouse's presiding spirit will be willing to accept such an
echo as heretical rather than blasphemous).

List of UK charitable and religious organisations in contact with CUTV and NVALA

National Council of Women of Great Britain; Christian
Social Action; The Royal Sailors' Rest; New Life
Foundation Trust; National Housewives Association
(whose headed notepaper boasted a snazzy rolling pin
logo); Southwark Diocesan Catholic Parents and Electors
Association; Cruse [The National Organisation for
the Widowed and their Children]; Action For Biblical
Witness To Our Nation; The International Care Relief
and Social Concern Department of Assemblies of God in
Great Britain and Ireland; Llandaff Diocesan Committee
for Social Responsibility; Derby Constituencies Catholic
Committee; Society for the Protection of the Unborn
Child [Derby Branch]; Swansea and District Free Church
Women's Council; Order of Friars Minor and Conventual;
National Pure Water Association [Southern Counties
Branch]; Wallasey Business and Professional Women's
Club; Reorganized Church of the Latterday Saints;
Preston Women Citizens Association, Merthyr Tydfil;
Labour Women's Association; Inner Wheel Clubs of Newark
and Spennymoor; The Women's Circle of Thetford; The
Farmer's Christian Postal Service Fellowship for Farming
Women (I didn't make this one up, honest); The Russian
Orthodox Church in Exile; The World Federation of
Doctors Who Respect Human Life (as opposed to the other
kind); The National Christian Endeavour Union of Wales;

The Brotherhood Movement; The Knights of St Columba;
The Bible Speaks Christian Fellowship; Abitillery Sunday
School Union; Glasgow Foundry Boys Religious Society;
Bangor Christian Trust; Antrim Women's Institute; The
Sussex Brotherhood and Sisterhood Federation; Union of
Catholic Mothers [Southern Diocesan branch]; The Order
of Unity.

With so much well-meaning competition out there, establishing a clear place for itself in British public life without treading on the toes of pre-existing rivals was always going to be a challenge for Mary Whitehouse's new model army. The first warning shot from an established social network had already landed by the late summer of 1964.

The smoking gun was held by the Mothers' Union, and the quietly exultant covering letter with which Charles Curran passed on the findings of their Television Watching Groups (a nationwide network renowned for the high quality of its nibbles) to a CUTV foot soldier was a measure of how gleefully any public dissension in the anti-permissive ranks would be exploited by the forces of dirt and doubt.

Reply from the Secretary to CUTV foot soldier

10th July, 1964

Dear Madam,
  Thank you for your further letter of 8th July about
the moral standards of television plays. I think you
will agree that the enclosed statement, issued recently
by the Mothers' Union, suggests that there are more
people who approve of the policy of the BBC's Board of
Governors than you are inclined to allow.
  Yours faithfully,
  (C.J. Curran)
  The Secretary

Edited version of Mothers' Union statement

THE MOTHERS' UNION (incorporated by Royal Charter, 1926)
SUMMARY OF DIOCESAN MOTHERS' UNION REPORTS ON REACTION
OF TELEVISION GROUPS TO THE MANIFESTO FROM 'THE WOMEN
OF BRITAIN'

Out of 13 dioceses, only two report that a majority of their
Television Watching Groups was in favour of the Manifesto. The
remainder, though sharing a common concern for declining moral
standards, were unwilling to hold the B.B.C. accountable.
This majority condemned the sweeping accusations made by
the Manifesto against the B.B.C, as 'grossly exaggerated',
'unreasonable', 'aggressive', 'unjust', 'too strong', 'unfair',
'harsh', and 'negative'.

In both the dioceses where most groups supported the
Manifesto there were dissenting minorities. In the case of one
diocese four groups agreed with the views expressed while one
disassociated itself; in the case of the other all three groups
agreed in principle but one of them thought that I.T.V. ought
not to have been omitted from the censures of the Manifesto.

Not only did most of the other 11 dioceses report that
groups did not agree with the accusations levelled at the
B.B.C., but they also seemed to feel that the writers of the
manifesto had invalidated it as a responsible or constructive
document by their use of intemperate language.

Every group in every diocese agreed with points 1 and 2 of the
Manifesto, namely that 'We women of Britain believe in a British
way of life' and want it for 'the children we bear and the
country we love'. And all joined the writers of the Manifesto
in deploring 'present day attempts to belittle or destroy'. But
from there on it was only a minority that was able to join with
the Manifesto in accusing B.B.C. Television of 'pouring into
millions of homes the propaganda of disbelief, doubt and dirt'.

Again all agreed with the factual statement that crime
and immorality were steadily increasing, but the majority of
groups not only declined to accept that the B.B.C. employs
people to peddle corrupt views and advice, but also seemed,
from their reports, to resent these allegations. Even the
call for 'a radical change of policy' was considered either
unnecessary or unrealistic.

The Mothers' Union was not the only potential rival which tried to make off with Mary Whitehouse's clothes while she bathed in the storm-tossed lido of public debate. The leading Methodist Kenneth Greet, who had been outspoken in his criticism of CUTV on earlier platforms, made a proposal at the British Council of Churches in the summer of 1965 which seemed designed to strangle the infant NVALA at birth. It would not be necessary to share Whitehouse's belief in divine intervention to see the tragicomic denouement of this presentation as a heartening instance of natural justice in action. Especially as this letter from one of the movement's most querulous and peremptory adherents indicates the extent to which fainter hearts than Mary's might have been tempted to let others pick up the gauntlet.

Letter from Harold S. Goodwin

July 7th, 1965

Dear Mrs. Whitehouse,

I think that Kenneth Greet's move with the British Council of Churches is very helpful to your cause. In case you didn't notice exactly what happened, this was it: on Kenneth Greet's motion at the Methodist Conference this week, the Conference agreed to urge the British Council of Churches to set up something in the way of a T.V. and Radio Watch Committee. He then walked out of the Conference and was knocked down by a motor vehicle, and is now in a Plymouth Hospital with a broken hip.

In my judgment you will get much further if you offer full co-operation to 'the Greet Committee' than you will by flogging the Viewers' & Listeners' Association. The Association is not making any real progress, and it is involving you in unnecessary hard labour.

Do you not agree that the Greet Committee provides a chance to drop the Association without any loss of face? I have sent a note to Kenneth Greet saying that I

think you are likely to co-operate to the full with the
British Council of Churches.
  My wife and I were glad to hear you were having a
short holiday at last.
  All good wishes from us both,
  Yours sincerely,
  Harold S. Goodwin

  Just a couple of months earlier, Goodwin had been a key
player in the formative ideological spat (outlined below) of
the CUTV-to-NVALA transition. It culminated in not only his
effective resignation but also that of his opponent B. Charles-
Dean. The fact that they were involved in a campaign which
presented itself as being the voice of 'The Women of Britain' did
not prevent these two gentlemen from comporting themselves
in the manner of rutting stags (veterans of female-led political
initiatives from the Trojan women to Greenham Common could
probably be forgiven a sardonic eye-roll and a muttered ''twas
ever thus' at this point). But behind the compensatory macho
bluster, there were real unresolved issues about the direction the
new organisation should take, as the ensuing epistolary triptych
makes abundantly clear.

Undated letter from Harold S. Goodwin, April 1965

Dear Mrs. Whitehouse,
(1) I did say, from the first, that I do not want to
be a member of the committee of the new Association,
but that I would do what I can to serve it. I do not
propose therefore to attend any further meetings, unless
you call upon me for some specific service. I have no
particular competence in the matter of creating or
running national movements, and indeed I think they are
far more bother than they are worth.
(2) Don't ever let Charles-Dean, or anybody else,
coax you away from your inspired amateurism to any

professional-pro piffle. Yes, he's right in saying that
that's the way things are sent out to the press: in such
vast quantities that they very nearly put themselves
into the w.p.b. You and Mrs. Buckland attract attention
just because you don't do things in the done way.
(3) Ration your own energies. Don't let anybody take
you off the vital things that you do well in order to
do routine things. Don't get involved in money-chasing,
sending out appeals and receipts, and keeping track of
hundreds of receipt books that have been put into the hands
of scores of people and likely to become uncontrollable.
(4) Go on strike. Tell the men with whom you have become
associated that when they will an end they must provide
the means. They must not make decisions that call upon
you to do costly things, assuming that the money will be
forthcoming as a by-product of your other campaign. Even
postage at 3d a time (shortly to be 4d) to 660 MPs comes to
over £8. Your treasurer, or somebody, must provide or raise
the money to pay for anything you do at their request.
Remember what I am saying to you: men will always impose
upon women in these matters if they get a chance. When I
was a child my mother used to say about our (Methodist)
chapel: 'Oh the men are having a meeting to decide that the
women shall have a bazaar'. Watch these men. Don't let them
impose upon you. You are already showing signs of overwork.
What will happen to the movement if you crash?
(5) Call on me if you need me, but only if you really do
need me.
(6) Consider adding another objective to your list. As
an alternative to a return to sanity by the BBC, demand
deliverance from their ill-manners and obscenities for
the millions to whom they are not acceptable. That
means abandonment by law of the monopoly principle,
and setting up of an alternative broadcasting system.
Nothing can justify a monopoly that disgusts a high
proportion of its clients. Greetings also from my wife.
   Yours sincerely,
   Harold S. Godwin

Letter from B. Charles-Dean

26th April, 1965

Dear Mrs. Whitehouse,

I am deeply sorry, but I feel I must resign from
further active part in the affairs of the Association.
This does not mean that I am not in sympathy with all
your ideals, I am, and hope I can be accepted as a
member, a foundation member perhaps.

I feel it would be unfair of me not to give you my
reasons for not wishing to take further active part,
and I trust you will not accept them as personal, but
I do believe in frankness, and it is my considered
opinion that the present handling of the affairs of
the Association are too amateurish to have a chance of
success in its aims and ideals.

You will of course feel from time to time that occasional
revisions in television and radio programme fare are
due to efforts of our Association, indeed some of them
might be, but for a total change of pattern, pleas and
the raising of voices (as has been proven over the past
thirty years to my knowledge) will have no effect.

Conservative M.P's will have little influence upon the
present Government, and being entertained by the former
at the House can mean little or nothing. As for the
invitation to meet Lord Hill in June, I assure you, this
is so much eye-wash, and you will find that you will be
received most sympathetically and given assurances by
Charles Hill that he has the moral welfare of the country
at heart and that you can rest assured that all your
desires and those of members of the Association will be
'carefully noted,' then life will go on as usual.

I think you are the one person who has a real
opportunity of bringing about a happy change of a sad
state of affairs in television and radio, but you will
be defeated at every angle by plausibility from those
holding the reins, and this I know would be a great,
indeed terrific, disappointment to you.

I do assure you that I am sending this letter after
only very deep and careful thought over the week-end.
Please tell the Chairman that I shall be quite happy
for the next Steering Committee to be held at my offices,
although I shall not be present, I feel it might be
embarrassing to change venue now and I would not wish to
be the cause of this.

Yours sincerely,

B. Charles-Dean.

Letter from Revd Basil and Mrs Norah Buckland

30th April, 1965

Dear Mary,

Thank you for your letter and enclosures. They
indicate a serious state of affairs in the ranks of the
Association; and show that we have reached a point when
some clear thinking is called for.

We need to discover how to give these men with
such varied viewpoints a share in the direction and
control of the Association in such a way that they feel
responsible; and that it really is their affair for
which they make decisions, together and operate in the
business-like way they understand — instead of merely
'lending a hand' occasionally.

Of course, they will be quite happy, as Goodwin says,
to leave it all to you — but we should not in that way
secure the active cooperation of those many organisations
which look for a truly representative committee, and
official office and a business organisation. At the
moment we are a collection of individuals rather than
representatives of official bodies.

Goodwin may not like receipt books, costly publicity,
etc: but there will be no National Association worthy
of the name without them — or if we limit the whole
association to what can be done from Postman's Piece —
or with the resources of money and manpower we have at

present. There has got to be a vast expansion. If we
give the business and professional men and women their
heads, they will take the job on, find the money, provide
the machinery and put it into operation. But they will
not attend meetings to rubber stamp what has already
been decided or written.

  This is the time to throw everything and everybody
into the attack. We have arrived very near to the moment
when we win or fail. Public opinion is roused, but will
quickly subside or be diverted into other channels. If
we don't succeed in the next few weeks, the BBC will
recover from the body blow which has for the moment
got them groggy. They will ride it out unless we strike
decisively soon — and we shall not get a second chance.

  All the best,

  Rev'd Basil and Mrs Norah Buckland

  For all its infectious sense of urgency, the last of these three
letters – written by the Revd Basil, but hand-co-signed by Norah
– makes it very clear that the mantle of leadership was now sitting firmly on Mary Whitehouse's shoulders. If she was to stride
on into the good fight, she was going to need people around her
she could rely on.

  Some of her most important long-term supporters – the apt-
ly named Birmingham GP Dr D. C. Sturdy, Mr J. Barnett the
chief constable of Lincolnshire – were already on the bus by this
point, but around this time the quest for the missing pieces of
NVALA's human jigsaw for a while took on the character of a
religious remake of *The Dirty Dozen*. Where Robert Aldrich's
classic war film featured a meticulously assembled gang of recid-
ivist desperadoes including Telly Savalas's fanatical misogynist
A. J. Maggott, Mary Whitehouse sought help from the Roman
Catholic Archbishop of Liverpool.

Reply from the Archbishop of Liverpool

June 25, 1965

Dear Mrs. Whitehouse,

Thank you for your letter of June 24, and the enclosure.

It is good of you to invite me to become a patron of the Association, but at least for the moment I should prefer not to do so. I was appointed last year a member of the Pontifical Commission for Social Communication, which has been established since the first session of the Vatican Council, and you will appreciate that I would not like to involve the Commission in any way, even indirectly, by my association with another organisation.

With all good wishes,

I am,

Yours sincerely,

Archbishop of Liverpool.

This was a disappointment – not least because the archbishop was apparently 'good with explosives' – but Air Chief Marshal Sir Theodore McEvoy ultimately proved a much more responsive option. At least, he did once he'd overcome his initial anxieties over his potentially controversial connections in the italic handwriting underground.

Letter from Air Chief Marshal Sir Theodore McEvoy

21st April, 1965

Dear Mrs. Whitehouse,

Thank you for your letter of 13th April and congratulations on having formed the Viewers' and Listeners' Association. It is kind of you to ask me to be a Patron but I hesitate to accept for two reasons: a) I would not be able to do very much for the Association and

b) I am associated with such things as Common Cause and
the Society for Italic Handwriting, which are commonly
regarded as Fascist and/or cranky, and a supporter
of 'lost causes' may not inspire much confidence in
prospective adherents.
  However, if you have scraped the bottom of the barrel
and feel willing to put up with these shortcomings, I
should be honoured to lend my name to your admirable
cause.
  With best wishes.
  Yours sincerely,
  Theo McEvoy

Once her crack team was in place, Mary Whitehouse could
carry on her mission more or less unhindered. A receipt from
her printer with the jaunty sign-off 'All the Jolly' (let's face it,
whoever else she did or didn't appeal to, Mary was good news
for printers) perfectly captures the upbeat 'Onward, Christian
Soldiers'-type mood which seems to have been the default setting of NVALA administrative transactions – at least, once the
looming shadows of Harold S. Goodwin and B. Charles-Dean
had banished themselves.

Whether by accident or design, a reasonably happy compromise seems to have been arrived at between the contrasting
Corinthian and professional approaches put forward by those
two warring rivals. Consider the can-do pragmatism on display in Mancunian treasurer H. Cobden-Turner's suggestion
that Mary should simultaneously approach every Anglican
priest in the country: 'To do so you need a list, and there is a
firm which specialises in this work and will send out circulars
for you. The name of the firm is British Industrial Advertising.
I see from their booklet that there are 19,769 clergyman in
England and they will send out circulars to all of them for the
sum of £48.'

That sounds like excellent value.

Whisper it softly, but there was more than a hint of the Marxist ideal of 'From each according to his [or her] abilities, to each according to his [or her] needs' about the way first CUTV and then NVALA addressed the practical obstacles in their path. The lack of a cumbersome bureaucracy to block lines of communication between Mary Whitehouse and her grass-roots support certainly seems to have allowed for a measure of creative improvisation on the latter's part.

Letter from a member of the Scottish Housewives Association

15th December, 1965

Dear Mrs. Whitehouse,
  I forgot to tell you, on the phone, that Mrs. Patullo is having a supply of Questionnaires duplicated, and collecting them back at her address: that Mr. Williams in South Wales is doing the same . . . the nucleus of a regional office system!
  All good wishes.

If there were any problems inherent in the total identification of a cause with the vision and aspirations of its supreme leader – as the blood-drenched examples of Stalin's terror and Mao's Cultural Revolution suggested there might be – they do not seem to have loomed large in the minds of the NVALA rank and file. Only in the communications of Mary Whitehouse's increasingly hands-off MRA handlers could a warning note be detected – 'On your own position,' one of them advised in July 1965, 'your strength has been that you are an honest woman working on strong conviction with nothing to gain from doing it. Guard this. There is always a temptation in public work to become enamoured of the figure one is cutting . . . Don't stop because of it, but watch it.'

22/8/72.

The Director of Public Prosecutions,
12 Buckingham Gate,
London WC1.

Dear Sir,

Yesterday I arranged to have delivered to your Office
a copy of the record "SCHOOL'S OUT" now being played by Radio
1 &2, and on B.B.C.1 "TOP OF THE POPS". You will also,I trust,
have received a telegram from me requesting that you take
action, the B.B.C. for playing this record on their programmes.

You will hear that the lyric contains the following
chorus -   "Got no principle,got no innocence,
              School's out for summer,school's out for ever,
              School's been blown to pieces - ah;
              No more books,no more teachers".

In our view this record is subversive. I hope you agree and
will take the appropriate action. It could also amount to an
incitement to violence.

Yours faithfully,
Mary Whitehouse.

Letter to the DPP regarding Alice Cooper's 'School's Out'

4. Mary vs. Pop

For someone as prone as Mary Whitehouse was to taking works of art at face value, pop music was always going to be a bit of a minefield. Songs about sex, drugs and youthful rebellion (all things to which she was apt to take exception) directed specifically at an impressionable teenage audience were never going to have any other effect than that of a red rag on a male bovine creature which, though largely colour-blind, is universally known to really hate red rags.

Whitehouse's early writings betray a clear understanding of pop's role as an outrider of broader social and cultural change. In an expanded version of the 'Tomorrow May Be Too Late' essay, quoted at length in Chapter 1 of this book, she broadened her range of alarming examples from 1963 pop lyrics to include the 'pornographic' sensibility of the Beatles' 'Please Please Me' as a corrupting influence on British youth. Not only can her rise to prominence be seen to have roughly shadowed theirs – in effect, she was the anti-Beatles – but perhaps her most significant success of the 1960s would be directly set in train by their increasingly central position in the nation's cultural life.

The battlefield on which Mary Whitehouse's killer blow seems to have been struck (although she did not know it at the time) was the proposal for a Boxing Day broadcast of the Beatles' *Magical Mystery Tour*. In her second volume of memoirs, *Who Does She Think She Is?*, Whitehouse gleefully passes on the account in a 1969 *Sunday Times* article by the erstwhile BBC executive Kenneth Adam of the falling-out between Sir Hugh Greene and the newly arrived BBC chairman of governors Lord Hill which would ultimately lead to the director general's retirement.

There was a widespread perception at the time that the former Independent Television Authority chairman (and before that Tory minister) Hill had been brought in to rein back the mercurial Greene. Adam's account – subsequently disputed by Hill, but not by Greene – suggests that a disagreement between the two over whether the line 'boy you been a naughty girl, you let your knickers down' should be cut from the song 'I Am the Walrus' before the Boxing Day broadcast led to the kind of executive face-off which, in the long term, only one party will generally survive.

'Hill wanted it to be taken out or the film cancelled altogether,' Whitehouse quotes Adam excitedly. 'Greene declined to do either. Hill asked what would happen if he gave an instruction. Greene said regretfully he would be unable to accept it.' The latter's principled defence of the Beatles' artistic freedom would cost him dear – within less than a year, he was left with no option but to announce his retirement as director general – but the person who'd initially alerted Lord Hill to the existence of the 'offending' line obviously didn't see it that way. There are no prizes for guessing what her name was.

The consequences of Mary Whitehouse's final victory over Hugh Greene are a topic for later chapters. Returning to the musical matter in hand, Whitehouse's vague but visceral suspicion of rock 'n' roll in all its forms (with the virtuous exception of Cliff Richard, winner of the second NVALA award – a marvellous annual institution of which more later) is neatly showcased by the following exchange with the chairman of Granada TV about the imminent threat of the Doors. The extent to which readers might feel inclined to challenge its assumptions about the 'inoffensiveness' of the band's music or the guaranteed veracity of statements in the *Sunday Telegraph*'s 'Mandrake' column will of course be very much up to them.

Letter addressed to 'Sidney Bernstein, chairman of Granada TV', but answered by his brother Cecil

4th September, 1968

Dear Mr. Sidney Bernstein,

We feel we must express to you our concern about the publicity Granada intend to give to the American group 'The Doors', in the forthcoming Saturday Spectacular.

You will perhaps have seen Mandrake's column in the 'Sunday Telegraph' of this week, and the report in to-day's 'Guardian' that this group was arrested in America for using obscene language and causing a riot.

You will not need us to point out to you the power of television and it is, in our opinion, highly undesirable that at this time publicity should be given to groups of this kind which have a strong political motivation.

Yours sincerely,

Mary Whitehouse

Reply from Mr Cecil Bernstein

3rd October, 1968

Dear Mrs Whitehouse,

Thank you for your letter of 4 September about the American Group 'The Doors'.

I wonder whether you have listened to the records made by 'The Doors' which are on sale in this country and one of which is in the Top Twenty? I wonder too whether you are aware or not of the circumstances under which 'The Doors' were arrested in America and of the nature of the charges, and of the evidence?

Yours sincerely,

Cecil G Bernstein

Further Letter to Mr Bernstein

8th October, 1968

Dear Mr. Bernstein.

Thank you for your letter of October 3rd, which I
received this morning.

I must confess that I did not find it very helpful,
nor did it convey to me that you understood the nature
and reasons for our concern. You must surely be aware
that I am most unlikely to have specific details of the
charges against 'The Doors' in America. Equally you must
know that the 'Sunday Telegraph' would not say that this
group had been arrested on charges of causing a riot and
for using obscene language unless it were true.

The fact that the records made by 'The Doors' in this
country are inoffensive is welcome. It in no way alters
our conviction that the building up of this group into
pop 'heroes' is an undesirable thing.

Yours sincerely,
Mary Whitehouse

Mary Whitehouse's antipathy to what she called (paraphras-
ing the title of a Christian polemic co-written by the MRA stalwart Garth Lean) 'the hippies and their cult of softness' was
instinctive and deep-rooted, to the extent that she was content
to take information received about the inappropriate behaviour
of the leading lights of 1960s counterculture entirely on trust.
The fact that she sometimes passed on complaints about things
she had not actually seen or heard herself is actually one of the
least interesting charges on Mary's rap sheet.

It was no more necessary for her to watch the Rolling Stones
performing 'Sympathy for the Devil' on *Frost on Saturday* to
know she would have disapproved of it than it would be for
us to do so. However, as a public service announcement, I
should point out that this (excellent) clip is now available to
all by the magic of YouTube.

What is slightly shocking about the following letter of protest is that Whitehouse wrote it just a few weeks after she and Jagger had appeared together on a different edition of the same programme and seemingly got on like a house on fire, to the extent that Mary's biographer Max Caulfield described them as establishing 'a rapport' (see plate section for photographic evidence). Those with a keen eye for Mary Whitehouse's own not inconsiderable showbiz tendencies might be tempted to consider the possibility that she was jealous to discover he'd been invited back on so soon.

Letter to the chairman of the Independent Television Authority

13th December, 1968

Dear Lord Aylestone,

A number of people have spoken to me about the behaviour of Mick Jagger on the 'Frost on Saturday' programme last week. They were affronted, not only by the obscenity of his actions — I am told that he used his microphone as a phallic symbol — but also by the references to Jesus Christ in a song in such a setting.

If my information is correct, may I put it to you that this programme must have offended against the statutory obligations under which I.T.V. works, namely that programmes should not offend against good taste and decency? Since the — perhaps too simple — explanation for Mick Jagger's behaviour is that he is an exhibitionist, could not the matter best be settled by him not being invited to appear again? Since it is becoming increasingly clear that there are some people in show business who will set no limits whatever upon their own behaviour, the onus is surely upon the Broadcasting Authorities to act on behalf of the public.

I look forward very much to your comment upon my remarks.

Yours sincerely,

Mary Whitehouse

Lord Aylestone's reply is a model of the amused tolerance for the 'sometimes extravagant capers of young musical entertainers' that seems to have characterised high-ranking TV executives' approach to rock 'n' roll in the late 1960s.

Reply from Lord Aylestone

17th December, 1968

Dear Mrs. Whitehouse,

Thank you for your letter of the 3rd December about Mick Jagger's appearance on a recent 'Frost on Saturday'.

As you know, there is an unavoidable subjective element in any judgment on questions of taste. Certainly the wild, sometimes extravagant, capers of young musical entertainers are not to everyone's liking. But this is, I would suggest, a quite different thing from finding them actively offensive to decency and good taste in the way you suggest. While accepting that the interpretation you quote of Mick Jagger's antics is a possible one, I can only say that we did not see them like that.

In these circumstances, you will understand that I can see no just grounds for adopting the course of action you suggest.

Yours sincerely,

Mary Whitehouse's most drawn-out bout with a sixties countercultural heavyweight was provoked by Tony Palmer's (subsequently) much-celebrated rock documentary series *All My Loving*. Beyond the problems both she and her supporters experienced in spelling either Jimi Hendrix's name or the title of the programme correctly, and the racial stereotypes that lurk just beneath the surface of some of their criticisms, the following correspondence is most notable for Whitehouse's attempt to enlist the help of the British legal system in her battle to restrict the freedom of the priapic guitar hero to influence impressionable young minds by 'using his guitar as the body of a woman'. Although it met with no success in the short run, this initiative would eventually provide the template for her subsequent move into the law courts.

The saga began, as so many did, with Sir Hugh Greene's refusal to respond directly to a characteristically tight-lipped epistolary overture.

Letter to the director general of the BBC

November 5th, 1968

Dear Sir Hugh Greene,

You are perhaps aware from press reports that we are taking legal advice to discover whether Broadcasting is covered by the Obscene Publications Bill following the screening last Sunday of 'All our loving' on B.B.C.1. The behaviour of Jimmy Hendrix in this programme was the most obscene thing I, at any rate, have ever seen on television.

We were concerned, too, at the use of psychedelic and hypnotic techniques which build up frenzy and eroticism. We would be grateful if you would clarify the policy of the B.B.C. in the matter of the use of techniques of this kind, and also if you would tell us whether expert psychological advice was taken before this film was shown?

The decision to show the film of the shooting of the Vietcong prisoner showed, in our opinion, an extraordinary lack of sensitivity, and took us straight back to the days of public executions.

I await your reply with great interest,

Yours sincerely,

Copy to Lord Hill

Perhaps wisely, Mary Whitehouse did not hold her breath for that reply. Instead, she carried out her threat and wrote to Quintin Hogg – formerly Viscount and later Baron Hailsham,

who would one day be Margaret Thatcher's Lord Chancellor –
for legal advice.

Letter to Quintin Hogg MP

November 5th, 1968

Dear Mr. Hogg,

I trust you will forgive me taking your time, but
we are greatly concerned about a programme broadcast
on B.B.C.1 last Sunday evening. It was called 'All my
loving' and dealt with the 'pop' scene. In the course
of the programme Jimmy Hendrix used his guitar as the
body of a woman, and he masturbated on the neck. There
was talk, too, of the fact that certain pop singers
masturbated during the course of their acts, and that a
pipe was fitted down the trouser leg.

You will be fully aware, I know, of the obligation
accepted by Lord Normanbrook on behalf of the B.B.C.
'as far as possible not to offend against good taste and
decency' etc, and I am sure that you are aware, too, of
the unceasing complaints over a minority of programmes
which offend against this obligation. It seems to us,
after Sunday night's display, that something more than
protest is called for.

I am wondering whether you are able to help us by
informing us whether broadcasting is covered by the
Obscene Publications Act, or whether there is any other
legal safeguard against behaviour of this kind? We have
tried, with no success whatever, to get the Attorney
General, and the Director of Public Prosecutions to take
action upon previous occasions. We are, therefore, most
anxious to discover whether there is any alternative
action open to us, and if you are able to give us any
advice in this matter we would be extremely grateful.

One problem is, of course, that we have very few funds,
and would not be able to launch an expensive private
action. Surely there should be some channel through which

the public can fight those who use a public broadcasting service for obscenity of this kind. If there is no provision at all, then the outlook is indeed bleak.

You may perhaps know that Lord Hill is abroad at this time and will be away until November 23rd. I cannot help wondering whether the programme would have been shown at all had he not been.

I know how busy you must be, but I am writing to you because I really do not know who else to turn to. In spite of Lord Hill's appointment, and considerable improvements in certain respects, the situation in certain areas of broadcasting seems to be getting out of hand.

With best wishes,

Yours sincerely,

On Hogg's say-so, Mary Whitehouse then approached the Director of Public Prosecutions for guidance on the matter, via her special envoy from the boys in blue, Lincolnshire chief constable John Barnett. It would be a mistake to regard Barnett as the lone anti-permissive voice within the fenland constabulary, as the following entertainingly detailed response to *All My Loving* supplied to him by a fellow officer makes clear.

Report on All My Loving *compiled by a chief constable from Grantham*

SUBJECT:

B.B.C. Television Programme 'All My Loving'.

I looked at this programme on B.B.C.2 on Sunday evening, the 18th May 1969. My personal comments are as follows.

The whole programme was, to me, in very poor taste; a disjointed series of crude flashes of conversation and performances by various people. There were several parts of it which, in my opinion, were likely to outrage public decency.

1. A cockney entertainment producer commented on the effect that 'pop' music had on the teenage public, especially the females. He appeared to say that the girls' main point of interest was whether a male singer had a big 'bump' or not, and he said that

when some singers were performing some of the audience had been known to masturbate in their seats and attendants had to go round slapping their hands with a ruler. He also went on to say that when Elvis Presley wore tight jeans he had a piece of rubber pipe down the inside of his trousers, and to demonstrate this the man drew an imaginary line down the inside of his crutch.

2. There was an American performer who was describing the effects of this type of music on people, and quoted how he had been performing along with a group of American Marines, who were a disciplined body, but he had sent out and obtained a large doll and invited these Marines to destroy it — pull it to pieces. This they had done and, this American said, in effect 'kicked the piss out of it'.

3. A coloured singer, Jimmy Hendrix, held his guitar whilst he was playing it directly in front of his groin and oscillated his body against it, and his strumming motion with his hand was exaggerated from time to time up and down the finger-board of the instrument in a manner which could be described as simulating masturbation. Also, he ended up with the guitar flat on the stage, kneeling astride it and appeared to be plucking at the strings and vibrating lever in such a manner that simulated both masturbation and sexual intercourse with the guitar.

4. There was a quick flash of a scene early in this programme where a North Vietnamese was shot through the head and he fell to the ground and blood was seen to be running from the wound. There was also a scene where an African youth was seen to be running whilst on fire.

I must add that I do not particularly like the most extreme types of 'pop' music such as this anyway, but the young people, knowing a programme about 'pop' music was being shown would wish to see it, and other people in the house at the time would put up with looking at it; therefore, seeing incidents such as I have described I am quite sure they were likely to outrage public decency affecting the majority of ordinary viewers.

As weighty as the evidence for *All My Loving*'s capacity to corrupt the innocent seemed to be, the DPP was not persuaded by it. But even though the reply the chief constable received was not entirely to his liking, it did at least supply some scope for future action.

Letter from Chief Constable John Barnett

9th January, 1969

Dear Mrs. Whitehouse,

I am sending herewith 3 copies of a letter from
the Director of Public Prosecutions relative to the
indecent material which was reported to me recently. I
am surprised at the attitude he has taken as I would
have felt there was sufficient evidence available to
warrant a charge. However, it is satisfactory to have
established the way in which the B.B.C. can be brought
to book should there be another instance where sufficient
evidence is available. I should be glad if you would
let me know of any such circumstance which comes to your
knowledge and I will arrange for statements to be taken
and a further report sent to the Director.

I hope that all goes well with you.

Kind regards,

J. Barnett

Enclosed letter from the DPP

6th January, 1969

Dear Sir,

British Broadcasting Corporation.

With reference to previous correspondence, I have now
received Counsel's Opinion, and the Director is prepared
to endorse the advice given by Counsel that where the
evidence is sufficient a charge of conspiracy to corrupt
morals or to outrage public decency could be considered.

There would appear to be avenues for proceedings
either at the source of the broadcast or in places where
it was received.

The Director would be prepared to consider whether he
should institute criminal proceedings in appropriate
cases, but in the instant matter, assuming that the
incidents referred to in your letter were, in effect,

isolated incidents in the course of the programme,
they would not of themselves be sufficient to warrant a
prosecution.
  Yours faithfully,

  Accordingly, by the time news broke of *All My Loving*'s
scheduled repeat, six months later, NVALA's legal eagles were
hovering.

Letter from NVALA solicitors to the BBC

16th May, 1969

'All My Loving'
  We are instructed by the National Viewers' and
Listeners' Association with regard to the proposal
to repeat a broadcast under the above title in a BBC
programme next Sunday.
  The programme in question contained a sequence
portraying Jimie Handrix which caused widespread disgust
when it was first shown. Our clients have, we understand,
already been in communication with the BBC. They have
been informed that it is intended that this sequence
should remain in the broadcast on Sunday, and they have
expressed their very great concern at this prospect.
  We are instructed to inform you that if there is
a further showing of this sequence our clients will
seriously consider bringing about a prosecution for
conspiracy to corrupt morals and outrage public decency.
Such prosecution might involve a considerable number
of people concerned with the broadcast, and we are
sending this by hand with a copy to the Producer and
to the Solicitor in order that if the broadcasting
of the sequence is not stopped, the BBC may have the
opportunity of passing on to all those concerned in the
broadcast this warning of the possible consequences.
  Yours faithfully,
  C.C Tony Palmer, Esq; The Solicitor, BBC

This threat, like many (but not all) of Mary Whitehouse's legal menaces, ultimately proved to be an empty one, the DPP responding to a further approach by noting acidly that 'there appear to be only four letters from the public expressing disapproval of either of the two showings of this programme'. Yet a precedent of recourse to the courts had (in theory, if not in practice) been established. The path was clear for her later accession to the self-appointed position of 'Director of Private Prosecutions', and one NVALA supporter at least was mightily pleased.

Letter from NVALA supporter

19th May, 1969

Dear Mrs. Whitehouse,
  All power to your elbow as VALA undertakes legal action against the B.B.C. for showing 'All My Loving'.
  My view of it is that it consisted mainly of an exhibition of symbolic masturbations. One can sympathise with those whose make up obliges them to this sort of exhibitionism. But as the symptom of a pathological disease of a sick society it ought not to have been pumped into people's homes. The film was depraved and depraving.
  I am writing to my M.P. and to the Postmaster General.
  Yours Sincerely,

Chairmen of the BBC are not people towards whom it is a natural human instinct to feel warmth and respect. Yet the experience of sorting through Mary Whitehouse's collected correspondence is sometimes liable to reveal them in an unexpectedly sympathetic light. For all the initial offence that any fan of Jimi Hendrix's 'hypnotic techniques' must initially register at the following summation of the *All My Loving* affair by the BBC chairman Lord Hill, his letter to Quintin Hogg might be taught

in TV executive correspondence courses as an object lesson in
how to combine distaste for popular culture with custodianship
of its best interests.

Letter from Lord Hill to Quintin Hogg MP, QC

16th June, 1969

In my letter of 6th June I promised to write to you
again after looking into the complaint from Mrs.
Whitehouse about the 'Omnibus' programme, 'All My
Loving'.

The BBC first showed Tony Palmer's film, 'All My
Loving', last November on BBC-1. Those responsible
considered it carefully before deciding to show it, for
they knew that it contained material which might offend
some viewers. But at the same time they considered that
'All My Loving' was a serious documentary study of the
world of pop music and its place on the contemporary
scene. Although some viewers complained at the time,
their numbers were not very great and the television
critics of the national press generally recognised the
programme's documentary value.

Mrs. Whitehouse is concerned about the sequence
showing a performer called Jimi Hendrix. I find sweaty,
gyrating and noisy performances like his repulsive; so
I imagine do you. But that, it seems, is what some pop
music is about and pop music was the subject of the
documentary. I did not, however, find the performance
objectionable in terms of sexual references. It is
certainly possible to interpret his performance as
sexually descriptive once the idea has been put into
one's head, but I should be very surprised if it were
interpreted by many viewers in a way which would justify
it being described as obscene.

Our own concern about the programme was related to
another aspect — its use of short sections of newsreel
film to illustrate the violent society out of which

pop music derives and which it, in some ways, reflects.
Personally I didn't like seeing that material used in
the way it was. However, this was Mr. Palmer's view of
the world of pop, not mine, and as such it was well
informed, honest and thought provoking. I would guess
that if you saw the film you would probably share my view
of it.

  Yours Sincerely,
  Lord Hill of Luton

To view the evolution of pop music through the filter of the
Mary Whitehouse archive is to be obliged to give reluctant
credence to the authorised (although at the time of writing
slightly unfashionable) version of our cultural history – widely
adhered to by those who were the right age to make the best
of the former decade's opportunities – which depicts the sixties as the time when the great battles were fought, and the
seventies as a grubby afterthought of novelty singles and glam
rock. From the insurrectionary heights of Jimi Hendrix, the
Doors and the Rolling Stones, New Year's Day 1973 found
Mary Whitehouse reduced to complaining about . . . Chuck
Berry's Ding-a-Ling.

Letter to the director general of the BBC

1 January, 1973

Dear Mr. Curran,

  Now that the controversy over the pop record, 'Ding-
a-ling' has died down, we feel it important that you
should understand our reasons for criticising the 'Top
of the Pops' presentation of this disc.

  Our complaint was based on the objections coming to us
not only from parents, but from teachers. One teacher
told us of how she found a class of small boys with
their trousers undone, singing the song and giving it
the indecent interpretation which — in spite of all the

hullaballoo — is so obvious. She was, by no means, the
only one with experiences of this kind. Parents too were
very upset by the stories their children were bringing
home about the actions which were accompanying the
singing of this song amongst their friends.
    I tell you this, not to justify our complaint,
but because I feel sure that in your position of
responsibility, you would wish to know. We trust you
will agree with us that it is no part of the function of
the BBC to be the vehicle of songs which stimulate this
kind of behaviour — indeed quite the reverse.
    Yours Sincerely,
    Mary Whitehouse

One of Mary Whitehouse's favourite tricks was to refer neu-
trally to 'controversies' that she herself had generated as if they
were simply historical facts of which all must take cognisance.
Another staple tactic – in some ways, the complementary opposite of the first one – was to modestly allow herself to be given
credit for changes in broadcasting policy which she had not in
fact been responsible for.

After almost a decade of answering her letters, Charles Curran was sufficiently wise to these ruses to call her out on both
of them in the space of a single communication. Although not
renowned as the wittiest of the BBC's director generals, Curran's
upcoming reference to 'My Ding-a-Ling''s 'clear account of the
contraption in question including bells' suggests the existence
of a drier sense of humour than he has previously been given
credit for.

Reply from the director general

21st December, 1972

Dear Mrs Whitehouse,
    Thank you for your letter of 27th November, already

acknowledged by my secretary, with which you enclosed
part of a letter from yourself to the Minister of Posts
and Telecommunications, with whom you had registered your
protest about the broadcasting of Chuck Berry's rendering
of the song 'My Ding-a-ling' in 'Top of the Pops'.

This record has been among the most popular of
the records on sale in recent weeks to the public
in this country, and it has held a similar position
of popularity in the United States; the BBC aims to
broadcast all the most popular records on current
release, and in programmes such as 'Top of the Pops'
there is a clear expectation that it will do so. We do
not, however, accept a record for broadcasting, if we
consider it to be in any way corrupting or frightening
or disturbing for young people.

'My Ding-a-ling' begins with such a clear account
of the contraption in question including bells, that
although the possibility of a double entendre was
recognised, we decided that it could be broadcast at
the discretion of producers according to the context
and character of their programmes. We did not think it
would disturb or emotionally agitate its listeners and
we believe that the innuendo is, at worst, on the level
of seaside postcards or music hall humour.

After you had made your public protest about this
song a number of other people wrote to the BBC to say
that they agreed with you. But more than twice as many
wrote expressing strong disagreement with your attitude.
Some of them, I should add, had gained the erroneous
impression that a change in the presentation of the
record in 'Top of the Pops' — the normal production
practice when the same record is featured for several
weeks running — had been brought about because of your
representations, and they were clearly very angry about
it. The Chuck Berry version was broadcast again in
'Top of the Pops' on 14th December. I have noted with
interest the question which has been widely asked as
to whether the record would have remained in a high

position in the charts for such a long time without
the publicity attendant upon the publication of your
comments.
  Yours sincerely,
  (Charles Curran)

Where the rock 'n' roll rebels of the sixties could conceive of
themselves as agents of social change with a relatively straight
face, by the early seventies an insulating layer of camp appeared
to have crept in between what they said and what they actually
meant. This process seemed to have somehow escaped Mary
Whitehouse's eagle eye, and in the new irony-friendly context of
the 1970s, her determination to take every word of every pop
song's lyrics at face value could often leave her looking a little
foolish, as in this communication with Bill Cotton (who was,
among his other accomplishments, Fearne Cotton's grandad's
cousin).

Letter to BBC head of light entertainment

21 August, 1972.

Dear Mr. Cotton,
  I am writing to express the gravest concern over the
publicity which has been given to Alice Cooper's record
'School's Out'. For weeks now 'Top of the Pops' has
given gratuitous publicity to a record which can only
be described as anti-law and order. Because of this
millions of young people are now imbibing a philosophy
of violence and anarchy. This is surely utterly
irresponsible in a social climate which grows ever more
violent.
  It is our view that if there is increasing violence in
the schools during the coming term, the BBC will not be
able to evade their share of the blame.
  Yours sincerely,
  (Mrs) Mary Whitehouse.

Mary Whitehouse's exaggerated perception of the potentially incendiary impact of Alice Cooper's 'School's Out' (the Director of Public Prosecutions does not seem to have felt it necessary to even dignify the letter printed at the start of this chapter with a response) can perhaps be explained in the context of her earlier experiences as a head teacher. However, she had no such occupational excuse when it came to her apocalyptic reading of Sweet's 'Teenage Rampage'.

Letter to head of BBC Radio

13th January, 1974.

Dear Mr. Trethowan,

I am writing with regard to a 'pop' record currently being played on radio, namely, 'TEENAGE RAMPAGE' sung by SWEET.

The words include the following —

'All over the land, the kids are out to get the upper hand, They're out on the streets, to turn on the heat, And soon they'll be completely in command.

Imagine the sensation at the teenage occupation. At thirteen they'll be learning, but at fourteen they'll be violent [the actual lyric stated 'Burning' — still an alarming prospect, but a much better rhyme]. Join the revolution NOW, NOW, NOW (crescendo) Get yourself a constitution, turn another page In the teenage rampage NOW NOW NOW' etc.

This record, thanks to the publicity given to it is now No 1. in the charts.

Yesterday I rang your duty officer about the matter and asked that it should be brought to your attention immediately. I hope you will agree that the playing of such a record is wholly inadvisable in present circumstances [by this Mary meant the beginning of the three-day week] and look forward to hearing that you have seen fit to ban any further transmission of this record.

Yours sincerely,
Mary Whitehouse

It is easy for pop-culture-literate readers to laugh at Mary Whitehouse's determination to perceive an actual revolutionary message in glam rock's pantomime posturing, and that is no reason for them not to do it. Yet isn't it also possible that the joke was on us?

Far from being alarmed at her attempt to censor his freedom of expression, Alice Cooper's autobiography told of him sending her a bunch of flowers in gratitude for all the extra exposure her campaigning had bought him. As funny as this cynical gesture was, might it not also be appropriate to be saddened by how far short rock 'n' roll was now falling of Mary Whitehouse's high ideals with regard to its capacity for political subversion? The easy cynicism of Ian Trethowan's reply rather compounds this impression – the line 'totally empty of real content' is especially devastating.

Reply from the head of BBC Radio

16th January, 1974

Dear Mrs. Whitehouse,
  Thank you for your letter of 13th January. Careful consideration has been given to 'Teenage Rampage', but we have not felt we would be justified in banning this record from the air. Nor do we feel it would have been right for us to have excluded the recent recording from 'Top of the Pops'.
  As you will know, we are not deterred from placing a ban on any record, however high it may be in the charts or however popular the group associated with it. Bans in the past have been placed on records by the Beatles and the Rolling Stones. However, in this case, although I doubt if anyone would think the lyrics

particularly distinguished (and you know I am given to
understatement), they do not identify any target for
'the revolution' and we believe that young people, while
possibly enjoying the easy beat of the music, will be
unaffected by the words, since they are totally empty of
real content — like all too much pop music.

This is by no means the first record of its kind and
certainly past examples have proved harmless in their
effect. Indeed, we believe that to ban this record would
have the sole result of making young people feel it <u>did</u>
have significance, as well as a meaning, which, in my
view, neither exists nor was intended.

Yours sincerely,

Ian Trethowan

By a further faint but satisfying irony, when a new musical
movement did finally come along that threatened (at least in
its own mind) everything Mrs Whitehouse stood for, she was
looking firmly in the opposite direction. In her eye-catchingly
titled 1977 volume *Whatever Happened to Sex?*, the Sex Pistols' fairly historic run-in with Bill Grundy merits only a single
line, while Mary concentrates her fire on the pop world's true
subversive enemy within – the sub-Bay City Rollers teeny-bop
act Flintlock.

To be fair, Mary Whitehouse was not the only cultural commentator of the time to overestimate the significance of the
latter superficially harmless ensemble's appearance on the ITV
kids' show *Pauline's Quirkes*. In support of her argument, she
quotes at length from the strangely splenetic contemporary
verdict of the *Times*'s TV reviewer Alan Coren: 'the leitmotif
of yesterday's miasma concerned the genitalia of a pop group
called Flintlock . . . I really do not know which I most hate,
the ruining of the language, the pandering to the lowest levels
of intelligence, the gods offered for idolatry, or the smut. All I
know is, I hate.'

If you were asked to try and represent the contemptuous mood of Coren's response to Flintlock in a song, the one you'd have to pick would be the Sex Pistols' 'Pretty Vacant'. By 1976–7, it seems, the anger and frustration to which punk gave vent was seeping from all sorts of unexpected faultlines in British society, and while it would be stretching the point a little to claim that Mary Whitehouse was something of a punk rocker herself, her fearless determination to get up the nose of the broadcasting establishment certainly struck a chord with one group of spiky-haired malcontents.

If you were asked to pick the song that best sums up Mary Whitehouse's relationship with pop music, the obvious choice would be Pink Floyd's 'Pigs (Three Different Ones)' – a track on the dinosaur rockers' 1977 album *Animals*. 'Hey you White-house, Ha-ha, charade you are,' spat Roger Waters contemptu-ously. 'You house-proud town mouse . . . all tight lips and cold feet . . . You gotta stem the evil tide and keep it all on the inside.' Mary took legal advice as to whether to sue, but was advised that a court case would have little chance of success, even if she could prove that the still more vitriolic previous verse (describ-ing an unnamed 'bus-stop ratbag' who was 'hot stuff with a hatpin') was actually about her.

There's another dark-horse candidate though, and that's the one my money would be on. The *Clockwork Orange*-inspired Ipswich punk band the Adicts would not be the first people you'd look to for a more nuanced interpretation of Mary White-house's life and work. Yet their 1981 debut album – coinciden-tally titled *Songs of Praise* (one of Mary Whitehouse's favourite TV programmes, even if it had initially been commissioned by Sir Hugh Greene) – contains what is undoubtedly Mary's finest pop moment.

Not only do the Adicts supply a fair and respectful summary of Whitehouse's life and work – 'She don't like pornography when it's on TV . . . when she sees all those nudes, she'll speak out and say that's very rude' – they cap it off with an unexpected emotional declaration. 'I love Mary Whitehouse,' insisted singer Keith 'Monkey' Warren, '[but] She don't love me.'

Copy of a telegram sent to The Prime Minister on
2/1/67 by Mrs Mary Whitehouse on behalf of the Clean Up
T.V. Camapign and the National Viewers and Listeners
Association.

SOMEONE ,SOMEWHERE HAS TO TAKE RESPONSIBILITY FOR STANDARDS
OF B.B.C. PROGRAMMES. IN SPITE OF THE GOVERNORS ACCEPTED
OBLIGATION TO " EXCLUDE FROM THE EARLIER PART OF THE EVENING
PROGRAMMES WHICH MIGHT BE UNSUITABLE FOR CHILDREN", 'TILL DEATH
US DO PART' 7.30 THIS EVENING WAS DIRTY,BLASPHEMOUS AND FULL OF
BAD LANGUAGE.
THE POSTMASTER GENERAL SEEMS POWERLESS TO TAKE ACTION. THE
DIRECTOR GENERAL SEEMS DETERMINED TO PROVOKE AND INSULT THE
VIEWING PUBIC. WILL YOU TAKE WHATEVER ACTION SEEMS NECESSARY.

Copy of telegram sent to Harold Wilson

5. Mary and Parliament

If Mary Whitehouse could have got what she would have regarded as satisfaction from Sir Hugh Greene, neither CUTV nor later NVALA would have ever needed to solicit the assistance of MPs. In the absence of any Damascene conversion on Greene's part to her gospel of deference and decorum, her approach to the House of Commons throughout the rest of the sixties would basically be the one she laid out in her speech at the Town Hall meeting of May 1964 – that the BBC was a rogue arm of government which needed to be given a disciplinary Chinese burn by more directly politically accountable rivals.

In the run-up to the general election of October 1964, she mobilised CUTV supporters to pressurise prospective parliamentarians. 'I have seen it in the papers that the votes of the women will decide which way this Election goes,' she had encouraged the faint of heart in that same Birmingham speech, 'and I am quite sure the vast majority of women are much more interested in people than we are in party.' The conclusion to which she carried this thought would help define a template still applied in Britain and especially (and often with fairly grim consequences) in America by single-issue protest groups.

'Over these next months,' Whitehouse continued, 'I feel that we could challenge our Members of Parliament and our respective candidates to come right out into the open on this question and to ask them straight out if they are going to be courageous and brave enough to deal with this thing in our midst.' The huge sheaf of replies Mary received from MPs in this and subsequent years inscribe an arc from wholehearted support (especially from

her local MP Jasper More and the subsequent NVALA stalwart
Major James 'Jimmy' Dance), through polite brush-offs, to the
toe-curling condescension of the Sheffield Labour MP Richard
Winterbottom (see below) and outright contempt from those –
like the Scottish Labour MP Norman Buchan (see further below) –
who seemed to take her criticism of the BBC as a personal affront.

Letter from Richard Winterbottom MP

1st December, 1964.

Dear Mrs. Whitehouse,
  Thank you for your letter of the 22nd November.
  Sorry I called you a dear old lady. Please eliminate
the word old and may I call you a dear lady?
  I am afraid I cannot agree with you on many of the
things that you advocate. There are enough avenues
to register complaints already and knowing Advisory
Councils of the BBC and what they say and do, prompts
me to say that I have not seen any of your literature
or heard anything about you that has not been already
debated and discussed in the Advisory Councils of
the BBC. Already your pamphlet points out some very
effective ways of protesting without going to the length
of another questionable type of democratic committee to
deal with the affairs of broadcasting.
  I am not satisfied with things as they are, but I am
not satisfied that your way will clear them.
  Yours sincerely,
  R.E. Winterbottom, MP

Letter from Norman Buchan MP

29th June, 1965

Dear Mrs. Whitehouse,
  Thank you for your letter. I must say that I find the
campaign which your organisation and others are waging

against the Director General of the B.B.C., at the
present time in extremely questionable taste. I feel
too that you might gain more support for your standpoint
regarding morality if what looks very much like a smear
campaign were conducted with rather more decency.
  Yours sincerely,
  Norman Buchan, MP

After her encouraging response from a Tory Postmaster General in the course of what she jauntily termed 'L'affaire Swizzlewick', Mary Whitehouse was disappointed to get a considerably frostier reception from the new Labour minister Anthony Wedgwood Benn. As is so often the way with the British constitution, the framework of institutional checks and balances within which the BBC operated was a complex network of overlapping spheres of influence, unspoken rules, and powers of last resort which in an ideal world (or pretty much any world in which people actually lived) would never be called upon.

Much to Whitehouse's frustration, Tony Benn regarded his theoretical capacity to interfere in the policy decisions of the nation's broadcasting networks as falling very much into the latter category. When she challenged him to reconcile the BBC's lack of accountability with democratic principles ('At present Audience Research – undertaken only on internal requests – remains unpublished; the number of complaints about any particular programme are not published; letters are ignored, or used as a vehicle to justify Producers' policy, and there is no established vehicle through which the voice of the public may be heard'), he countered by raising the spectre of a far more serious threat to democracy.

Extract from Hansard, 10 November 1964

Oral Answers (by The Postmaster-General, Mr Anthony Wedgwood
Benn)

WIRELESS AND TELEVISION PROGRAMMES

MR SHEPHERD asked the Postmaster-General whether he is aware that television programmes continue to give offence by reason of the use of questionable material; and if he will use his powers under the Television Act to require the British Broadcasting Corporation and the Independent Television Authority not to send programmes containing such material.

MR BENN: The powers of the Postmaster-General have always been regarded as reserve powers, for use only in the last resort. Both broadcasting organisations are independent in matters of programme content; and their independence has been repeatedly reaffirmed by successive Governments. I regard the maintenance of this fundamental principle as essential.

MR SHEPHERD: Is not the right hon. Gentleman aware that much of the material broadcast in recent years has been damaging to our national prestige? Will he make these organisations realise that they are national institutions and that we do not want our national image to be damaged by pandering too much to the long-haired young men?

MR BENN: I think the hon. Gentleman will agree that it is very unlikely that everyone could agree about the quality of certain programmes. The governors of the B.B.C. and the members of the Independent Television Authority are appointed for the purpose which the hon. Gentleman has in mind. It would be wrong for me to use my powers, though I have them, as any Postmaster-General has, in matters of this kind.

SIR G. NICHOLSON: There is a real problem here. There are occasions when the most offensive language is used, and no possible redress can be obtained. We are told that this matter is outside the scope of Government intervention, and that script writers must be given free rein for their artistic urges. Nonetheless, great offence is caused, and some scandal. Will the right hon. Gentleman see that something is done about this matter?

MR BENN: If, by asking whether I will see that something is done, the hon. Gentleman means will I exercise personal censorship over B.B.C. and I.T.A. programmes, the answer is 'No'.

SIR G. NICHOLSON: I did not say that.

MR BENN: The question could mean only censorship over things which I, in the exercise of my judgment, thought to be undesirable and worthy of censorship. If the hon. Gentleman thinks more about the problems involved in trying to do what he wants me to do, he will realise that it is much better to leave it to the board of governors of the B.B.C. and members of the I.T.A.

A week later, the threat of 'pandering too much to the long-haired young men' was no longer specifically in play, but the willingness of Conservative MPs to echo Mary Whitehouse's battle cries (in this case, the demand for the creation of a 'Viewers' Council') was very much in evidence. Tony Benn's resolute defence of the status quo – and this is not a sentence one gets to write every day – showed no sign of faltering.

Extract from Hansard, 17 November 1964

Oral Answers (by the Postmaster-General, Mr Anthony Wedgwood Benn)
WIRELESS AND TELEVISION PROGRAMMES (CONTENT)
MR DEMPSEY asked the Postmaster-General if he will establish a viewers' council to advise on the suitability of television programmes; and if he will make a statement.

MR BENN: No, Sir. Programme content is the responsibility of the Board of Governors of the B.B.C. and members of the I.T.A. The establishment by me of a viewers' council would tend to diminish the authority of the two broadcasting authorities and, in consequence, their capacity to discharge their responsibility. Also, it would raise doubt as to where responsibility lay: with the broadcasting authorities, or with the council. Each authority has already its own General Advisory Council, and other advisory committees, through which it can sound opinion on its services.

MR DEMPSEY: Yes, but is the Minister aware that these so-called advisory councils have in no way halted the growth of suggestive entertainment and of the glorification of thuggery in television, or the unsuitability of programmes at school holiday times? Would he not agree that it would be far more effective if we established a council from a very good cross-section of the British community to advise these organisations and my right hon. Friend's good self on television presentations?

MR BENN: No, Sir. The fact that an advisory council does not give advice of the kind the hon. Gentleman would like it to give is not a prima facie case for setting up another advisory committee.

MR JENNINGS: Would it not be advisable if the right hon. Gentleman were to look a little closer at some of the programmes which are broadcast on television? Has he, for instance, seen the reputed successor to 'That Was The Week That Was'? Does he realise that some of that programme is in extremely bad taste and in some cases is almost blasphemous, and that in an incident last week—

HON. MEMBERS: Speech.

MR DEPUTY-SPEAKER: Order. This supplementary question is getting a little long.

MR RANKIN: Too long.

MR BENN: I think that the hon. Gentleman had better think this through to its logical conclusion. There are reserve powers invested in the Postmaster-General. If they are to be exercised by the Postmaster-General that means that whoever occupies my office would have the power, on the hon. Gentleman's suggestion, to censor individual programmes if he thought, in his judgment — for it could not be anyone else's judgment — that they were offensive to taste, or biased politically. If I were to exercise my judgment in censoring a programme which I thought politically biased or offensive, one of the first people, I think, who would object would be the hon. Gentleman himself, for our views would not coincide.

Over the next few years, Mary Whitehouse would continue to badger Tony Benn and his Labour successors Edward Short and John Stonehouse, but with very little success. While they proved stoically resistant to the allure of her traditional ice-breaker – a copy of the *Viewer and Listener* – she also reached out to a succession of other government departments in a sustained attempt to convince them that in lieu of the Postmaster General or the director general of the BBC having any willingness to do their duty, surely the urgency of the current situation demanded that [insert name of politician concerned] must now take the matter out of their hands?

Whether this meant arguing that the Home Office should take responsibility for the question of whether Peter Watkins's terrifying post-nuclear drama *The War Game* should be shown, or the Minister of Health ought to intervene to stiffen the BBC's resolve in the matter of the 'pre-marital experience', her approach was a characteristic blend of persistence and urgency.

Copy of telegram to the Home Secretary Sir Frank Soskice

6th October, 1965

In view of the reported statement ('The Sunday Express', 5/9/65) by Mr. Leonard Lozman, Civil Defence officer of Tonbridge, Kent, that the B.B.C. film 'The War Game' would 'have a terrible effect on the public morale', we urgently submit that the decision as to whether or not this film should be shown is one which should be taken by the Home Office and not by the B.B.C.

This would seem too serious a matter to be treated as entertainment. For a producer to be allowed, as now appears possible, to prejudge the effectiveness of our Civil Defence Services, or the ability of the British people to re-act with courage, initiative and control in a crisis, surely goes far beyond the responsibility which should be taken by, or given to, anyone in such a position.

This programme could have a serious effect upon the morale of people at home, and, should it later be shown abroad, upon the image of the British public throughout the world.

However, if a statement could be issued showing that this programme has the approval of the Home Office, and is indeed a fair and factual representation carrying official approval then the public would, we believe, accept its necessity and be re-assured.

Yours faithfully,

Mary Whitehouse

Letter to Kenneth Robinson, Minister of Health

2nd November, 1965

Dear Sir,

  We would ask you to consider making a direct approach
to the B.B.C. to support Sir George Godber's appeal for
an all-out attack on the problem of venereal disease.

  There has been a considerable 'cleaning up' of the
plays on the B.B.C in response to public demand, but
there is a trend developing towards presenting near-
pornographic material under the guise of education and
culture, as in 'The American Way of Sex' and 'Picasso'.

  Last night's programme in '24 Hours' on contraceptive
clinics was strongly biased towards pre-marital
experience, and exercised censorship against the doctor
taking part in the programme, and so against the great
majority of young people who wish to live clean and
straight, and know how to do so.

  The social and political consequences of promiscuity
on the health of the nation could be so grave, that
we are of the opinion that the time for drastic action
has come. We believe that the urgency of the situation
is such that responsibility for the policies of the
Director General of the B.B.C can no longer be side-
stepped by Ministers of The Crown.

  Yours faithfully,
  Mary Whitehouse

  As if this situation was not already urgent enough, the BBC
decided to make it far worse by broadcasting one of the most
celebrated (alongside the same director's *Cathy Come Home*) of
all the Wednesday Plays – Ken Loach's adaptation of Nell Dunn's
Up the Junction (not to be confused with the film version of a
couple of years later, in which Dennis Waterman starred). Viewing figures were a stratospheric ten million, and the BBC received
almost four hundred complaints. Where most critics applauded

a vivid and compassionate docudrama highlighting the dangers posed by backstreet abortionists and the consequences of unprotected sex, Mary Whitehouse – along with a good many of her four hundred fellow complainers – saw a shocking slur on the good name of British working-class womanhood.

Further letter to Kenneth Robinson

November 4th, 1965

Dear Sir,

Following our previous letter to you (2/11/65) in which we drew your attention to the failure of the B.B.C. to adopt an attitude of responsibility towards the problem of venereal disease in the country, we would urgently bring to your notice last night's play 'Up the Junction'.

It would appear that the B.B.C. is determined to do everything in its power to present promiscuity as normal.

Having given the impression in Monday's '24 Hours' that the intellectual cream of our young people are overwhelmingly promiscuous, the play 'Up the Junction' last night made the same point about the working girl.

The parents of this country are not prepared to stand by and watch young people exploited for the indulgence of dirty minds. The continual denigration of womanhood is disastrous to our national life.

We would respectfully suggest that no matter how much public money you pour out in an attempt to counteract the physical results of moral decadence, the responsibility of the B.B.C. in these matters will undercut all your effort.

We are anxious to lay our concern and constructive suggestions before you personally and would be grateful for the opportunity to bring a delegation of responsible people to meet you.

Yours faithfully,

Mary Whitehouse

Perhaps unsurprisingly, such an invitation was not forthcoming – not even the promise of 'a delegation of responsible people' could quite swing it. This is not to say that the Houses of Parliament proved entirely resistant to Mary Whitehouse's wiles – quite the reverse, as it was intervention by her new friends in the political elite that would ultimately help her unlock the doors of Broadcasting House.

From the very beginning of her campaign, Whitehouse had found that high-level BBC executives – Hugh Greene in particular – were much more likely to respond positively (or, indeed, at all) to communications that had passed through a parliamentary filter. The contrast between the clubbable courtesy of Sir Hugh Greene's reply to Quintin Hogg and the stonily patrician gaze with which he looked upon Mary's direct letters could hardly be sharper.

Letter from Sir Hugh Greene to Quintin Hogg, QC MP

16th December, 1964.

My dear Hogg,
  I have now been able to look into the circumstances of the programme about which you wrote to me on 7th December after having received correspondence from Mrs. Mary Whitehouse.
  The programme to which she and Mrs. Daley refer was the ninth in a television series addressed to students of between 16 and 19 years of age attending engineering courses at technical colleges. The series is broadcast under the title 'Living in the Present'. Its general intention is to encourage these students to think about various important problems which face people in modern society and this programme on the subject of 'Belief' was intended to stimulate thought about the relevance of religious belief to social behaviour. I think you would agree that this was a worthwhile objective.

   I am not entirely happy about the way the intention
was put into effect, but nothing that was said or
suggested could justify the accusation made by Mrs.
Whitehouse that the original intention was corrupt.
Mrs. Daley makes some fair points, though I think she
goes too far when she infers that this programme was
'propaganda for a definite, and attractive, form of
atheism'. It was not.
   I have arranged for the attention of the producer to
be drawn to the genuine criticisms which could be made
of this programme.
   I return the letters of Mrs. Whitehouse and Mrs.
Daley.
   Yours sincerely,
   (HUGH GREENE)

   The standard BBC and Postmaster General's line – that Mary
Whitehouse was the self-appointed spokeswoman of an organisation that represented no one but herself – was harder to
hold when her criticisms were forwarded by elected representatives. The following letter to Tony Benn from her local MP
confirmed the opening of a second front in NVALA's assault on
Lord Normanbrook's inner sanctum.

Letter to the Postmaster General from Jasper More MP

8th October, 1965

Dear Mr Benn,
   I am writing to you on behalf of a constituent of
mine, Mrs. Whitehouse of Claverley, near Wolverhampton,
to whom you wrote on the 22nd September in reply to a
letter of hers of the 11th September.
   Mrs. Whitehouse, as I think you are aware, is one
of the organisers of a campaign for improving the
quality of television programmes — a campaign which has
attracted enormous support throughout the country.

The object of Mrs. Whitehouse's letter was to ask for
a meeting. Your reply suggests that a meeting would
serve no useful purpose because apparently you cannot
accept Mrs. Whitehouse's letters as reflecting anything
but the personal opinions of the organisers.

I must express my regret that you should think it
sufficient to write in such terms. Obviously in a
movement which has attracted the support of, I believe,
hundred of thousands of people, there may be many who
have given their signature without much thought to the
issues involved. But it is really insulting to one of
the chief organisers to suggest that she knows so little
about the movement and the broad views of its supporters
that her letters can only be regarded as representing
her individual opinion.

It is, however, now up to me to decide whether it
would, in fact, serve any purpose if I were to agree to
meet Lord Normanbrook myself. Have you any views?

Yours sincerely,

Jasper More, MP

By this time, Whitehouse had already heard the good news
from one of her most stalwart allies in Westminster – the
Bromsgrove Tory MP James Dance – that a parliamentary delegation to put what was essentially her case to BBC top brass
was looking increasingly practicable.

Letter from James Dance MP

20th July, 1965

Dear Mrs Whitehouse,

I was so sorry to hear you have not been too well, and
I do hope you are feeling better now. I can understand
the strain of all your hard work and organising, but it
must help when you see the success of all your efforts.

In confidence (not for publication) we in the House
are in touch with the B.B.C. and I am hopeful that in

the near future we will have a meeting with Sir Hugh
Greene, with a view to having a heart-to-heart with Lord
Normanbrook when we return after the summer recess. We
do, however, feel that it would be wrong to invite Lord
Normanbrook to meet us unless we have all the facts
thoroughly marshalled. So before we meet him I will get
in touch with you for first-hand eye witness information
on the type of programme which is causing offence.
  Yours sincerely,
  James Dance, MP

As if Jasper More, James Dance and Quintin Hogg did not
make up a sufficiently potent troika of parliamentary allies,
Mary Whitehouse could also call upon the affable advise-
ments of William Deedes. Widely (albeit perhaps erroneously)
thought to be the journalistic inspiration for Evelyn Waugh's
Scoop, and later less disputably identified as the addressee of
Private Eye's 'Dear Bill' letters, Deedes was the perfect person
to tell her how best to go about getting articles in the national
papers.

Reply from William Deedes MP

January 16th, 1966

Dear Mrs. Whitehouse,
  Many thanks for your letter. I will certainly agree
to help on April 30th, and short of some political
cataclysm I undertake to come to Birmingham on that day.
  About the enclosed piece, which I agree is good and
ought to be used. My own view is that your best bet is
to await provocation in one of the National newspapers
and then weigh in with it. They all, from time to time,
have pieces on this subject, and some attack your
movement. If you send it 'dry' so to speak to the 'Daily
Mail' or anyone else, the chances are they will thank
you politically and return it. But if you await a chance

provided by some criticism they print, then you start
some points up. I do not think you will have long to
wait! Anyway, that is my advice.
    All good wishes,
    William Deedes, MP

Deedes was as good as his word and spoke to general acclaim
at NVALA's inaugural annual convention. His justification for
stinging the organisation for the cost of a first-class rail ticket is
a masterclass in *noblesse oblige*.

May 3rd, 1966

Dear Mrs. Whitehouse,
    Thank you so much for your nice letter and even more
for your kind telephone call. I greatly enjoyed the
event and it was really an excellent thing we none of
us said just the same thing. There were some exchanges
today in the House with the Prime Minister about setting
up a Council. They were not memorable, but I cannot help
thinking these will be included in the Government's
white paper [on broadcasting], when it comes. I know
the Post Master General thinks favorably of such a
Council. What part your people played would be difficult
to decide. I sense a good many would prefer to stand a
little back and maintain strict vigilance independently.
I will reflect on this and let you have any thoughts as
they occur.
    The cost of my journey was simply the rail fare
London—Birmingham which was £4 10s. 6d. I considered
traveling second class. In view of the heat and the
crowd you may consider it fortunate I did not!
    Warmest regards,
    William Deedes, MP

With the help of such urbane counsellors, Mary Whitehouse
was learning the ground rules of doing business in the corridors

of power. She would never fully make the transition from out-
sider to insider, but by the time of Lord Normanbrook's death
in June 1967, the BBC's chairman of governors had softened
his stance towards NVALA to the extent of taking confidential
soundings about the possibility of implementing their proposal
for a viewer's council. If only his replacement could be someone
a little more sympathetic (although as one of Winston Churchill's pall-bearers, Lord Normanbrook was hardly an anti-estab-
lishment figure), who knew how much they could achieve?

Letter to the Prime Minister, Harold Wilson

24 June, 1967

Dear Sir,

May we suggest, with respect, that the appointment of
a new Chairman of the Governors of the B.B.C. offers a
most timely opportunity to reconsider the nature of this
most important position.

It is vitally important, for the sake not only of
broadcasting, but of the country as a whole, that there
should be a man in the Chair at the B.B.C., independent
of political pressures, capable and determined to
control the excesses of the present Director General
and a closely connected section of his staff. We would
ask you therefore to appoint a full time Chairman
with a salary sufficiently in excess of the Director
General's as to leave no doubt in anyone's mind who
holds the senior position, and on whose shoulders
the responsibility for the standards and future of
Broadcasting rests.

Finally we feel that it is imperative that you should
understand the far reaching repugnance which exists
in the provinces for much of what has come to be known
as 'swinging London', and for which the B.B.C. appears
to have a predisposition, thus moulding the climate
of opinion rather than reflecting it. It will indeed be

a wise politician, and wise Party, who realises that
the future lies with whoever has the courage to grasp
this nettle, thus ensuring that the B.B.C. remain a
democratic institution serving the best interests of the
nation, and having special concern for the needs of the
growing generation.

  Yours sincerely,

  Mary Whitehouse

The subsequent appointment of Lord Hill – with whom she
had already established a (relatively) harmonious relationship
in his previous job at the Independent Television Association –
left Mary 'delighted'. She was not naive enough to imagine that
her letter had swayed Harold Wilson on its own, speculating
in her diary, 'Why did Harold Wilson do it? Was he afraid that
Greene was gaining power the PM was not prepared for him to
have? . . . Maybe Wilson means to settle the scores which have
been mounting up against him on the screen.'

Whitehouse saw the advent of Lord Hill as the first stage in
a conservative resurgence, but before the great work of rolling
back the frontiers of the permissive society (or at least stopping its seemingly inexorable advance) could begin, a change of
occupant at number 10 Downing Street was going to be called
for. Harold Wilson had always been too shrewd a politician to
treat her with the outright rudeness that had been the BBC's
default setting – 'You have always treated our approaches to
you seriously and with courtesy,' Mary blandished him shame-
lessly in a letter dated New Year's Day, 1968 – but she was
under no illusions about the lack of common ground between
them, otherwise she might have made more effort to tailor the
following sentence from the same festive communication to the
linguistic requirements of its profoundly worldly recipient.

'The coverage given to the "Back Britain" campaign launched
by a group of Surrey typists', Whitehouse informed Wilson

piously, 'has strikingly demonstrated what a mass media can do to spread the new mood and sense of purpose to which the Archbishop of Canterbury has called us.' She might just as well have added 'Put that in your pipe and smoke it.'

The general election of June 1970 brought the Conservative victory she had been waiting for since 1964. Edward Heath showed every sign of being the kind of man Mary Whitehouse could work with, as did Chris Chataway, the former Olympic middle- and long-distance runner turned Tory MP Heath had appointed as the new Minister of Posts and Telecommunications (a rejigged version of Tony Benn's old job as Postmaster General). Very much the Sebastian Coe of his day, Chataway had just pipped Roger Bannister to be voted the inaugural BBC Sports Personality of the Year in 1954.

Letter to the Rt. Hon. Edward Heath

27th June, 1970

Dear Mr. Heath,

May I offer you most warm congratulations on your election victory? It was a wonderful and almost miraculous event. It was surely the result not only of your own policies and personal integrity, but of the deep longing in the hearts of so many people to have done with the tawdriness and compromise of the last years.

I think I have mentioned to you before that my experience traveling and speaking around the country has taught me that concern over the libertarianism of the 'permissive' society ran even deeper than anxiety over our economic state. I doubt if people have ever prayed so sincerely about the result of an election as they did over this one, and it is a matter of enormous gratitude that you now hold the office you do.

Thank you very much indeed for your encouraging and thoughtful reply to my election letter. Now that Mr. Christopher Chataway's appointment has been announced we

are hoping that it will be possible to meet with him at
an early occasion. Perhaps you would be interested to
see a letter which I have sent to him to-day?
  With very best wishes for the future.
  Yours sincerely,
  (Mrs) Mary Whitehouse.

Unfortunately, Mary then made a tactical error to which
she was often prone at moments of great optimism and excite-
ment. She released an overconfident briefing (transmitted to a
national audience via a *Daily Telegraph* article entitled 'Plan to
cut Television Obscenity'). Just three days had passed, and the
honeymoon already threatened to end before it had even begun.
Luckily, Mary Whitehouse had a strategy already in place
for dealing with these kinds of tricky situations – she denied
all knowledge of the intimations she had given the press and
blamed the whole thing on the media.

Further letter to the Rt. Hon. Edward Heath

30th June, 1970

Dear Mr. Heath,
  I was rather troubled by the reports in the 'Sunday
Telegraph' and yesterday's 'Daily Telegraph' regarding The
Government's attitude to the work of this Association. We
would like to assure you that at no time did I say that
we had arranged to meet Mr. Chataway as reported in the
'Sunday Telegraph', and I did manage to get that corrected
in yesterday's 'Daily Telegraph'. Neither did I infer that
you had expressed specific support for the four points
raised in our Election letter to you though, of course, I
did express my satisfaction at the last paragraph in your
letter to me as quoted in yesterday's 'Daily Telegraph'.
  I would be sorry indeed if either you, or Mr.
Chataway, felt that we were in any way responsible for
the assumptions in these articles.

I am enclosing the current issue of 'The Viewer &
Listener' in which we have set out, in toto, the text
of your letter to me. I shall be sending a copy of
this letter to Mr. Chataway in order to put the record
straight with him also.

Yours sincerely,

(Mrs) Mary Whitehouse.

Crisis duly averted, Mary took the utmost care to ensure she
didn't make the same mistake again.

Letter to Chris Chataway MP

25th August, 1970

Dear Mr Chataway,

I am very grateful to you for sparing the time to meet
me on the 7th September.

You will, I think, be aware that the press took
some interest in the fact that we had asked for the
opportunity to meet you. I have not told the press that
we are to meet, though they are anxious to know if, and
when, this is likely to happen.

I realise, of course, that our discussion will
be confidential and that no statement would be made
afterwards, except by mutual agreement. I would,
however, be grateful for your permission to tell the
press that this interview has now been arranged.

Yours sincerely,

(Mrs) Mary Whitehouse

Reply from Chris Chataway's private secretary

26th August, 1970

Dear Mrs Whitehouse,

The Minister has asked me to thank you for your letter
of 25 August.

He agrees that you may tell the press, if they ask,

that you are meeting him on 7 September for a confidential
discussion. But he is against any general press release
either before or after the meeting.
  Yours sincerely,
  (J. M. ELLIS)
  Private Secretary

  Once the minister had been assured of her discretion, the
meeting could finally go ahead. The gates of the Palace of Westminster (or at least the Ministry of Posts and Telecommunications on Waterloo Bridge) opened up before her, and Mary
Whitehouse was in. The legislative phase of NVALA's national
clean-up operation could now begin.

  On 11 December 1970, she wrote to tell Edward Heath how
'tremendously impressed' she had been with the TV broadcast
of his speech to the Conservative Party conference. Sweetening
the deal with a copy of the *Viewer and Listener*, she concluded
with the upbeat assertion that 'the 70's could turn out to be a
most stimulating, as well as challenging, decade.'

20/8/70

The Producer,
"Survival",
Anglia Television.
Norwich.

Dear Sir,
    May I express our very great pleasure in your truly
delightful programme on the beaver? This was a wonderful
effort and it is a great pity that we are not treated to many
more programme of this nature and calibre.

    Our only regret is that it was placed so late at
night - a number of people, who heard from friends about the
programme - have asked me to express the hope that it will be
possible to re-show it at peak viewing time. There is little
doubt,I think, that the audience appreciateion for programmes
of this kind is far higher than is realised by programme makers.
We do hope this will be possible- it would surely be of enormou
interest to viewers of all ages and would fit perfectly into
family viewing time.

                    With best wishes for the future,
                        Yours sincerely,

                            (Mrs) Mary White

Copy of letter from Mary Whitehouse to the producer of Anglia TV's *Survival*

6. Mary and ITV

Where NVALA's activities in the 1960s had been largely driven by Mary Whitehouse's titanic battle of wills with Sir Hugh Greene, the next two decades would see a gradual evening-up of the balance in terms of the relative number of complaints she made to the BBC and to Britain's independent TV companies. The Women of Britain's decision to focus their attention on the former to the virtual exclusion of the latter had been one of the most controversial aspects of CUTV.

The apparently infallible (and in some ways politically progressive) logic of Mary Whitehouse's argument – that as licence-payers the BBC's viewers were essentially shareholders in the organisation, which gave them a particular right to have their views heard – did not stop the occasional angry Labour MP from calling her an ITV stooge. However, no conspiracy theory was necessary to explain the generally more cordial nature of her relations with the recently formed independent companies (commercial television having only arrived in the UK in 1955).

Basically, they were just nicer to her. The following letter from ATV chairman Lew Grade (not only the man who brought Britain *The Prisoner*, *The Muppet Show* and *Jesus of Nazareth*, but also uncle of the subsequent BBC and ITV chairman Sir Michael) is a case in point.

Letter from Lew Grade

April 8th, 1970

Dear Mary Whitehouse,

I am enclosing a reply to your letter of the 6th April.
    I want to say how much I appreciated your telephone
call to me advising me that you were going to write
to me. This meant a great deal to me and I am deeply
grateful.
    Yours sincerely,
    Lew Grade

He doesn't just reply to her letter, he thanks her profusely for
her phone call telling him she was going to send it. To say that
the former Lev Winogradsky was no pushover would be putting
it mildly. Among other things, this cigar-chomping showbiz buc-
caneer will be eternally remembered for saying of his flop 1980
film *Raise the Titanic* 'It would have been cheaper to lower the
Atlantic' (though no thumbnail sketch of his showman's personality would be complete without his reported – albeit possibly
apocryphal – observation to the director of *Jesus of Nazareth*,
Franco Zeffirelli: 'Only twelve disciples? Didn't I tell you I want
this thing to be BIG, BIG, BIG!').
    The actual reply promised above turns out to be an impec-
cably polite and carefully worded rebuff to a Whitehouse complaint about a dangerously liberal-minded new religious affairs
programme. Younger readers may struggle to come to terms
with the fact that they did once have those on ITV.

Reply from Lew Grade

8th April, 1970

Dear Mrs. Whitehouse,
    Thank you for your letter of the 6th April, 1970 and I am
sorry that our programme 'BEYOND BELIEF' has upset you.
    The language used in the 'Good Samaritan' sketch was
strong but not inappropriate to the circumstances. The
words you will recall, were used by a white worker to a
coloured immigrant.

The white man was retelling the Samaritan parable. The
language was, as you say, sometimes robust. So was the
character using it, and I think we were right to allow
it as an essential part of the characterisation. As
a result the man was believable and the message which
emerged of 'Love Thy Neighbour' was loud and clear. A
commendable objective that was excellently achieved.

The programme, in my view did not 'make a mockery
of the Christian Faith'. It exposed the people who
are truly mocking it by their racial prejudice and
intolerance.

You also say the programme made a mockery of
clergymen. I strongly feel it did not, but it did
criticize clergymen who use the pulpit for political
propaganda calculated to increase racial intolerance,
and this I am sure we both agree is undesirable.

I do not think that anyone, of any faith can support
the kind of wickedness embodied in racial prejudice and
racial intolerance.

If any programme made by ATV did attempt to encourage
racial intolerance, religious prejudice, or man's
inhumanity to man, I would act immediately and
decisively, but I guarantee that no programme in the
'Beyond Belief' series will do so.

Above all, we all here feel that the format of this
programme can do a great deal to increase the audiences
of religious programmes and as a result will get its
message over to a group of people who would normally not
watch a religious programme in its more stylised form.

Again thank you for writing because I know, and
appreciate the conviction that motivates you.

Yours sincerely,

Lew Grade.

Treating Mary Whitehouse with respect wasn't just a question of good public relations. Executives at independent TV
companies had a uniquely multifaceted system of accountabil-

ity to negotiate. As well as keeping viewers and shareholders happy, they also had to please the advertisers and – particularly after Lord Hill tightened up franchise renewal procedures in the aftermath of criticisms made by 1962's Pilkington Report – take care not to fall foul of their regulatory network the Independent Television Association (changed to the IBA from 1972 onwards) for fear of losing their regional franchise.

When one Granada TV drama producer – driven over the edge by endless complaints about the use of the word 'bloody' from a particularly tireless Liverpudlian correspondent – replied that the only blight on his horizon at the start of a new series was 'the thought that I am going to get a letter from you every week for the next two months', Mary passed the letters on to ITA chairman Lord Aylestone. While diplomatically pronouncing himself 'as little attracted as you' to the 'wholly inappropriate tone of the letter', Aylestone did allow himself the qualification that her correspondent was 'a very persistent writer . . . not easily satisfied . . . So perhaps it is understandable that in his replies he receives a range of reactions.'

The higher levels of decorum that prevailed in Whitehouse's relationship with ITV did entail certain obligations. In NVALA's ongoing war of words with the BBC, the nuclear option – often called for at annual conventions, to the alarm of more pacifically inclined delegates – was a mass refusal to pay the licence fee. When dealing with ITV, the deadliest weapon in Mary's armoury was to threaten a boycott of advertisers, but she called upon this at her peril, as the following letter makes clear.

The relevant communication with Sir Paul Chambers, then chairman of ICI, is sadly not to be found within the capacious box files of the Whitehouse archive (perhaps an undercover ITV operative broke in and destroyed it). Yet from the irate response it obviously provoked from ITA director general Sir Robert Fraser, one could reasonably assume that this letter threatened a

boycott of ICI products advertised during ITV's 'controversial'
1969 gangster drama *Big Breadwinner Hog*. The first episode
– with its beguiling Portobello Road Market opening sequence
– can now be viewed in full online, for those who wish to make
their own minds up about this strangely compelling piece of
Notting Hill noir.

What's interesting is that Mary Whitehouse's reply eschews the
combative stance she normally adopted in response to any kind
of direct criticism in favour of a far milder – almost poignant –
brand of self-justification. Her stance is very much that of the
democratic politician who seeks to capitalise on the threat posed
by paramilitary elements by presenting him- or herself as a more
responsible channel for their legitimate feelings of grievance.

Reply to the director general of the ITA

20th May, 1969

Dear Sir Robert,

    I very much appreciate your frankness about my letter
to Sir Paul Chambers. I was sorry indeed to read that
you felt it to be a great mistake, though I think I can
understand why you should feel so.

    May I just say, in order to clarify our approach to
the matter, that we are constantly under pressure from
our members — and even others — to launch a campaign to
boycott the goods of firms who seem to be advertising
during what people consider to be undesirable
programmes. This we will not do, but it was against a
background of pressure of this kind, and the extremely
strong reaction to 'Big Breadwinner Hog', that I
wrote my letter to Sir Paul Chambers. People feel very
desperate sometimes. I do hope you understand.

    Yours sincerely,
    (Mrs) Mary Whitehouse,
    Hon. Gen. Secretary.

The most obvious distinguishing feature of commercial TV's output in terms of the kinds of complaints it would prompt was the existence of advertising. The following very concerned response to an enquiry about a potentially terrifying snack-food ad shows the lengths ITV companies were prepared to go to in reassuring concerned viewers that their complaints were being taken seriously.

Letter to Mary Whitehouse from a worried mother in Bristol

3rd October, 1974

Dear Madam,

I have got a 27 months old little boy who has been an advert fanatic of [West Country commercial channel] H.T.V. until the latest advert of Smiths Fangs which has been disturbing of late. In fact I have even had to take him to the doctor's through this advert giving him nightmares.

I have been in touch with H.T.V of which I have had no satisfaction what so ever after numerous phone calls I was advised by I.B.A. to get in touch with you to see if you can help me in this matter.

I am sorry I have had to draw your attention to this but my little boy is so petrified that it is making him a nervous wreck. I hope you can help me.

I have also sent a similar letters to the makers of 'fangs' and am looking forward to a favourable reply.

Reply from the IBA's advertising control department to viewer's letter forwarded by Mary Whitehouse

24th October, 1974

Dear Madam,

Mrs. Mary Whitehouse has sent on to us the letter you wrote to her about the advertisement for 'Smith's Fangs'. You can of course always write to us direct if you have

any problem or complaint and I am sure that our regional
office in Bristol would have been able to give you a
satisfactory reply if you had asked them to help you.

  With regard to the commercial you mentioned we did
reject the advertiser's first proposals because we
thought that these might result in children being
frightened. After changes had been made we felt that
we were safe in approving the film because it featured
a light-hearted comedian, Frank Thornton, in a comic
strip situation which was not at all horrific and which
we believed would make children laugh rather than be
frightened.

  We are therefore surprised and concerned that your
little boy should have been so affected by the film but
his does seem to be an exceptional reaction as we have
had no other complaints, although the film has been shown
for some time.

  I do not think that we should be justified in having
this film withdrawn, but I hope that you believe that
comments such as yours are not unnoticed and will help
us in making difficult decisions on matters of this sort.

  I am grateful to you for writing to us about this.

  Yours sincerely,

  PETER WOODHOUSE

  To twenty-first-century eyes, one of the most striking lessons
of the commercial TV shelf of the Whitehouse archive is the
extent to which the balance of power in broadcasting has shifted
towards advertisers. From the 1954 Television Act (which paved
the way for ITV's existence) onwards, concerns about what was
perceived at that time as 'American-style vulgarisation' ensured
very strict regulation, not only in terms of product placement
but also of any subtler forms of overlap between advertising and
programme creation.

  Even as late as the mid-seventies – if the next letter is anything to go by – the opportunity to effectively foot the bill for

the TV shows that surrounded the ad breaks was still seen as a privilege which might be withdrawn at any moment. The same song would later be used in adverts for PlayStation and Adidas (among others), but it is strangely gratifying to know that such boundaries between the sacred and profane were ever formally patrolled by an IBA director general.

Reply from Brian Young

18th February, 1975

Dear Mrs. Whitehouse,

Thank you for your letter of 5th February and for sending me the postcard from one of your members about the television advertisement for McVitie's biscuits featuring the sung words 'You've got the whole world in your hands'.

It is certainly our practice not to permit religious music and hymns to be associated with the advertising of commercial products and we have often refused to accept background copy and music based on these.

We have now looked into the history of this particular song and enquired into the reasons why the advertiser chose to use it. It seems that it was originally a negro spiritual but was first published nearly fifty years ago as a popular song. There have since been many versions and arrangements of the work by various pop groups over the years. Copyright was acquired by Chappell & Co., in 1957, of an adaptation by Geoff Love and this was recorded by Laurie London and acquired by Chappell's as part of its 'popular' repertoire. Subsequently this has been recorded by such pop artistes as Wayne Gibson, the Isley Brothers and Count Basie, and it was also included last year in the album 'Alan Freeman's History of Pop'. It has always been promoted as part of Chappell's 'popular' repertoire and not as part of their religious music section. It does not appear in Hymns Ancient and Modern nor in the Baptist or Methodist hymn books.

The advertiser assumed that it had been so secularised
that it would be considered as a popular song and we
certainly accepted it on this basis. The advertiser is
genuinely concerned that the use of the song could cause
offence to some people who recall the original basis of
the song and has not, I believe, acted irresponsibly.

We consider that it would be going too far to refuse
to allow currently approved commercials to continue for
their normal life but in view of the comments received
we would not propose to permit further commercials to
perpetuate this theme song.

Yours sincerely,

A further point of difference between ITV and the BBC (at
least in the mid-sixties) was that Mary Whitehouse had not been
informally banned from the former network. By the time of her
1968 appearance on *Frost on Sunday* (not to mention later
encounters with Michael Parkinson, David Dimbleby and Dame
Edna Everage, to name but three), Whitehouse had become a
fairly accomplished TV performer, yet her early brushes with the
medium were not happy ones.

After Lord Normanbrook refused to grant her the opportunity for a 'serious discussion' of her first book *Cleaning Up TV* on
the BBC (although Alf Garnett did supply a favourable capsule
review – 'You should read this, she's got the right ideas, she'd
clean up the place'), Mary Whitehouse was more than happy to
accept an opportunity to appear on the ITV consumer affairs
show *On the Braden Beat*. This formative foray into the realm
of 'the tele' was something less than a howling success.

Well, there was howling, but not of the kind that denotes success. The gales of slightly forced defensive hilarity with which
Mary Whitehouse's remarks were greeted would become all
too familiar a sound as she made her way around the country from one university speaking engagement to another.
For someone who was often accused of channelling sexually

repressed hysteria, she had an uncanny knack of eliciting just such reactions from those who considered themselves more liberated.

Letter from Sir Robert Fraser, director general of the ITA

23rd March, 1967

Dear Mrs. Whitehouse,

Since your telephone call to me, we have had a number of talks among ourselves and with ATV about the interview with you in the Braden programme on 11th March.

We are all rather distressed, both in this office and in the company. From my own part in these conversations, I am really left in no doubt at all that there was no intention on anyone's part other than that the programme should give you, however briefly, the opportunity to have your say and to treat the interview as a serious one with a serious purpose.

As I told you, I did not myself see the programme, but I have read the transcript. While I agree that abbreviation has made some of your remarks read rather raggedly, I do also feel that you managed to say a good deal of what I think you would have wished to say. Indeed, when one remembers that television interviews often have a habit of not going exactly as was intended, I doubt whether one could reasonably find fault with the programme if one were judging it from the transcript alone. Anyhow, I enclose a copy of the transcript as it was broadcast, and will leave you to judge.

To me it is obvious that the question with which Mr. Braden concluded was rhetorically intended, and that his own answer, had he given it, would have expressed his genuine respect, however much he had also expressed his disagreement.

A view given by members of our own staff is that what went wrong, and what no one was prepared for, was the behaviour of the studio audience. Reading the

transcript, I am baffled to know what it was they thought
they were giggling about. If you show the transcript
to anyone and ask them if they thought that there was
anything in it that would make an audience giggle, I
am sure they would have said they did not. Maybe they
just felt that laughing was the thing in the Braden
programme, of which parts are comic and parts are
serious. Maybe some members of the audience thought it
a seemly way to express their disagreement with you.
Whatever the reason, I am inclined to think that this is
where the trouble lay.

Be that as it may, we all feel regret that you had
cause to complain. It was the last thing anyone wanted.

Yours sincerely,

Robert Fraser

Mr Braden's 'rhetorically intended' final question was 'You
aren't laughing at Mrs Whitehouse now, are you?' And there
were times in the politically charged atmosphere of late-1960s
Britain when to be laughed at was the best she could hope for.
The traumatic personal impact on her of becoming what Braden
(not entirely unsympathetically) termed 'a figure of fun' – not to
mention the subject of physical threats and attempted tabloid
stings – will be dealt with in the next chapter, but by the early
years of the next decade there was definitely a sense that the
wheel was turning.

Bernard Braden was sacked from the BBC for taking a large
sum of money to advertise margarine, and later saw his former
researcher Esther Rantzen go on to have huge success with *That's
Life* – a TV vehicle so clearly based on Braden's that a comedy
sketch programme of the time came up with a spoof called 'That's
Bernard Braden's Show, Really'. Whitehouse meanwhile – while
never anything other than a controversial figure – had become
almost an institutional presence within British public life.

No longer fighting quite such a lone battle, she found herself

joined in the certainty that (to quote a *Sunday Times* poll mentioned in the letters below) '"things" had gone far enough' by
some allies more uncompromising even than she was. When the
Guinness Book of Records founder and Conservative campaigner Ross McWhirter (who within two years would be assassinat-
ed by the IRA after offering a £50,000 reward for information
leading to the capture of the gang whose members ultimately
killed him) managed to persuade three judges to place an injunction on the late-night ITV broadcast of an arts documentary
– David Bailey's profile of Andy Warhol – which none of those
concerned had actually seen, new IBA boss Brian Young felt confident enough in Mary Whitehouse's common sense to challenge
the legitimacy of her attempts to drum up support for them.

Letter from IBA director general, Brian Young

23rd February, 1973.

Dear Mrs. Whitehouse,
  As I am writing about another matter, may I send you a
private note about the Warhol programme? I cannot help
feeling that the National VALA circular, of which a copy
was sent to me yesterday, can only diminish National
VALA's credibility. Genuine reactions to our output, from
all kinds of people, are valuable. But does not soliciting
responses in this way rather debase the currency?
  Just as an illustration of what I mean, can I ask
you how you would react if I told you that the British
Humanist Society was urging all its members to watch
a Sunday service (even though they wouldn't do so for
choice), strongly suggesting to them that they would
dislike it, and saying that they should then write to
the IBA, the local company, their M.P., the advertiser?
You would, I think, be inclined to give less credence
to letters which then came in, and to rely wholly
on researches into the reaction of people to church
services in general.

You won't think this a fair analogy, and in fact
there is no such lobby on the humanist, or indeed the
permissive, side, though I know that National VALA and
[the allied moralistic campaigning organisation] the
Festival of Light believe that there is.

As I say, this is a personal and a candid letter. I
write it, as you will realise, not out of hostility to
National VALA.

Yours sincerely,

Brian Young

Her conscience evidently pricked by this eloquent appeal to
her sense of fair play, Whitehouse deflected the anxiety it might
otherwise have caused her into first an anti-secularist rant and
then a display of umbrage at an insulting implication which it
really is very hard to discern in Young's original letter. She also
mooted the threatened boycott of advertisers in a far less apolo-
getic way than she had done four years before.

Reply to Brian Young

12th March, 1973

Dear Mr. Young,

I appreciate the frankness with which you wrote to
me concerning our letter to members regarding their
reaction to the Warhol programme. I know you would
expect me to be equally frank in reply.

I have to confess I find it hard to believe that you
are not aware of a humanist lobby, though I realise you
would not have said this if you were. The incredibly
powerful lobby of the British Humanist Association
is a social phenomenon of no small significance. Even
a cursory reading of their publications in regard to
Abortion, euthanasia, the doing away with religious
instruction in schools, Sunday Observance, etc, etc,
leaves no doubt whatsoever of their use of every vehicle

of persuasion as far as broadcasting is concerned. 'If
ever you see a programme that you think will draw a
complaint from Mary Whitehouse, write and appreciate
it'. (Humanist News)

Secondly, I feel your implied assumption that members
of VALA are unlikely to be interested in Arts programmes
is really unacceptable. VALA membership is extremely
broadly based, and many of our members — and I am one
of them — resent the implication, which one meets in
many quarters, that 'experimental' arts material is
somehow too 'intelligent' and esoteric for people with
a concern for the moral quality of broadcasting. In
any case, VALA members are highly sophisticated viewers
who are well aware that no programme can be isolated
in its own category but inevitably affects standards of
presentation across the board, sooner or later.

I trust you will understand when I tell you that I
was appalled at what appeared to be a suggestion that
letters coming in about the WARHOL programme may well
not be taken into account because we had suggested to our
members that they should write! I could better understand
if we had issued some particular format which people were
invited to sign. This we have never done and never would
do. In fact, we did no more than many national newspapers
did — tell our members to express their views.

As far as advertisements are concerned, I would ask
you to understand how deeply frustrated and angry people
feel about certain aspects of broadcasting — and how
helpless to affect them. You will perhaps have seen
the very recent 'Sunday Times' opinion poll, in which
all but less than 5% of people thinks that 'things'
have gone far enough, if not already a great deal
too far. Even within the weeks since, the 'bounds of
acceptability' have been pushed even further back! One
can well understand the concern of the Authority over
our action regarding the advertisers, but pressure upon
them is one of the very few options left to the viewer.

As I think you know, this Association has greatly

valued the open and mutually respectful relationship
which has existed between it and the IBA. Our ability to
be frank, one with another, is indicative of this, and I
trust that it will continue.

  With kind regards,

  Mary Whitehouse

The vision of the director general of a commercial TV network as an authentic repository of moral authority may be a tricky one for twenty-first-century readers to come to terms with, but the measured wisdom of Young's reply leaves us few other options.

Reply from Brian Young

<u>Private and confidential</u>
15th March, 1973

Dear Mrs. Whitehouse,

  Thank you for your letter of 12th March. I must have
expressed myself very badly: for I would certainly
not take the view that members of VALA would not be
interested in arts programmes and do not know how I gave
that impression; moreover, the Authority is not in any
way worried about the advertisers — it is a myth that
programming decisions taken here are in any way affected
by the expectation of a good response from advertisers
or the fear of a bad response.

  My sole point was this: unlike one or two special
lobbies, National VALA has been distinguished by the
fact that it reports to us, through you, spontaneous and
unprompted reactions to programmes seen. It has not in
the past, I think, attempted to prejudge programmes or
to whip up a reaction based on newspaper reports. The
ironical thing about Warhol is that the entire affair
stems from pieces written in the 'News of the World' and
the 'Sunday Mirror' — not, I think, papers which are
normally taken or respected by your members.

Once their prurient writings had led McWhirter and three judges to take up a particular attitude, it was understandable that there should be a certain amount of smoke and dust when the position was restored to normal. But this does not mean that the Warhol programme 'extends the bounds of permissiveness' in any way at all. Frankly, I fear that encouraging people to prejudge the programme will diminish National VALA's credibility and will make the Association seem to be propagandist and even foolish in the eyes of many whose reaction to the Warhol programme will be 'What on earth was all the fuss about?'.

Up to now, you have conveyed to me from VALA genuine, unprompted responses, and I value that: I should be sorry if you put your members in the position of those stirred up by another lobby who telephoned the Authority recently with the charming and simple admission 'I've been urged to complain to you about something, but I'm not sure exactly what I'm supposed to be complaining about'. I am sure you will agree with me that, when people are in this position, they lessen the value and effectiveness of their comments, and I wrote to you frankly and confidentially because I didn't want VALA to take this road. This was more for VALA's sake than for the Authority's.

With kind regards,
Brian Young

The early seventies was certainly a time when ethical vigilance was called for from those in positions of power in TV, as this letter from a NVALA member in Hull makes clear.

Letter from NVALA member, forwarded to Brian Young by Mary Whitehouse

18 November, 1974

Dear Sir,
I wish to complain about an incident in the football match which was televised on Sunday November 10th.

The match in question was the Sheffield/York match, and during the game, a middle-aged man was shown running across the pitch naked.

As this is a clear case of indecent exposure, and since the match was a <u>recorded</u> <u>programme</u>, I wish to complain in the strongest possible terms about your permitting this incident to be televised.

The act itself constituted a police offence and by 'aiding and abetting' — i.e. showing the incident, I feel that the television company is certainly not blameless in this respect.

As there are innumerable children of both sexes viewing on a Sunday afternoon, I consider this a deplorable lack of foresight on the part of a) The producer and b) The Company.

I am a member of the National Viewers and Listeners Association and a copy of this letter has been sent to them.

The Whitehouse archive has no record of Brian Young's reply, but it would be nice to think that the questionable practice of including footage of streakers in recorded football highlights would not have survived for too much longer. It's hard to be sure, though. This was the seventies after all, and to say that not all of the British public's tastes were developing in ways that Mary Whitehouse approved of would be putting it mildly.

Reply from Thames TV's controller of light entertainment

10 January 1974

Dear Mrs Whitehouse,

Thank you for your letter of January 3 regarding THE BENNY HILL SHOW.

You have already noted that Benny Hill has a 'particular type of humour' and I am happy to say that this brand of humour pleases and entertains the very large majority of our viewers. In point of fact, Mr

Hill writes his own material and I can assure you that
there is no desire on his part or ours to produce a show
as narrow as you suggest. I believe that Benny Hill's
comedy is honest and is no more to be denigrated than
saucy postcards or, for that matter, Restoration comedy
which is so respected at the National Theatre.

  As in the previous instance on which we have
corresponded, I will certainly send copies of our
letters to the Producer and to Mr Hill. But it is
interesting that as I write this letter we have just
received the Christmas week ratings in which THE
BENNY HILL SHOW is once again top! Not necessarily
conclusive, I agree, but at least it is a pointer to the
general appeal of this programme.

  With best wishes,

  Yours sincerely,

  Phillip Jones

  The crisp tone of the above letter was already some way from
the old-world courtesy that characterised Brian Young's communications with Mary Whitehouse, and as the decade progressed, the brasher sensibility which might always have been
anticipated in a commercial channel came increasingly to the
fore. The complaint about lewd dancing on *The Kenny Everett Video Show* which inspired the following faintly sarcastic
response would find itself the centrepiece of the advertising for
the following week's edition of the programme.

Reply from Thames TV's controller of light entertainment

12th July, 1978

Dear Mrs Whitehouse
  THE KENNY EVERETT VIDEO SHOW

  Thank you for your letter of 5 July to which I am
replying on behalf of David Mallet, Producer of the
programme.

After receiving my copy of your letter, I looked
at the tape again. I have to say that I was rather
surprised that you found the dance sequence so
offensive. It is, after all, 'Modern Dance', and very
little different, if at all, from much that has been
seen recently on, for example, TOP OF THE POPS.

I agree that it might have been considered 'coarse and
degrading' some years ago (as was the waltz when it was
first introduced in the last century), but I believe it
is widely accepted nowadays, and can have no harmful
effect on young people who constantly practise something
very like it in their discotheques.

However, the dance sequences in future episodes of the
show will be carefully watched, to ensure that movements
which might go beyond what is normally accepted are avoided.

Yours sincerely,

Phillip Jones

Mary was not going to let that waltz crack go unanswered.
Two weeks later she wrote again, briskly acknowledging 'No
doubt you will use this letter as publicity for the "Kenny Everett
Show", as you did my last', but having been left with no alternative than 'to place on record my amazement and great dismay
at the decision to dress up one of the female dancers as a young
schoolgirl in a sequence using prostitutes'.

Whether they were actual prostitutes, or just dancers dressed
as prostitutes, the essential point was the same. 'You must know
perfectly well', Whitehouse counselled sternly, 'that the fetish of
a woman dressed as a schoolgirl is a feature of sex perversion,
and that it was "the bridge" which led from adult pornography
to child pornography.'

In another letter of three years later – complaining about a
'deliberately titillating' Hill's Angels segment in *The Benny Hill
Show* (presumably as opposed to their other, more artistically
motivated, dance sequences) – she raised the spectre of a violent

feminist backlash. 'May I also make the point that shots of the kind used in this programme are precisely the type of "explosive" material which is now arousing the anger – in some cases – violent, of the feminists. It would be encouraging to know that you take equally seriously the objections of those who would never resort to illegal demonstrations.'

In the course of the decade, the broadening of Mary Whitehouse's zone of operations from TV to the cinema to the fight against pornography had seen her make a number of new ideological connections, of which a notional alliance with radical feminism was not necessarily the most unexpected. Yet there was a reassuring continuity to the kinds of televisual scenes that attracted her ire. Those who remember the TV series *Brideshead Revisited* will not have to rack their brains too hard to guess which was the one scene in that landmark literary adaptation that Mary Whitehouse felt was out of place.

Reply from the producer of Brideshead Revisited

5th Feb, 1982

Dear Mrs. Whitehouse,

Thank you very much for your letter and your kind remarks about BRIDESHEAD REVISITED which are greatly appreciated. It is obviously very gratifying when audiences show such a sympathetic and generous response to a television adaptation which has attempted to do some justice to an original novel of great beauty and power.

I was obviously unhappy to hear from you, however, that the love-making scene in Episode 9 had caused offence and distress to some viewers.

I would only like to say that the scene appeared finally in this form only after much careful thought and debate. It was included in this way only for the reasons indicated above — namely, we were endeavouring to be as faithful as possible to the spirit of the original. In

the novel the love-making scene is described as being
a somewhat harsh and selfish act on the part of Charles
Ryder and one which accounts for much of Julia's later
sense of sin and for her desire for expiation.

BRIDESHEAD is not an entirely romantic novel and we
wanted viewers to respond as much to the story's sadder
and darker and more sombre aspects as to its charming
and glittering surface. In the end I feel in this case
we were right. But I am grateful for your letter. For no
one, however carefully a decision to include 'difficult'
matter of this kind is made, can be absolutely sure that
the decision is correct, and no responsible producer
wants to upset or alienate viewers without good cause. So
it can be very useful and helpful in the making of future
decisions of this kind to take into account the obviously
equally sincere views expressed in your letter.

Again thank you for your warm remarks and with my very
real regret that members of the National Viewers' and
Listeners' Association were given cause to be upset.
That was as far from our intention as was the desire to
titillate.

Yours sincerely,
DEREK GRANGER

Brideshead Revisited aside, 1982 would prove to be a red-letter year (perhaps a 'red-triangle year' would be a better way of putting it) for Mary Whitehouse's relationship with British commercial television. The long-awaited advent of a second ITV channel – a Conservative Party manifesto commitment since the early seventies – would ultimately take a form which might have been drawn directly from Mary Whitehouse's worst nightmares. And while the gory details of her interaction with Channel 4 must wait a few more chapters yet, her earlier non-meeting of minds with the ambitious young producer of an award-winning Thames TV documentary series is included at this point to sound a suitably ominous note.

Letter to the producer of The World at War

30 April, 1974

Dear sir,

  I know that your series 'THE WORLD AT WAR' has
been highly praised in many quarters, and rightly so.
However, we have received some complaints about the
episode on 27 March, entitled 'Genocide'.

  Yours sincerely,

  Dictated by Mrs. Mary Whitehouse, but signed in her
absence

Reply from the producer of The World at War

2nd May, 1974

Dear Mrs Whitehouse,

  I have your letter of 30 April about the WORLD AT WAR
episode 'Genocide'.

  I was interested to read and have taken careful note
of the letter of complaint you have received.

  You will not be surprised, I know, to have me confirm
that we considered very carefully indeed whether it
was right to include in this episode the scenes and
the narrative which we did. But, however difficult they
were for some viewers, we came to the conclusion that,
although by no means over-emphasising the grim detail of
the Nazi murders, we had to make quite clear what human
beings serving their ideology had done to their fellows.

  And we took more than the usual precautions in warning
prospective viewers of what they were going to see.

  Thank you for your interest in writing.

  Yours sincerely,

  JEREMY ISAACS

BRITISH BROADCASTING CORPORATION

TELEVISION CENTRE WOOD LANE LONDON W12 7RJ

TELEPHONE 01-743 8000 TELEX: 265781

TELEGRAMS AND CABLES: TELECASTS LONDON TELEX

22 November 1979

Mrs Mary Whitehouse
National Viewers' and Listeners' Association
Ardleigh
Colchester
Essex CO7 7RH

Dear Mrs Whitehouse

<u>Play for Today - COMEDIANS</u>

I take note of your objections. You quote as
typical of the language used in the play
"prick of a brothel". It seems that even your
typewriter is infected by your prurience
and your vision of universal corruption for
"brothel" should, of course, read "brother".

Yours sincerely

RICHARD EYRE
Producer
Play for Today

Reply from Richard Eyre

7. Mary vs. the Playwrights

What was Mary Whitehouse's attitude to creativity? Without the resources to conduct a proper opinion poll, it would be fair to assume a consensus across a fairly broad spectrum of the late-twentieth-century British showbiz establishment – from the former head of the National Theatre Richard Eyre, to one of her most reliably splenetic adversaries, Alf Garnett's creator Johnny Speight – that she was the implacable adversary of authentic artistic expression.

While Whitehouse's objections to particular plays, films, or TV shows were most often couched in terms of 'bad' language – by which she meant swearing of any kind, but particularly with a religious or sexual connotation – she was not afraid to underpin that moral 'bad' with an aesthetic foundation. 'An alibi for poor script-writing or character delineation' was how she introduced the issue in the complaint about Trevor Griffiths' play *Comedians* which inspired the angry response opposite.

'Typical of the language used in this play were the following,' she continued: 'Filthy bastard, moody bugger, prick of a brothel, piss off, shit, "Oh Christ", suicidal pisshouse Jesus, and an obscene "joke" about bestiality . . . It is perhaps a measure of the disregard for public feelings which exists that viewers are driven to use such language in a letter.'

The mutually abusive (in both the linguistic and emotional senses) character of Mary Whitehouse's relationship with the people who wrote the scripts of the dramas and comedies she complained about had been set in stone by the advent of *Swizzlewick*. In January 1967, listeners to the BBC's *The World at One* (includ-

ing Whitehouse herself) were surprised to hear Johnny Speight –
interviewed live in the studio and working up a considerable head
of steam – implying that her organisation was 'neo-fascist' and
(rather more bizarrely) allied with 'the killers of Christ'.

After taking legal advice from the ever-helpful Quintin Hogg
MP, QC, Whitehouse sued the BBC and came away with her
second successive courtroom victory (the first was over Ned
Sherrin via the *Daily Mail*). This time, the settlement was a
handsome £300.

Of all the long-term antipathies that underscored Mary Whitehouse's time in public life, her ongoing war of words with Johnny
Speight was the only one that came close to rivalling her ideological dispute with Sir Hugh Greene in its intensity. It is probably no
coincidence that, initially at least, the two conflicts overlapped,
because the common ground between the urbane and patrician
director general and the self-consciously rough and ready Can-
ning Town comedy writer and playwright was exactly the territory Mary Whitehouse was most determined to fight for.

Extract from 1967 NVALA briefing re Till Death Us Do Part

'TILL DEATH US DO PART'
Writing of B.B.C. Television on March 10th, TIME magazine described the programme series 'Till Death us do Part' as follows:

'Its protagonist is a sort of Every slob, an odiously vulgar
xenophobe named Alf Garnett. Every Monday night at 7:30, old
Alf gets on and starts sputtering away. West Indian cricket
players? "It's amazing how them sambos have picked this game
up." The Labour Government? "Right load of pansies they are."
Prince Philip? "Well, he's a different sort of Greek; he isn't
one of your restaurant Greeks."'

'There is not a sponsor in all U.S. television who would
countenance that sort of gritty billingsgate, but in Britain Alf
is not only on the air but is also the most popular character
on television. Or rather the most talked-about, for he either
outrages viewers or spills them laughing on the floor. "The

amusing thing about Alf," says B.B.C. Director-General Sir Hugh Greene "is the intense fury aroused among those who share his prejudices. The programme offends a great many people — but those one is glad to offend."'

So now we know, and we have it from Sir Hugh Greene himself. Those who hold certain 'prejudices' he is glad to offend. This is 'amusing'.

To see exactly what prejudices Sir Hugh finds so funny, turn to the <u>Radio Times</u> of June 2nd, 1966 where Sir Hugh Greene's own paper tells us:

'Alf Garnett. He is working class, skilled at his trade, three generations behind the times and is well endowed with most natural human failings . . . He is also a Tory and a Monarchist, but has never forgiven Edward Heath for trying to get us into the Common Market. It need hardly be said, therefore, that Harold Wilson and the Labour Party are utterly wrong as far as he is concerned. The same goes for General de Gaulle, the Russians, the Chinese . . .'

'But what wounds Alf's permanently hurt pride most is his young son-in-law Mike. Young, good-looking, virile, strictly of this new generation which rejects all the lovely traditional shibboleths in which Britain has wallowed since Queen Victoria, he tears down every belief that the older man depends upon.'

Sir Hugh has certainly declared himself with a vengeance, Working class, skilled at his trade, Tory and a Monarchist, against the Common Market, against Harold Wilson and the Labour party, the Russians the Chinese . . . one does not need to be an expert on aversion therapy to understand the game. The series started off quite well; even the vulgarity was well done and humorous, and there was a genuine attempt to hold the balance. Then came the change, Alf's ideas must <u>always</u> be ridiculed. He <u>always</u> shouted, <u>always</u> swore, <u>always</u> got drunk, <u>always</u> lost the day as when he threw something at his nice sensible young Socialist son-in-law and hit the Queen's portrait instead.

To imagine that Mary Whitehouse's dislike of Alf Garnett was based solely on his propensity for swearing would be to greatly underestimate the sophistication of her understanding of both the character and his creator. 'Johnny Speight has made it perfectly clear, on a number of occasions, that the motivation of this series is political,' she explained to a new BBC chairman, Sir Michael Swann, in January 1974. 'He portrays Alf as he does in the hope that the public, in rejecting Alf, will reject also these things which he holds dear. That it has not worked out that way is no fault of Mr. Speight's.'

You don't have to look too hard to discern a trace element of admiration in Whitehouse's feelings towards her sworn ideological adversary. The critique of *Till Death Us Do Part* in her second book *Who Does She Think She Is?* expresses Whitehouse's anxieties about Alf Garnett's treasonous implications – 'the man we were supposed to hate . . . a loyal patriot who believed in God and was devoted to the Queen' – through still more explicit approval of the show's positive qualities.

'The characterisation and the acting of the series was brilliant,' she insists, before coming up with what is actually a very shrewd and interesting response to the anxieties later expressed by the show's producer, Dennis Main Wilson, that people might have been laughing 'with' Alf's prejudices rather than against them. 'He and Johnny Speight', Whitehouse argued, 'then made the mistake of interpreting as sympathy for Alf's ideas what was in my opinion sympathy with him as a person, for the way he was treated by his wife and family, and for the way in which week after week whatever he did he came out the dog's body.'

The logical implication of this statement – that a positive response to a fictional character does not automatically necessitate support for their views – challenges the validity of some of Mary Whitehouse's most cherished beliefs about the inevitability of viewers emulating antisocial or immoral behaviour on their TV screens. The capacity to demolish your own arguments is the hallmark of a more flexible and intuitive thinker than the honorary general secretary of NVALA is generally given credit for being, and yet – as this further anti-Alf letter of complaint written almost a decade and a half later (and giving a new chairman of the IBA the chance to hit the ground running) demonstrates – Mary was nothing if not consistent.

Letter to Lord Thomson of Monifieth

6th January, 1980

Dear Lord Thomson,

I am sorry indeed that my first communication with you as Chairman of the IBA should be one of such great concern and I believe shame.

I do not know whether you personally watched the 'Thoughts of Chairman Alf' on Boxing Night. If you did you will be aware that in addition to its foul language and its offensive references to God and Jesus Christ, the following episode was transmitted.

After describing Mr. Foot as a 'bastard' Warren Mitchell said that the Queen said 'Excuse me. Black Rod, where is the Leader of my Opposition?'. Black Rod, we were told, then explained to the Queen how Mr. Foot had fallen over and broken his leg. 'Oh ho' said her Majesty 'pissed was he?'

I hope you will agree that to put such words into the mouth of the Queen was a gross insult and totally unacceptable to her subjects. Certainly it shamed us all and, speaking for this Association, I believe the least the IBA can do is make a public apology to the Queen and I trust that you will decide to do so.

May I finish by offering you our warmest good wishes for your time as Chairman of the IBA. I don't doubt there will be many problems — I hope there will be much pleasure also.

Yours sincerely,

Mary Whitehouse

The default position of the BBC and the British theatrical and cinematic establishment was that Whitehouse and her supporters were hopeless philistines with no understanding of the history and development of drama. Sometimes – in fact, often – the complaints she passed on without critical comment from NVALA members (and, indeed, the ones she wrote herself) did little to counteract this impression. The following letter – from a qualified child psychologist who was one of Mary's most oft-quoted scientific sources – was sent on to the BBC with the recommendation 'This letter came to me from a Doctor and, therefore, I accept the report as both accurate and objective.'

Letter forwarded to head of BBC radio drama

17th December, 1971

Dear Mrs. Whitehouse,
  I listen habitually to the 'Wednesday Play' on the Home Service of the B.B.C. After 30 seconds of last night's ('It Pays to be Frank') I would have turned it off as being far too inferior to trespass on my mind, but I kept it on for the statistics! In three-quarters of an hour there were 25 'bloody' expletives, 6 'damns', 2 'blasts' and 2 coarse expressions, one of which was taught at great length to the listeners. I think that the expression 'put a bun in you' would not be comprehended by the average woman listener, but by the time the references had finished, it was quite plain what the meaning of this expression was.
  It seems to me that if the B.B.C. cannot maintain standards of drama, they should have the courage to leave that three-quarters of an hour free rather than put on something that even a fourth form child would have been ashamed to produce. The theme was very scanty and the depiction was that of selfishness in all its forms, the whole being most unedifying.
  Somebody ought to tell the B.B.C. that there is a

multitude of one-act plays by classic authors, Chekhov,
Strindberg, Shaw, which are good theatre and could well
be used in this Wednesday play period if they have not
got a new one of a sufficiently high standard.
  Yours sincerely,
  Louise F.W. Eickhoff, M.D., D.P.M.

  The reply from Martin Esslin – a leading academic authority
on absurdist drama – is a collector's item of well-informed disdain, especially in its final paragraph. It is an interesting reflection of the gender hierarchy of the BBC at the time that the
professional standing of Whitehouse's correspondent has led
Esslin to identify her as male, even though the name printed at
the bottom of the letter clearly suggests otherwise.

Reply from Martin Esslin

22nd December, 1971

Dear Mrs. Whitehouse,
  Thank you very much for your letter of 17th December.
I have looked into the question of the play 'It Pays
to be Frank' which was transmitted on Wednesday, 2nd
December, and repeated on the afternoon of Thursday, 3rd
December.
  The play in question is a harmless little northern
comedy about a steam engine enthusiast who wanted to
turn an old mill into a steam engine museum. His wife is
the secretary of the local business tycoon who in turn
wants to use the site to make it into a caravan park. In
the end the Council buys the site and converts it into a
reservoir.
  From the above summary you will see that there could
hardly be a more innocuous subject for a play. The
fact that the characters occasionally use the expletive
'bloody' (I didn't count them in the script but your
correspondent's estimate seems to be exaggerated) is to

my mind entirely justified in characterising these people
as rough and ready northerners.

  As regards the other phrase your correspondent was
upset about: first of all he misheard it. The phrase is
'He accidentally put a bun in your oven'. This is a
widely used and, to my mind by no means a more obscene
euphemism for pregnancy than 'putting someone in the
family way'. Moreover, the phrase is spoken about a
husband and wife. I feel that the obscene connotations
were entirely in your correspondent's own mind through a
mishearing.

  I was amused to see that your correspondent recommends
Strindberg, Chekhov and Shaw as more wholesome fare.
I can only conclude that he may not be very well
acquainted with authors like Strindberg.

  Yours sincerely,

  Martin Esslin,

  Head of Drama, Radio

  A further letter in the archive – not from, but about Esslin
– gives a telling glimpse of the darker backwaters of NVALA
support (which Mary Whitehouse herself generally – in public
at least – did a pretty good job of steering the organisation away
from). A NVALA member and former colleague of Esslin's, who
had worked alongside him in the German Service at Bush House
during the war years, wrote to congratulate Mary on her fight
'not just against bad television, but against a diabolical conspiracy against our country and Christianity itself'.

  She supplemented this general expression of goodwill with a
series of libellous accusations directed at Esslin, backed up with
a supposedly clinching detail. 'I don't know whether you know
that Mr. Martin Esslin's name, until recently, was Jules Peres-
zlenyi . . . What in my opinion is so outrageous is that this man,
who is NOT an Englishman, and who accepted the hospitality
of this country when he had nowhere else to go (he came from

Czechoslovakia) . . . should corrupt OUR children . . . In my opinion no foreigner has a right to dictate in somebody else's country, however many times he changes his name.'

The man originally known as Julius Pereszlényi (before he anglicised his name – an integrationist gesture common among East European immigrants of that period) was in fact Hungarian, and being of Jewish descent had left his homeland for Britain after the Anschluss. Still, why let a little detail like 'he was fleeing for his life from the Nazis' get in the way of a good racist conspiracy theory?

Once you start trying to square the circle of Mary Whitehouse's often very perceptive assessments of the motives and talents of writers and performers and her movement's stubborn adherence to an anti-art agenda, a very interesting question begins to ask itself. Rather than the problems she experienced in her relationships with Britain's TV screenwriting fraternity being based on her not having enough in common with them, is it possible these tensions might have derived from an *excess* of overlap?

As a pat psychological explanation for Mary Whitehouse's extraordinary and enduring dynamism, the notion of frustrated artistry certainly makes considerable appeal. Not so much for Mary herself – though she did begin her professional career as an art teacher – as for the family background that shaped her. It's certainly true that a clear faultline between art and commerce ran through the previous two generations of her paternal bloodline.

Her grandfather Walter Hutcheson had tested the patience of his own wealthy businessman father by marrying a 'humble Highland girl' and becoming an illustrator for the *Glasgow Herald* (for whom he would make engravings from on-the-spot sketches of major news events). After the advent of photographic reproduction robbed him of this journalistic livelihood, he embarked on a modest career as an oil and watercolour painter, and made ends meet by teaching at art school.

Rather than being delighted when both his own children showed signs of artistic talent, Walter decided to protect them from themselves, apprenticing the son who would later become Mary's father to a gentlemen's outfitter in England, to insulate him against the material privations of the artist's life. Unbeguiled by the life of a draper, James Hutcheson sold his shop and became a cattle-feed salesman – an unromantic-sounding career shift which, Whitehouse wrote in *Who Does She Think She Is?*, 'at least took him out into the country'.

Her father, she continued, was 'a very gifted artist . . . never happier than when he could help me with my school illustrations'. Yet as a consequence of being pushed into a more prosaic (not to say manure-strewn) field than he might have chosen, his daughter adjudged him 'in many ways, an unhappy and frustrated man, and it has been looking back at the wastage of his talents that made us always determined to give our own children their "chance"'.

Although willing to acknowledge the sadnesses in her family background, Mary Whitehouse was never one to overplay them. This characteristically pithy correction to an article in *The Listener* reflects the concern with maintaining a respectable front which is so often the hallmark of those who have not lived lives of luxury.

Letter to the editor of The Listener

5th July, 1979

Dear Sir,

  Without implying any disrespect for gypsies and in the name of accuracy I have to correct your statement that my Father was 'an itinerant cattle-feed merchant'. He was, in fact, the Cheshire sales representative of a long-

established and highly respected firm supplying cattle
medicines, vaccines, etc. And the only time there was 'no
money at all' was when the then not infrequent outbreaks
of foot-and-mouth disease meant that he was met at farm
house after farm house by a 'NO ADMITTANCE' order.
  Yours sincerely,
  Mary Whitehouse

  The need to keep up appearances seems to have been every bit
as significant a factor in Mary Whitehouse's family background
as thwarted artistic ambition. The second of four children whose
older sister was confined to a bath-chair by polio, the headstrong
and fun-loving Constance (though she'd dropped the first name
long before changing her surname on marrying Ernest) Mary
Hutcheson was 'expected to help a great deal' despite being 'a
rebellious child who resisted pleas to "speak nicely"' and was
'constantly in trouble for mischief of one kind or another'.

  It would be reasonable to assume that such an upbringing
might have inculcated a strong sense that freedom must necessarily be balanced by a sense of responsibility (an idea which
was inevitably going to put her out of step with the children –
not to mention the parents – of the 'swinging sixties'). However,
to suggest that Mary Whitehouse channelled the thwarted creativity of three generations of her family into a sustained attack
on the artistic freedom of others would be a grotesque oversim-
plification.

  Far from expressing frustration through her role as the aveng-
ing angel of respectable Middle England, Mary Whitehouse
seems to have found it an immensely satisfying channel for a
considerable array of creative talents. Her knack for self-presentation was apparent from her earliest journalistic forays in the
forties and fifties, and once she became a public figure, Whitehouse's aptitude for the creation of a coherent persona would
have been the envy of any sharp-witted dramatist.

Impeccably turned out in her instantly recognisable uniform of horn-rimmed spectacles and tightly coiffed hair, Mary White-house offered herself to the British public as a repository of moral certainty sharply at odds with the more mutable beliefs of the broadcasters and politicians she harried with such relentless determination. Inevitably, her high public visibility and willingness to identify herself with unfashionably prescriptive positions came at a considerable price.

Shouted down at meetings, publicly derided, the subject of physical threats and endless attempted Fleet Street stings (including a concerted tabloid campaign to lure her sons into sexual indiscretion), in the months after the 1966 publication of her first book she had just about reached the end of her tether. It was at this lowest ebb that her faith was most important to her.

She wrote in her diary of being 'almost overwhelmed by the speed and power of the enemy'. By this time, her perfectly understandable persecution complex was developing in an almost mystical direction: 'This is the Cross – to realise there is no glamour, no appreciation to be asked or expected, nothing but ridicule, pain and loss . . . it is in this loneliness, and in this alone that one finds Christ.'

Mary Whitehouse's talent for orchestrating a narrative with herself at the centre (although obviously in the above extract she shares the limelight with Jesus) did not end with her diaries. The titles alone of the six volumes of memoirs she completed in her lifetime (and unlike many celebrities and other figures in the public eye, she did actually write these books herself) testify to Whitehouse's sharp eye for the aspects of a dramatic situation most likely to capture an audience's attention.

Those (remorselessly readable) books were – covering a historical arc of twenty-seven years from first till last – *Cleaning Up TV*, *Who Does She Think She Is?*, *A Most Dangerous Woman?* (my favourite title for the extent to which it echoes the work of

Barbara Taylor Bradford), the ruthlessly exploitative *Whatever Happened to Sex?*, 1985's self-explanatory *Mightier Than the Sword* and (saving the most obvious title till last) 1993's *Quite Contrary*. Closer to home than even her own multi-part auto-biography, Mary Whitehouse's storytelling instincts seemed to be at work in the addresses she wrote at the top of every letter.

The first of these – Merridale Road – sounded like the kind of place J. R. R. Tolkien's hobbits of the Shire might have hung out on their weekends off (although it was actually quite near the middle of Wolverhampton). At this time in the post-war years – in an instance of dramatic irony so blatant even the most ill-intentioned filth-peddling screenwriter might have hesitated over it – Mary Whitehouse lived next door but one to the local Tory firebrand Enoch Powell.

'His two daughters were then very tiny', she remembered in *Who Does She Think She Is?*, 'and could be seen at their nursery window watching our children build their "tree house" in the big old apple tree at the end of the lawn.' There was clearly mutual admiration between the two households in this Black Country suburban idyll, and the Whitehouse family 'watched with fascinated interest and respectful awe the care with which he [Enoch] planted out his lettuce seedlings'.

Not everyone was so taken with the gardening techniques of the ultra-conservative ideologue. The vigour with which he shook the apples off his own tree elicited 'almost unprintable remarks' (perhaps a 'Damn!', or even a 'Blast!') from a group of workmen helping the Whitehouses with some alterations. 'We didn't share their dismay, because, to us, the falling apples simply demonstrated the direct Powellite approach to an immediate problem.'

Well, that's one way of putting it. If only the Whitehouse family could have continued to live next door to Enoch Powell for a little while longer, they might have been around to see the construction of his celebrated 'Rivers of Blood' water feature, and imagine the sagas that might have ensued if the two families had stayed neighbours into their children's adolescence. It would've been like an incredibly right-wing low-budget remake of *Seven Brides for Seven Brothers*.

After Merridale Road, Mary and Ernest's next move was to 'Postman's Piece' in the rustic-sounding enclave of The Wold, Claverley. Thence – just as she was becoming really well-known – they relocated again to the fairy-tale location of Triangle Farm House, Far Forest, Kidderminster. History does not record whether Whitehouse renamed those properties herself – or was perhaps drawn to them by their resonant ceramic nameplates – but either way, their scenic-sounding addresses were seamlessly incorporated into her innately theatrical self-presentation.

The idea of home and hearth as a sanctuary from the depredations of the outer world was central to Mary Whitehouse's world-view. This was why the threat of immorality stealthily poisoning that personal haven through the box in the corner was so horrifying to her. And yet, those who saw her as the inhabitant of some kind of unblemished domestic cloud cuckoo land were greatly underestimating the levels of turbulence that seemed to prevail in her immediate domestic environment.

In an article called 'When Mother Falls Ill' – written unbylined for a West Midlands local paper in the mid-fifties – Whitehouse told of the family pressures which led to her taking to her bed for three months with chronic kidney trouble. In just fifteen years of her and Ernest's marriage they 'had five children of our own [three living sons and the twins who had died in infancy], one adopted child [Mary's niece, who she and Ernest nursed through a sickly infancy after the child's mother died when she was just three months old], two evacuees and [briefly] one unmarried mother and her baby'.

One of her sons spent several years out of school after contracting chronic rheumatism brought on by a streptococcal infection (with her trusty eye for a telling detail, Mary recalled that a local bus conductor had turned her son's plight into a local landmark, announcing the stop from which his room could be viewed with a cheery cry of 'Anyone for the little boy in the bed?'). Another almost lost his sight to an exploding spirit-level – a nasty accident in whose happy ultimate resolution his mother clearly discerned divine intervention.

All this was some years before she was being pilloried by the nation's satirists or called a 'hypocritical old bitch' by a man with a handlebar moustache. Yet those doubts and fears which would continue to assail Mary Whitehouse throughout her three and a half decades in public life were already gnawing away at her – 'It isn't as though I haven't tried to keep calm,' she berated herself anonymously in 'When Mother Falls Ill'. 'I have, desperately, but time and again I've failed, and suffered terribly from a sense of defeat and failure.'

Mary Whitehouse was not afraid to admit weakness in public. In fact, she would often put her vulnerabilities to use in an unabashedly pragmatic way. As close to the start of her media career as the anonymous 'Mothers & Sons' article for the *Sunday Times*, she was already soliciting early payment directly from the editor on the basis of her son's unfortunate run-in with the exploding spirit level.

CUTV and NVALA's accounts are one realm of the archive to which access is forbidden, but 'the Lord will provide' does seem to have been the mantra of those organisations in terms of funding. Although her husband Ernest's family copper business had been a source of financial stability early on, the income it provided was far from being on a Denis Thatcher level, and the combination of his nervous collapse in the early sixties and the need to support his wife's campaigning meant that the money she brought in was increasingly important to the household.

From the time she gave up her teaching position to focus all her energies on CUTV in late 1964, Mary Whitehouse's professional life was basically that of a jobbing journalist and public speaker (not to mention occasional beneficiary of libel judgments). As such, she knew many of the same anxieties and frustrations as those whose work she publicly pilloried. Her correspondence finds her chasing up payments for unpublished articles commissioned by the *News of the World* with the rigour of the hardiest freelance stringer, and receipts for TV and radio appearances glow with the satisfaction of payment well earned (a February 1971 covering note from ATV's *Personally Speaking* delivers an appearance fee of £25, together with another cheque for expenses of £5, 8 shillings and 6d 'in the old currency!').

Viewed purely in the context of her struggle to maintain her hard-won public prominence through the operation of her own wits, Mary Whitehouse's profound ambivalence towards those whom she might – had the circumstances been slightly different – have regarded as her professional peers could start to look like the expression of a straightforward competitive instinct. Yet if you consider her fetishisation of home and hearth as a creative response to the emotional pressures of her own domestic life (rather in the same way that Brian Wilson's songwriting genius proceeded partly from his lack of ability at surfing), a vastly more satisfying and human picture emerges.

If some part of her envied the artistic and personal freedoms which writers and artists around her were claiming as of right in the early 1960s, perhaps Mary Whitehouse found an equivalent satisfaction in giving the fullest and most eloquent possible expression to an opposing viewpoint. As such, her career in public life might almost be defined as a kind of evangelical Christian performance art.

One of her most reliable targets – in fact, the only writer to challenge Johnny Speight for the title of Mary's arch-nemesis –

seems to have himself intuitively grasped this possibility. Dennis Potter's standing as one of Britain's most prolific and talked-about (not to say 'controversial') dramatists ensured that he often found himself on the wrong side of Whitehouse's sharp tongue. And yet, like Spike Milligan (another frequent target who supplied the quote 'I thank God for a woman like Mary' for the jacket of one of her books), Potter apparently had a warm appreciation for her sincerity and seriousness of purpose.

'He loves the idea of Mary Whitehouse,' the *Guardian* journalist Stanley Reynolds wrote of Potter. 'He sees her as standing up for all the people with ducks on their walls who have been laughed at and treated like rubbish by the sophisticated metropolitan minority.'

Potter's own combination of religious and sexual themes (not to mention his artistic preoccupation with the loss of childhood innocence) was always going to set him and Whitehouse on a collision course, and it is no surprise to find her sending the then BBC drama chief her 'warmest congratulations' on the decision not to film Potter's adaptation of the Cinderella story in 1966. She didn't want him 'twisting the magic stories of childhood into perverted fantasies of sexual behaviour'. The following is a typically damning critique of one of his many ITV productions.

Letter to Sir Robert Fraser

4th June, 1970

Dear Sir Robert,

I have received quite a number of letters about Dennis Potter's play of the 23rd May. The person who wrote and described it as 'vile' was pretty typical.

In particular the language was much objected to and a number of people enclosed in their letter the phrase used 'God all bloody mighty'. Such language is surely blasphemous and quite inexcusable.

I would appreciate it very much if you could pass on
our complaint to the company concerned, and I would be
grateful for your own comments so that I can pass them
back to our members.
Yours sincerely,
(Mrs) Mary Whitehouse

Her delight at the BBC's decision not to broadcast Potter's
Play for Today Brimstone and Treacle suggests nothing would
please her more than to see the writer and his works expunged
entirely from the earth.

Letter to BBC programme controller

8th April, 1976

Dear Mr. Milne,
I am writing, somewhat belatedly, owing to my absence
abroad, to express appreciation on behalf of this
Association of your decision to ban Dennis Potter's
play 'Brimstone and Treacle'. I do not doubt that you
in particular and the BBC in general will come under
considerable pressure, not least from TV critics, to
reverse your decision. We trust you will not do so.
While it is difficult to prejudge a programme, I can
only assume that 'Brimstone and Treacle' was more
offensive than Tuesday night's Dennis Potter play
'Doubledare'. In that case, it must indeed be bad.
Yours sincerely,
(Mrs) Mary Whitehouse

And yet, when the BBC broadcast the third part of what had
been intended by Potter as a trilogy (but was now missing its
middle part), Mary Whitehouse's response to his 'loose' adaptation of Edmund Gosse's memoir *Father and Son* was (to put it
mildly) somewhat more favourable.

Letter to the producer of Where Adam Stood

23rd April, 1976

Dear Sir,

It would, I think, be difficult to put into words my appreciation of the play 'Where Adam Stood'. The acting, production, timing, photography, were superb. If I had to pick out anything for special praise, I think I would mention the timing, which seemed to me exquisite.

I have written a personal note of thanks to Dennis Potter but I would be very grateful if you could pass on to all concerned my very grateful thanks. It is too soon yet to make a full assessment of its impact on our members, but some have already spoken to me, and all are as deeply appreciative as I am myself of a most memorable experience. I am writing to Alasdair Milne to see if it can be repeated on BBC1.

Yours sincerely,
Mary Whitehouse

Perhaps it was the subject matter – a boy growing up in a strict religious environment – perhaps it was simply the fact that it wasn't *Brimstone and Treacle*. Either way, there was something about *Where Adam Stood* which Mary Whitehouse liked so much that she wrote a personal note of thanks to the man whose work she'd been brusquely excoriating only two weeks before.

Letter to Dennis Potter

8th April, 1976

Dear Mr Potter,

I would like to tell you how wonderful I thought your play 'Where Adam Stood' was. Everything about it — the characterisation, timing, photography, production, was superb.

I shall long remember and treasure the memory. I
am writing to Alasdaire Milne to ask if it could be
repeated on BBC1.
   Thank you very much indeed.
   Mary Whitehouse

The expression on Potter's face when he opened that letter
must've been a picture, although it should be noted here that he
also considered *Where Adam Stood* to be among his 'most satisfying' pieces of television – further evidence of potential common ground between the writer and his most tireless critic. As
to the precise location of this shared terrain, an interview the
playwright gave to Melvyn Bragg on the *South Bank Show* in
1979 probably gives the clearest directions.

Somewhat to Bragg's surprise, Potter said that he refused to
'join in the chorus of abuse about Mary Whitehouse, because I
think that at least she acknowledged the central moral importance of – to use the grandest word – art'. Resisting the idea that
her puritanical strictures thwarted creativity by causing artists
to limit themselves, Potter argued that 'self-censorship, far from
being the worst [form of censorship], is the best'. (If only he'd
practised what he preached when the time came to write *Black
Eyes*.)

The unlikely ideological coming together of Mary Whitehouse
and Dennis Potter was to have a brutally ironic dramatic climax. In her 1990 interview with Anthony Clare for the Radio 4
series *In the Psychiatrist's Chair*, Whitehouse was discussing her
objections to *The Singing Detective*, that landmark TV production which she insisted (not entirely groundlessly, although one
might argue that this was exactly the effect the writer intended)
'made voyeurs of us all'. During the interview, she inadvertently
conflated the character of the mother in the drama (whose son
catches her in flagrante in the woods) with Dennis Potter's actual mother.

Given the substantial autobiographical elements in the story – and Whitehouse's own tendency to literal interpretations of works of art – this mistake was not perhaps a very surprising one, but it was to have horrendously embarrassing consequences. Understandably aggrieved at the (wholly unwarranted) slur on her long and faithful marriage, Dennis Potter's mother sued the BBC, *The Listener* (for reprinting a transcript of the interview) and Mary Whitehouse herself.

Not only would this have seemed a wildly improbable trio of defendants in the early days of CUTV (when *The Listener* was habitually cited as the in-house journal of the secular communist pre-marital activity conspiracy), but the nature of the offence – impugning the sexual integrity of someone's elderly mother in a national radio broadcast – could hardly have been further from the kind of public act Mary Whitehouse would wish to be associated with.

Statement of Claim by Margaret Potter

IN THE COURT OF JUSTICE QUEEN'S BENCH DIVISION
BETWEEN:
MARGARET C POTTER <u>Plaintiff</u>
And
[1] BRITISH BROADCASTING CORPORATION
[2] LISTENER PUBLICATIONS LIMITED
[3] Mrs MARY WHITEHOUSE

<u>Defendants</u>
STATEMENT OF CLAIM
1. The Plaintiff is the widowed mother of the well-known playwright Dennis POTTER. She was married on 7 July 1934 and her husband died in November 1975. Dennis Potter was born on 17 May 1935.
2. The First Defendant was originally incorporated by Royal Charter on the 20 December 1926. It transmits for general reception wireless and television programmes under Licence from the Minister of Posts and Telecommunications.

3. The Second Defendant is a limited company which publishes
'The Listener', a weekly magazine widely read by people with
an interest in the arts and current affairs.
4. The Third Defendant is a married woman.
5. On 9 August 1989, the First Defendant broadcast a programme
entitled, 'In The Psychiatrist's Chair', in which the Third
Defendant was interviewed by a Psychiatrist, Dr Anthony Clare.
During the course of this broadcast, the Third Defendant said
and the First Defendant broadcast the following words which
are defamatory of the Plaintiff:

'The heart of the problem was the fact that Dennis Potter,
the reason for all his skin trouble was shock. You see as a
child he had seen his mother having sex with a strange man in
the grass.'

This broadcast was repeated on Saturday 12 August 1989 and
the Second Defendant published the same words in the 10 August
1989 issue of 'The Listener'.
5. The said words meant and were understood to mean that the
Plaintiff who was then married, her husband having died in
November 1975, had, when a married woman, committed adultery
with a strange man and that the shock of witnessing this had
caused her son to be afflicted with the painful skin disease
known as Psoriasis which Dennis Potter suffers from.
6. By the publication of the said words, the Plaintiff has
suffered great personal distress and embarrassment and her
reputation has been grossly injured and brought into public
scandal, odium and contempt. The injury to the Plaintiff's
feelings has been aggravated by the repetition of the libel.

AND THE PLAINTIFF CLAIMS:
1. Damages for libel;
2. An Injunction restraining the Defendants and each of them
by themselves, their servants or agents or otherwise howsoever
from publishing the said or similar libels of or concerning
the Plaintiff.
3. Interest pursuant to Section 35A of The Supreme Court Act
1985.
4. Costs.

Rather than the rapid and fulsome apology which might – in retrospect – have been the best option to go for, Mary opted to run the full gamut of evasive strategies. Total denial (of course she would never have said such a thing) was followed – when evidence to the contrary was presented – by obfuscation (the BBC must have edited the tapes) and then bluster (even if she had said such a thing, she obviously wouldn't have meant it). Finally, at the prompting of Whitehouse's legal advisers, the poignant mitigating circumstances came out.

After recently sustaining the serious spinal injury which would ultimately hasten her exit from the public eye, and enduring an unusually long and arduous journey to the studio, the now eighty-year-old Whitehouse had been so discombobulated by the time the recording began that there was audio evidence of her blacking out earlier in the interview. In the light of this revelation, Mrs Potter accepted a handsome five-figure libel settlement from the BBC and *The Listener* and graciously let Mary off scot-free, once she'd agreed to put her name to the following (under the circumstances) very mildly worded statement.

Extract from statement read in open court

Anyone listening to the broadcast or reading the article in 'The Listener' would have inevitably concluded that Mrs Margaret Potter, Dennis Potter's mother, had, as a younger woman, committed adultery with a strange man and that the shock of witnessing this had caused her son to be afflicted with a terrible disease.

Such a serious allegation, as the Defendants readily acknowledge, is wholly without foundation. Mrs Potter remained faithful to her husband throughout their married life. The skin disease from which Mr Potter suffers started after he had left university and was due entirely to hereditary factors and had nothing to do with mental trauma. The scene in question was written by Mr Potter entirely from his imagination.

Not surprisingly the publication of the allegation in two

separate broadcasts which must have reached a wide audience
and the further publication in 'The Listener', a magazine
widely read by people with an interest in the arts and current
affairs has caused the Plaintiff considerable distress and
embarrassment and she felt that she had no option but to
bring these proceedings to clear her name. The Defendants
appear today by their solicitors to apologise unreservedly
to the Plaintiff and they have in addition agreed to pay
a substantial sum by way of damages, to carry a fair and
accurate report of this statement in the next edition of 'The
Listener' and to meet her costs in full in bringing these
proceedings. In these circumstances the Plaintiff is prepared
to let the matter rest.

Under these circumstances, Mary Whitehouse's subsequent
attempt to solicit a contribution towards her legal costs from
Mrs Potter's libel settlement met with the disdainful response
it probably deserved. What is truly remarkable in reading the
former's correspondence with her legal representatives over this
matter is that for all her lifelong concern with privacy – particularly in the sexual arena – and the many unwelcome media
intrusions to which her own family life had been subject over
the years, there is no evidence anywhere that Mary Whitehouse
felt a moment's actual compunction for the wrong she had done
Mrs Potter. If such singular self-interest isn't the province of the
true artist, I don't know what is.

TIPS ON LETTER WRITING

A. LETTERS TO POLITICIANS - about anything of concern to you

a) Start with a draft ~~following~~ Make a few pencilled notes. ~~Discipline yourself to what you want to say and stick to it.~~ and then a draft

b) Be as brief as possible. Short sentences ~~make a much easier - unless you have the gift of writing and making it flow (few have!)~~ are ~~SHORT~~ paras make easier reading too.

c) Put a heading to your letter, e.g. "TV STANDARDS"

d) Look at your draft critically and see if you can delete unnecessary words. e.g. If your draft says, "It occurred to me the other day that if the government . . ." I glance at that sentence and then realise that I can start: "If the gov't .."

e) Write legibly and space well. Always be courteous - even if you express annoyance.

f) Don't be tempted to mention or interlink too many issues. This will help you to keep it simple and you'll have more chance of the contents being noted.

g) ~~Your letter would start, "Dear Mr. X" then pitch right into your subject without beating about the bush. e.g., "I would like to draw your attention to ..." or, "referring to your comment in The Press/on TV/on radio on Wednesday, regarding the TV standards, I would like to point out that ..." or, "I think that the proposed Bill on . . . would cause . . ."~~

h) ~~Don't ever send a formal sounding letter. Your simple language will have far more effect. Don't be careless about spelling. It may convey an idea that you are careless and ignorant in other areas too, so where in doubt use a dictionary.~~

i) Always keep a copy of your letter - even if handwritten. Buy carbon. (give a sheet to friends and encourage them to write too!)

j) Don't have dozens of signatures on one letter. The effect of several letters - no matter how brief - have a far greater impact.

X) ~~XXXXXXXXXXXXXXXXXXXXXXXXXXXXXXXXXXXXXXXXXXXXXXXXXXXXX XXXXXXXXXXXXXXXXXXXXXXXXXXXXXXXXTheXXXXXXXXXXXXXXXXXXXX XXXXXXXXXXXXXXXTheXXXXXXXXXXXXXXX~~

~~XXXXXXXXXXXXXXXXXXXXXXXX~~   ~~XXXXXXXXXXXXX~~

k) A ~~newly-elected~~ MP ~~acquires~~ should have just those two letters after his name. e.g. ~~Address the envelope:~~ 'James Jones Esq., MP'
                              House of Commons
                              LONDON SW1A 0AA.
~~Or writing to your own Member? 'Mr. James Jones, MP'. Or:~~ 'Sir Gerald Jones, MP'. If he happens to be a Privy Counsellor, then he acquires the title: 'Right Honourable'. This is abbreviated to 'Rt. Hon.' - and appears at the start of his name on the address - but not when you are writing the letter itself.
Thus: 'The Rt. Hon. Sir Gerald James, PC, MP' (the PC is for Privy Counsellor). Start your letter: 'Dear Sir Gerald'.

l) ~~XXXXXXXXXXXXXXXXXXXXXXXXXXXXXXXXXXXXXXXXXXX.~~

Rough draft of NVALA's advice to letter-writers

8. The Poetry of Prurience

One of the most unexpected treasures yielded up by the Mary Whitehouse archive (and this includes the special playing cards) is a sequence of poems. Neatly typed out, with no attribution in terms of their authorship, these impassioned verses are a kind of Hallmark *cri de cœur* against the tyranny of an unfeeling national broadcasting network.

There is no way of knowing whether they were written by Whitehouse herself or a particularly zealous acolyte (the latter seems more likely, as if the former they would presumably have got an airing in one or other of Mary's memoirs), but either way, these poems offer such a pure distillation of the voice of NVALA that it would be a crime to deny them what is – at least, to my knowledge – a first official publication.

Two anonymous poems from the Whitehouse archive

TELEVISION PLAYWRIGHT

I wish you could see the contract I've signed:
They pay me for my filthy mind;
I simply drain
The cesspit of my brain,
And pour it over you.

A public demonstration
Of my degradation;
I just write reams
Of jottings from my dirty dreams;
That's all I do.
Then sometimes for an hour,

I have millions in my power;
I bury them in slime,
That breeds sadistic crime;
If they only knew.

What do I care if a girl is raped,
Or an old woman killed?
What are children's fears,
Or old men's tears
To me?

Nothing.
I just turn on the flow;
It's easy you know,
For I'm shameless and unclean,
Really obscene,
You know.

So I don't care if you whine;
You're all only swine.
I've nothing but contempt
For you.

NEWS FLASH

We're stopping our programmes to say,
There's been a terrible crash today;
To pretend that we care,
Our cameras are there.

Smashed limbs in the mud,
Close-ups of blood,
Now you can stare
At numb despair;
We're always the first
To show you the worst.

And the more that it's gory,
The better the story.

There's something about both the style and the message of these poems – the sarcasm, the willingness to take on the voice of the enemy, the way the anger is focused through an unapologetically direct rhyme scheme – that will seem strangely familiar to readers of a certain vintage. Effectively, they're punk rock songs.

No wonder the Adicts liked Mary Whitehouse. Declaim the opening two lines of the next (similarly TV-current-affairs-inspired) NVALA protest number in the voice of Johnny Rotten or the Dead Kennedys' Jello Biafra, and they are certainly rendered no less effective.

Another anonymous poem from the Mary Whitehouse archive

TV NEWS

Children, while we're having tea,
How many corpses shall we see?
As the cameras slowly pan,
Let's count the corpses while we can.

Perhaps we'll see them as they die,
And watch their children scream and cry;
How lucky we are.

We can watch a crowd of thugs,
Or homeless derelicts crazed with drugs;
And children, what a lot we learn,
From seeing how well hospitals burn;
There's always something good to see.

And children, when you reach an age,
When you may want to earn a wage,
You'll have such sick and morbid views,
You too can work in television news.

The extent of punk and Mary Whitehouse's shared obsession with the impact of the mass media and the corruption of

youthful innocence is just one intriguing aspect of this unexpected crossover (the Sex Pistols' 'Who Killed Bambi?' for
example would have made a great title for a CUTV newsletter).
How satisfactorily 'Infiltrators' – the last of these four pieces
of impassioned doggerel – translates the agenda of Moral Re-
Armament into a format Wattie from the Exploited could have
worked with not only tells us something about Mary Whitehouse, it also tells us something about punk.

At its best, punk *was* a kind of moral rearmament – a 'change'
(to use MRA jargon) which would inform every subsequent decision new adherents ever made. In Sid Vicious's predilection for
the swastika armband, it even had a nominal figurehead willing
to flirt unabashedly with Nazism, just like the MRA's founder
Frank Buchman brown-nosing Hitler at the Berlin Olympics.

*One more anonymous poem . . . but sorry, this has got to be
the last*

INFILTRATORS

I used to wonder who had defiled
The innocence of my child,
And how he'd come to worship thugs,
And rupture his mind and body with drugs.

I used to wonder where
He'd learnt to be so wild.

But now I know.
Here in his home,
Before my eyes,
Worthless people come
And tell him lies.

Their sneering faces fill the screen,
Their hands gesticulate and jerk;
Glib and insincere,

With cunning leer
And fraudulent compassion,
They talk about the growth of crime
That they themselves have caused.

For all his life
My child has watched men die:
Shot in the head;
Murdered in bed.

Blood-stained corpses in the dust;
Sweating bodies squirm with lust;
They're all the same:
It's just a game.

And lechery's the thing
About which all his idols sing.

While the brutal morons of the BBC,
The self-appointed jailers of our souls,
Talk pompous garbage.

And now it's too late.
Reared on their hate,
His life is ruined.

OK, maybe 'self-appointed jailers of our souls' might have been a bit flowery for the Exploited, but Jimmy Pursey could have got away with it. The important point here is not so much that – as the Ramones might have put it – 'Mary was a punk rocker', but rather that punk and NVALA were in many ways apples that fell from the same tree, this particular arboreal specimen being a crabbed and slightly withered post-war Britain with its roots sunk deep in social exclusion and disillusionment.

As if the parallels between the two movements were not already striking and numerous enough, there was also their shared fascination with bodily functions and swearing to be considered.

Letter to the controller of Radio 4 from NVALA member in Surrey

29 April, 1977

Dear Sir,
    <u>Radio programme</u>
    I wish to make a strong protest regarding offensive
words in 'Morning Story' broadcast on 28 April at
10.45 am. This was called 'The Deep End', by Bernard
Maclaverty.
    Owing to the broad Irish accent of the reader, I
did not hear every word, but managed to catch the
following:-
    TITS AND GENITALS
    FARTING NOISE
    ON THE WALL 'TONY LOVES JIMMY'.
    Not pretty, is it?
    Once again, a deplorable example of radio 'entertainment',
which we can well do without. It seemed all the worse as it
followed immediately after 'Morning Service'.
    Yours faithfully,

    The conjunction of inappropriate language and an iconic
repository of respectable virtues – Radio 4's *Morning Service*
in the letter above, Bamber Gascoigne in the one below – was
a lapse in editorial judgement NVALA letter-writers found
especially provoking, although the BBC's representative does a
stalwart job of questioning the etymological credentials of the
eminent-sounding Edgar G. Westlake in his reply to the following communication.

*Letter from Swindon NVALA member, forwarded to the BBC
by Mary Whitehouse*

29th March, 1968

Dear Mrs. Whitehouse,

<u>For your information</u>

I would draw your attention to an interloper on radio, B.B.C., T.V. and I.T.V. programmes. It is the German equivalent of a four-letter word (Shit), i.e. 'SCHEISS'. I have heard the word 'Scheisster' (equivalent to 'Shit-house' on each of the above three mediums in recent weeks, and, on Wednesday of this week (March 27th) on the Midlands I.T.V. programme, 'University Challenge', Bamber Gascoigne introduced the mascot of the University of Kent team by the name of Lieutenant Scheisskopf (Shithead). He repeated the name — apparently, so that there should be no misunderstanding — amidst sniggers and applause.

I am sure that Gascoigne (one of the most erudite of T.V. personalities) was under no illusions as to the meaning of the word.

It will be interesting to see if the use of this word and its variants increases, or whether either of the authorities sees fit to clamp down on this latest example of licence.

Yours sincerely,

EDGAR D. WESTLAKE.

Reply from the Secretary of the BBC

22nd April, 1968

Dear Mrs. Whitehouse,

Thank you for your letter of 10th April.

Mr Westlake has invented a new word and provided his own etymology for it. If, instead, he had consulted a dictionary, he would have found the harmless American slang term, shyster. Though its derivation is a matter for speculation, the word is over a hundred years old, and it has been used in the cinema and on radio and television many times, particularly in Westerns. It meant, originally, a crooked lawyer, but more recently has come to be applied to almost any kind of trickster.

As for Scheisskopf, no-one here thought it more than
a nonsense name for a mascot: nor, as far as we know,
did anyone but Mr Westlake. In any case, the linguists
on the staff tell me that in German usage, the word is
vulgar but not obscene.

I have no objection to your making known the contents
of this letter to your members.

Yours sincerely,

The Secretary

As zealous as NVALA members were in their pursuit of
broadcasting impropriety, none had sharper nostrils in hunting
down even the vaguest scent of a double entendre than Mary
Whitehouse herself. Sadly, her archive contains no record of a
reply to the following devastating critique of declining standards in the closing items of news broadcasts, but it is hard to
see how the recipient could have resisted her call to administer
the sternest possible admonishment to those responsible.

Letter to BBC newsreader Richard Baker

7th May, 1973

Dear Mr. Baker,

I am sure I speak for very many people when I say how
much your work both as a newsreader and as the compere
of 'These You Have Loved' is appreciated. It always
seems to me, if I may say so, that your work has real
quality.

It is because of this that I venture to make two
criticisms. The first, and most important, was the remark
you made recently at the end of a news bulletin which
carried, as its last story, a feature about the antics
at the opening of a new lavatory. As you signed off you
made some remark about having 'to go' yourself. Watching
the screen, your own expression of embarrassment led
up to the conclusion that these lines had been prepared

for you, and were not spontaneous as these final 'punch
lines' are obviously meant to appear.

Mr. Baker, we have a high regard for you, but remarks
of this kind are not only an intrusion into our privacy,
they are an intrusion into your own. I feel quite sure,
from the impression of your personality which comes over
the screen, that you would not normally publicly inform
a gathering of your friends that you were going to the
lavatory, you would just go!

I have intended writing to you ever since that
particular episode, but was moved finally to do so by
your remarks about 'feathered birds' in 'These You Have
Loved' on Saturday night. I know this is a small matter,
but feel sure that the people who gain so much enjoyment
from listening to this programme are unlikely to think
of women and girls as 'birds'. I know we felt irritated
by it, and are rapidly coming to the conclusion that
there are no programmes which one can watch or listen to
without meeting this general cheapening of culture and
people.

Could you have a word with the people who prepare your
scripts?

With best wishes, and again many thanks for so much.

Yours sincerely,

(Mrs) Mary Whitehouse

For all the high levels of linguistic squeamishness that prevailed at the top of the NVALA command chain, the organisation was not afraid to get its hands dirty when the situation
demanded. The formative experiment with programme monitoring that Patricia Duce presented to the Town Hall meeting
in 1964 evolved over the decades that followed into an exhaus-
tive (not to say exhausting) mechanism of evaluation, where-
by potentially 'controversial' elements – whether in terms of
language or sexual and violent content – would be carefully
removed from their dramatic contexts by industrious groups

of NVALA volunteers, and presented en masse in the form of official-looking brochures.

The resulting documents are strangely ambivalent artefacts – originally designed to induce outrage and alarm, but now just as likely to elicit a very different reaction. What child of the seventies who ever managed to persuade their parents to let them stay up to watch *The Sweeney* or *Target* could fail to experience a Proustian rush at the sight of the following Anglo-Saxon smorgasbord – laid out for the delectation of all in NVALA's 1978 brochure 'Law and Disorder'.

Extract from NVALA monitors' report on The Sweeney

THE SWEENEY 12/10/88
'Bloody point'
'Bloody money'
'Bloody silly'
'Bloody nightmare'
'Nasty bastard'
'Mind your own sodding business'
'Put the bastard away'
'Piss off!'
'Stupid mare'
'Bloody copper'
'Sort the slag'
'Playing silly buggers'
'Bleedin' fiddler's elbow'

Not all NVALA's targets are so fondly remembered. Consider this monitors' digest of one episode of a largely forgotten (by me, at least) mid-eighties Channel 4 TV show called *What Now?* Like small chunks of pottery found at the site of a Roman ruin and displayed in the boring anteroom of a small-town museum, these sharp-edged linguistic fragments somehow take on a deeper poignancy in their complete isolation from the broader narrative that once gave them meaning.

Extract from NVALA monitors' report on What Now?

'WHAT NOW?' 1/5/86 Channel 4 9–9. 30pm
'For shit's sake, Derek'
'Always pissed off at school'
'Sod off, no-one seen us did they'
'Soft bastard shouldn't have parked there'
'Christ! it bloody stinks in there'
'Ow Christ'
'Christ! will you stop leading him on'
'Tell her to drop 'em or piss off'
'Act like a shit'
'You're acting like a shit'
'You're a prick to tell her in the first place'
'Piss off'
'You're a pair of wankers you two'
'Christ a couple of woman . . .'
'You don't have to settle down with the first bit you get your
leg over'
'Christ! if I had done that I'd have been married at twelve'
'We're not talking about that, soft arse'
'Don't give me that shit'
Gang fight
'Bastard'
'Shit'
'Shit'
'Mucker me 'ole scum bag'
'Bastard'
'Arse hole'
'They're really gonna be pissed off when . . .'
'Not 'arf as pissed off as me mum'
'Bollocks'
'Knock the shit out of him to knock the shit out of him'
'Christ! you remember that walkman I lost?'
'Piss off will ya Derek'
'A bloody miracle worker'

At times like these, the insanely forensic record-keeping of
NVALA foot soldiers produces a kind of dirty-mouthed *musique
concrète*. The pseudo- (or even authentically – sometimes it's a

thin line) scientific framework of volunteer monitoring at once
required and created its own corporate language. This is the
official version of what it seems only respectful to call the Poetry
of Prurience.

The best way to understand how NVALA's way of talking
about film and television developed is to delve into the mechan-
ics of a monitoring project. The chosen sample – in which sixty
members in various parts of Britain agreed to watch all TV programmes on the four UK channels that then existed between the
hours of 6 p.m. and close-down from Saturday 17 January to
Friday 30 January 1987 – has been taken from quite late in the
Whitehouse archive timeframe to show the process in the final
stages of its evolution, but fundamentally similar schemes had
been in operation since 1964.

Extract from NVALA monitoring project

MAIN FINDINGS

More than one-third of peak-time TV programmes monitored were
concerned with human relationships. This amounted to 162
(37%). Of these programmes, monitors noted that:

More than three-fifths (62%) featured relationships involving
sex outside marriage. The majority of these programmes were
films, plays or comedies. Nearly half (47.5%) of programmes
monitored featuring sex outside marriage or references to it,
were broadcast before 9pm.

The following chart illustrates number of monitored programmes
featuring, joking about or accepting as normal, sex outside
marriage.

BBC1   21 (58%)
BBC2   18 (78%)
ITV   42 (69%)
CH4   20 (48%)

TYPES AND INSTANCES OF BEHAVIOUR PORTRAYED

	BBC1	BBC2	ITV	CH4	ALL
Extramarital	11	10	18	12	51
Living together unmarried	8	4	14	6	32
Promiscuous	10	8	14	10	42
Homosexual	4	5	3	3	15
Dialogue taking such behaviour for granted	11	7	16	6	40

As an example of how a familiar televisual landmark would look when viewed through the NVALA filter, I have picked the much-loved US cop show *Hill Street Blues*.

Extract from NVALA monitors' report on Hill Street Blues

DATE 26/1/87 CHANNEL FOUR TIME (from 10.00pm) (to 10.55pm)
PROGRAMME Hill Street Blues
Characterised by extra-marital, promiscuous and homosexual
relationships.
Dialogue:-
1. 'I was with Celestine all night and all morning. We live
together.'
2. Police officer to his Chief Officer 'Just imagine, a woman
wanting to take it outside.' He is talking about his second
wife, having an affair.
3. 'I broke up with a guy in July. We'd been together for 3
years' (homosexual)
4. Woman police officer to the Chief Officer inviting him to
spend the night with her. 'Do you want to give your angels a
night off?'

Beyond such individual incidences of 'bad' language and pub-lic defender Joyce Davenport's legendary come-to-bed dialogue, the stringing together of long chains of decontextualised violent events in the next extract creates a new narrative with a strange, dreamlike quality (an overall effect uncannily similar to that hip

hop sampling had on the back catalogue of James Brown). When
followed by a list of the advertisers whose products appeared in
the show's three commercial breaks (information stockpiled as
weapons of mass destruction in case NVALA ever decided to go
for that nuclear advertiser-boycott option) the consequence is a
cut-up effect of which William Burroughs would certainly have
approved.

Further extract from NVALA monitors' report on Hill Street
Blues

DATE 1/3/86 CHANNEL 4 (10pm to 11pm)
PROGRAMME Hill St. Blues (Modern Setting — New York)
Police car crashes into back of shop-raider's car in car
chase man flys over bonnet of car on collision of vehicles.
(On screen). Two police officer's found shot after surprising
burglars (off screen). Police officer provoked into physical
and verbal attack by barman. He takes hold of barman by his
neck. (On screen). Jumps over bar. Murderer of two policeman
refuses to surrender — fires shotgun wildly and is shot down by
police. (Camera slowed down as shotgun explodes and he falls
to ground). Programme emphasises throughout the increased need
for the police to arm themselves in fighting armed villains.
e.g. 1. Great variety of guns on show to police for orders 2.
Woman lawyer confesses that she has armed herself in case she
is attacked in the street. 3. Police officer says, 'It seems
like every "nut case" is armed.'

Advertisers:

beginning	middle	end
St. Helens Glass	Cidal	International
Batchelors Cup a	Sunday People	Volleyball
Soup	Danepack	Today Newspaper
Mail on Sunday	Platinum Key	Cadbury's Caprice
Abbey Habit	T.V. Times	biscuit
Yorkshire Building		A.A.
Soc.		Stones Ginger Wine

Would the word 'nutcase' have appeared in an American TV drama? It seems unlikely. Happily for the dependability of the rest of their microscopic analysis, NVALA volunteers were not required to make their assessments of the levels of violence in a programme entirely from scratch, but were given a checklist of things to look out for.

Extract from guidance given to NVALA monitors

```
ACTS OF VIOLENCE (Indicate here if no violence_____)
(It is possible that a combination of all options below may
occur in one programme. Please indicate whatever occurs.)
a) Was it a single blow (include gunshot or throwing of
missiles) YES / NO
b) Was it a sequence of blows YES / NO
c) Were two people involved YES / NO
d) More than two i.e. gangs etc. YES / NO
e) If possible state number of acts of violence _____ (e.g)
if two men engage in fight or brawl count as one act of
violence.)
f) Who was involved? Was it 'good' characters or 'bad'
characters?
g) Any other comments: (please refer to briefing notes
enclosed)
```

When the results of the monitors' work were gathered together, they were often – as in this slightly earlier survey from 1983–4 – presented with no distinction made between factual and fictional violence. On the one hand, this is completely insane, on the other, it gives a fairly accurate reflection of the fluid, random character of the remote-control-driven TV viewing experience which would increasingly become the norm as channels began to multiply.

Edited extract from earlier NVALA monitoring report

PROGRAMME	DATE	TIME	REMARKS
Spyship	7/12/83	8.05pm	Excess of violence used. Macabre concentration on dagger and blood.
Frankenstein; The True Story	18/12/83	10.15pm	This showed 1) an amputated arm crawling across the floor of its own volition; 2) A man's head being battered against a wall leaving a trail of blood down to the floor; 3) A woman's head being wrenched off and rolled along the floor.
Rollerball	20/12/83	9.00pm	Brutally violent film — many examples in guise of 'sport' e.g. one player is fatally comatosed after vicious attack with spiked glove on unprotected head.
Dirty Dozen	23/12/83	10.05pm	Brutal commando type film. Sadistic knife killing of woman. Two to one fist and kicking attack.
News	5/1/84	9.00pm	Angola — two dead bodies close up shots. Eyes wide open of one victim — bloodied neck wound of other.
News	5/1/84	5.40pm	Violent clashes — strike — Poissy near Paris. Two groups throwing bolts, spanners etc. at opposite ends of factory close up of eye injury. Face held close to camera. Angola — bloodied neck wound on corpse.
The Mechanic	8/1/84	10.40pm	A film with various explosions and fires causing death. Again the background music heightened the tension. It was even explained that the time it took to die after cutting wrists depended on weight of person concerned.
The Carey Treatment	15/1/84	10.25pm	Two flick knife attacks, broken bottle threat. Car driven thru' occupied 'phone box victim — face injuries and piece of glass stuck in throat.

Remington Steele	27/1/84	9.25pm	One strangling with doctors stethoscope and one attempted strangling.
Cannon for Cordorba	29/2/84	9.00pm	A man is strung up head downwards over fire then shot for refusing to give information. Camera dwelt on him.
Day of the Triffids	14/3/84	7.40pm	One man beating woman with a stick, group of football supporters threaten young woman. One says 'I want a woman'. Her defender gets beaten up. Looting. Whip lash violent attacks by triffid plant forms. Blind people hammering on occupied car — their attitudes menacing and frightening.
Crosstalk	18/4/84	10.05pm	Film about an almost human computer which tries to tell operator about a gruesome murder in which husband killed his wife then chopped her up and put pieces down disposal unit except for the blood covered head which he put into a paper bag to take away. Horrible, eerie background music.
The Omega Man	12/5/84	10.00pm	Supposed results of germ warfare. Zombie like people white hair, white eyes. Paranoid loador. Docomposing bodies — horrific close ups. Looting. Violent attacks. Smashing up of property and possessions — fatalistic attitude to life, use of knives, axes and spears.
Across 110th Street	14/5/84	10.05pm	Harlem, New York. Extremely violent brutal film, Strong racist element, sadistic killings including police brutality Close up of fatal throat wound Mafia action — victim is castrated (off screen). On screen victim is hoisted up on top of skyscraper. After interrogation by Mafia he is released to fall to his death. Many attacks with furniture, kicking and violent abdominal fist beatings, gun and machine gun killings.

Starsky & Hutch	25/5/84	9.25pm	Screaming girl thrown (whilst scantily dressed) into car, long drawnout shootout on roof, murderer slips and falls several hundred feet. The camera follows all the way. Film speed slowed down.
The Young Ones	12/6/84	9.00pm	Some lines were funny, but unnecessary violence and vandalism, obscene phrases and gestures, childish references to excrement, phlegm, masturbation etc. made it extremely bad taste. An appealling thing for children to follow as an example.

The Freudian slip is not an uncommon phenomenon in the Mary Whitehouse archive, but the coinage of the new adjective 'appealling' – presumably a conflation of 'appealing' and 'appalling' – in the above entry for *The Young Ones* is probably as eloquent a paraprax as any. While there is something almost heroic about the striving for an appearance of objectivity in the collective voice of NVALA, that didn't mean the movement allowed no room for individual self-expression.

Although the four poems printed at the start of this chapter are the only recorded instances of members (or indeed the hon. gen. sec. herself) corralling their sense of outrage into formal verse form, there are plenty of other documents in her archive that might reasonably be said to merit the adjective 'poetic'. Consider for example this anguished circular letter from a London pastor, inspired by a trailer for Dennis Potter's adaptation of the story of *Casanova*:

Copy of letter sent to parishioners of a London gospel ministry

10th November, 1971

URGENT ACTION REQUIRED NOW
Of all the filth on TV! We saw a trailer on BBC 2 on

Monday of a programme to be shown next Tuesday, Nov.
16th. It is the first of 6 on CASANOVA. I'll be blunt.
 The trailer showed a naked woman in bed, exposed from
the waist up, shaking her breasts before a man. With
his back to us he dropped his dressing gown, and stood
naked. We then saw his bottom as he climbed on the foot
of the bed. The next shot was of a woman with a sheet
held up. She dropped this to expose her breasts. There
was another similar shot. Then we had a woman in bed
eagerly awaiting Casanova. We switched off, having been
too stunned before.
 It's on the front of the Radio Times for next week.
 I BEG YOU TO DO ALL YOU CAN TO STOP IT, please
please please. How bad do you want it to be before you
act? In Jesus' name, isn't this bad enough. Write to
the B.B.C., your M.P., the Queen, the Home Office, the
Archbishop of Canterbury.
 PLEASE,
 Yours, for souls,

The last and perhaps most important parallel between
NVALA and punk was that both advocated a DIY ethic as a
means of taking on the British establishment. Mary Whitehouse's
equivalent of 'Here's three chords, now form a band' was the
following NVALA guide to best epistolary practice – 'Always
keep a copy of your letter, even if handwritten. Buy carbon. Give
a sheet to friends and encourage them to write too!'

*NVALA guidance on letter-writing (the finished version of the
draft printed on the opening page of this chapter)*

LETTER WRITING
Thank you for kindly undertaking to write letters on the
issues raised by National VALA.
We hope that the following will help you:-
** Do some cool thinking and perhaps a little research
before you start, but don't let procrastination set in!

** START by enumerating your points, then decide which
you will major on.
** BEGIN with a draft of well-spaced lines. This will
make it easy when you go over it to substitute words
above those scored out or changed.
** WRITE as you speak.
** A short sentence is like a short message — quickly
understood.
** THE vast majority of people are Mr. or Mrs. Ordinary,
so don't over-reach yourself but say it simply.

This guidance was certainly sensible, but as with much of the
good advice given on creative writing courses or by screenwriting gurus, sometimes the best results were achieved by ignor-
ing it. How much less rich in idiosyncratic character would the
Whitehouse archive have been if all NVALA's outriders had
followed her injunction to 'Always be courteous – even if you
express annoyance'?

What were the defining characteristics of the Poetry of Prurience as expressed by those who took Mary Whitehouse's template
and made it their own? The practice of using a sledgehammer to
crack a nut was certainly widespread, or to put it another way:
of the three musketeers, NVALA members' favourite would be
Bathos.

*Letter from NVALA supporter to BBC managing director's
special assistant*

30th July, 1982

Dear Mr. Cary,
  Is this the kind of 'More Daring' the new Director
General (Designate) had in mind when he was interviewed
by Sue Lawley on his appointment? I know the ready
answer will be that it is a simple matter to switch off
one's set when a programme such as this gives offence.

Nonetheless, this is the very fear I expressed at the
time, remembering the proverb 'One cannot touch pitch
without being defiled.'
Yours sincerely,
Mrs McGregor-Craig

Enclosed was a clipping of a *Radio Times* listing for an ano-
dyne-looking (were there any other kind?) edition of the Saturday night variety show *Summertime Special*.

Reply from BBC managing director's special assistant

10 August, 1982

Dear Mrs McGregor-Craig
Thank you for your letter of 30 July. No, 'The
Summertime Special' is of course not the sort of
'daring' programme that Alasdair Milne had in mind when,
before he became Director-General, he was interviewed
by Sue Lawley on 'Nationwide'. 'Summertime Special' is
simply a series that BBC-1 is offering viewers in August
and September on a Saturday evening, remembering that
the BBC is absolutely required to entertain, as well as
inform and educate. By entertaining, we mean here family
entertaining. So even if you do not find it particularly
funny or enjoyable, I hope that it will not contain
anything that will give you offence and so cause you to
switch off.
Yours sincerely
(Roger Cary)
Special Assistant to
Managing Director, Television

At its classical peak of absurdity, a NVALA member's communication would erect a marble temple of aggrieved eloquence
only to bring forth a child's fluffy Shaun the Sheep toy to sacrifice upon the altar.

Letter from NVALA member to the director general

5 March, 1982

Dear Sir,
  Surely the team producing 'NOT THE NINE O'CLOCK NEWS'
must be one of the most inane imaginable. To destroy
appreciation for national monuments (the remark last
Monday about Nelson's column) couldn't really come any
lower in taste . . .
  Yours sincerely,

Letter from another NVALA member to the same lucky recipient

October 18th, 1982

Dear Sir,
  Art knowingly depraved to serve the lowest levels
of human response is most hurtful when broadcast to
ordinary homes by television.
  Topics near to treason — the ridicule of a child-
bearing woman, the debasement of courage, decency,
goodness . . . all represent an evilness which bring
shame to artistic capability and technical skills.
  Jasper Carrott's deplorable effort on the evening of
Saturday 16 October, 1982 comes close to as nauseating
an occasion as TV has ever produced.
  Is this programme to continue?
  Yours sincerely,

  Mary Whitehouse's greatest achievement was to give these
people a collective voice without impinging on their individu-
ality. The accolade (my own – the actual NVALA awards were
given only to TV shows Mary liked) of 'NVALA's ultimate correspondent' is shared – appropriately enough – by two letter-
writers with names Monty Python might have made up.
  The first, Leslie C. Spikesman, wrote a letter about the declin-

ing propriety of common English usage to the BBC's head of
religious programming in October 1975 that was so long this
book would need to run to a second volume to include it all.
Leslie's epistle concluded with a rousing rallying cry to 'the millions of us who still hold fast to the view that "we do not have to
become dirty because the other fellow doesn't wash"', and the
following touching postscript:

Postscript of letter from Leslie C. Spikesman

Although four-score years of my life-span are already
behind me, I still hope to see signs that the downhill
drift has been reversed, and if all those to whom my
criticisms are directed will have the courage and
humility to say 'Stop! We have gone too far' and take
immediate steps to repair the ills they have wrought,
then the hopes and the lives of younger and future
generations of people will be the happier, and my living
will not have been in vain.

As a final measure of the power of the forces that Mary
Whitehouse managed to channel, I call – in conclusion – upon
the indefatigable Dorothy Crisp. After a BBC employee had the
temerity to suggest to this prolific correspondent that no purpose would really be served by her writing to the corporation
again, she issued the following magisterial response. Anyone
who attempted to silence the voice of Dorothy Crisp would do
so at their peril.

Letter from Dorothy Crisp to BBC chairman Sir Michael Swann

June 6th, 1978

Dear Sir Michael Swann,
   Her Majesty The Queen (whom your organisation now

gracelessly refers to as 'The Queen' — 'She — she — she') has just commanded that my (copy) correspondence with the Church Commissioners and the Bishop of St Albans, concerning the projected sale of a Christian church to the Sikhs, be sent to the Home office.

At the moment, I reserve a decision to send Her Majesty my correspondence with you, and those under you.

The Right Hon. William Whitelaw and Mrs Mary Whitehouse, in her capacity as honorary secretary of the National Listeners and Viewers Association, have independently asked for copies of your reply to me, and will receive copies in a day or so together with copies of this my answer the Right Honble Enoch Powell intends to work my information dated May 11th into a parliamentary debate; Mrs Jill Knight M.P writes: 'I am sure you are right to write to the B.B.C. when you find that they are broadcasting misleading information, and indeed it seems your letters are very clear on the subject.' ETC, ETC.

I charge the B.B.C. with broadcasting slanted information, and perversions of truth — and all you can reply is 'Please don't write again'!!!

This goes beyond the extremes of puerility, and confirms the impression that you intend to reduce politics to the same anarchic, undisciplined mush as your present 'religious' broadcasts.

Your Corporation is very fond of quoting Dickens. Let me commend to you 'A Tale of Two Cities'. When Miss Pross was confronted with the self-proclaimed wife of a revolutionary, she commented, 'You might — from your appearance — be the wife of Lucifer. Nevertheless, you shall not get the better of me. I am an Englishwoman.'

Now: exactly what do you intend to do about the fact (which you do not deny) that the B.B.C. is tampering with the news and with the truth?

What is not reformed from within is going to be reformed from without, and you, and others, will continue to receive my report. Whatever is necessary

will be done, inside and outside correspondence, and,
as a matter of courtesy you will be kept constantly
informed.

  Yours sincerely,
  Dorothy Crisp

UNITED INTERNATIONAL PICTURES (UK)

Distributors of MGM, Paramount, United Artists and Universal motion pictures.

23 August 1988

Mrs Mary Whitehouse
Blachernae
Ardleigh
Colchester
Essex

Dear Mrs Whitehouse

On behalf of United International Pictures, I should
like to invite you to attend a special screening of Martin
Scorsese's new film "The Last Temptation of Christ". The
preview will be held at United International Pictures,
37 Mortimer Street, London W1 at 6 for 6.30pm on 30 August.

We are keen that you should have an opportunity to view the
film, in order to draw your own conclusions, before it goes
on general release. A number of other invited guests will
also be in attendance on this date. If you would like to
attend or you would like to fix another date, please call
Liz Thompson, Chris Guyver or Simon Moore at 24-28
Bloomsbury Way, London WC1 on 01 831 6262.

"The Last Temptation of Christ" has generated a great deal
of interest in Britain, and UIP would welcome your views
after you have seen the film.

Yours sincerely

Liz Thompson

Mortimer House, 37-41 Mortimer Street, London W1A 2JL. Telephone 01-636 1655. Telefax No. 01-6364118. Telex: 261818.
Registered Office: Mortimer House, 37-41 Mortimer Street, London W1A 2JL. Registered No. 1580904 England.

Invitation to distributors' screening of *The Last Temptation of Christ*

9. Mary at the Movies

Left to her own devices, Mary Whitehouse would not have gone to the cinema very often. As a young woman, tennis had been her favourite form of recreation. However, by the early 1970s her campaign had been drawn out of its initial focus on the impact of TV on the domestic environment into a series of broader debates about the social responsibilities of the artist and (in the wake of Lord Goodman's Arts Council working party on censorship) the possible removal of all censorship controls.

During these years, when the cinema was – rightly or wrongly – seen as the front line of a permissive bridgehead, Mary Whitehouse was never going to be far from the fight. After all, when it came to knowing which films would and which films would not have a pernicious impact, the vigilance of the young could not always be relied upon (although it could in the following case).

Letter to Mary Whitehouse from a regular correspondent

11th August, 1970

Dear Mrs. Whitehouse,

  I asked my child, a 13 year old, if he would like to go to see the film 'Kes'. He replied that he would not and he asked me in return if I realised that it was full of swear words put in to make it realistic because it was about a delinquent boy, and therefore it had to have swear words to be realistic.

  This film is advertised in such a way as to make intending viewers think that it is primarily a nature film, one which would attract the good parent and the well brought-up child, and did actually so attract my secretary, who was dismayed to find that it did indeed contain a number of swear words and was essentially a film about an episode in the life of a delinquent boy of 14—15, and as such could have a very corruptive influence.

Undoubtedly this film will become part of television's repertoire unless a stand is made against it in time.

Yours sincerely,

Louise F.W. Eickhoff, M.D., D.P.M.,

Consultant Child Psychiatrist.

The possibility of particular films – potentially more 'corruptive' even than *Kes* – becoming a part of television's repertoire was always going to be Mary Whitehouse's primary concern in her dealings with the medium of cinema. Because she lacked the personal contacts in the film industry that she had spent years cultivating in TV, she had to take her information in this area where she could get it.

Letter to Brian Young, director general of the IBA

10 September, 1975

Dear Mr Young,

This morning I received a letter from someone who had got into conversation with a man who said he worked for a firm of film distributors. He told her they had sold 'Last Tango in Paris' to ITV for distribution as soon as the five-year embargo was ended.

I would be grateful for your comments on this.

Yours sincerely,

(Mrs) Mary Whitehouse

Hon. Gen. Secretary

Enclosure from Mary's informant

9th September, 1975

Dear Mary,

  My daughter, Julie, was working at a club last Saturday night and got into conversation with a man.

  They were discussing films and the man said he worked for a firm of film distributors. He said he had sold 'Last Tango' to ITV for distribution in five years time. He added that he had had considerable trouble with Mary Whitehouse 'in Worcester', and Julie said she supported Mary's views. The Man said 'Mary knows about this and is already fighting us'.

  Julie asked him why he distributed this filth which the majority of decent people were very much against, particularly for showing in our homes and he replied 'It's my job, Ducky'.

  It is possible that it was a pure invention by a pompous man who was trying to impress Julie, but I thought you should know about it.

  The man was of medium height, blond hair turning silver and a neat beard.

  If you have any ideas on how to find out who he was, I should be glad to hear.

  Yours sincerely,

Reassuring reply from Brian Young

23rd September, 1975

Dear Mrs. Whitehouse,

  Thank you for your letter of 10th September.

  I can assure you that there is no truth in the rumour that 'Last Tango in Paris' has been acquired for showing on Independent Television.

  Yours sincerely,
  Brian Young

Have you seen that mystery man, readers? It's probably not just the blond hair that has turned silver by now, the beard may well have done so, too.

One problem that came up repeatedly in Mary Whitehouse's correspondence on cinematic matters was the impact of 'art' films – especially as presented in those BBC2 international seasons that were such a lifeline to budding cineastes in the pre-video era – on the perceptions of a non-specialist TV viewing audience. It is perhaps not surprising that a late-night screening of *Un Chien Andalou* should have caused a certain amount of consternation in a wider public, given that this is exactly the effect Luis Buñuel and Salvador Dalí intended it to have, and any teenager whose parents have returned home during a particular sequence of Nicolas Roeg's *Don't Look Now* can tell you how awkward these instances of perceptual overlap can be.

Anyone with a passing interest in the celluloid art form might enjoy trying to guess which film by the same garlanded British director the following letter-writer blames the BBC for 'spoiling' with 'crudeness and vulgarity'.

Letter to the BBC Correspondence Section from husband-and-wife NVALA members

24th January, 1979

Dear Sir,
   With ref. to Monday Film B.B.C.I at 9.25pm Jan. 22nd. The general scenery was superbly photographed, but WHY must you spoil a good film by crudeness and vulgarity.
   You seem to delight in talking close-up pictures of the following:
(a) A young girl putting on her panties.
(b) A native boy's buttocks.
(c) A close up of breasts belonging to a native whilst she was climbing up a tree.
(d) And please don't tell me it was not done intently:

the branches of a tree, photographed in such a way as to resemble the lower part of a woman's body.

(e) The naked girl swimming under WATER all right one can accept that, but <u>WHY</u> a photograph of her standing absolutely naked, was there any need for that?

(f) The scientist scene, was there a necessity to show a close up the legs of the woman sitting there?

(g) And was there an excuse to show men gloating over a gap in the woman's blouse?

It is disgusting that you cannot make some stand to stop these sort of scenes, especially when family viewing includes young men about 15 to 16 yrs old watching with parents. Their minds get corrupted enough by newspapers etc. without you putting on such unnecessary close ups.

Actually I think the beginning was very unwise, fancy filming a father shooting at his own children. Children watching, and don't say they should not be watching at that time of night, because you know full well that a certain percentage of children would be watching.

Just imagine the thoughts in these children's minds, wondering if ever their father would do that to them?

We had settled down to what we thought was going to be a good film, but turned it off in disgust, before it ended.

And you have the cheek to increase our licences! WHAT FOR? To receive rubbish like this in our homes?

Yours sincerely.

Reply from BBC Programme Correspondence Section

7th March, 1979

Please accept my apologies for the very long delay in replying to your letter in connection with the film 'Walkabout'.

This feature film, originally made in 1970 received a general release in the cinemas and considerable critical acclaim. We are naturally sorry to note that you thought

poorly of it, but it is only fair to point out that
we have in fact received an unusually large number of
telephone calls and subsequently letters from viewers
who had enjoyed the film very much.

We cannot agree that the camera shots you list were
included gratuitously. May I assure you too that all our
feature film presentations are carefully viewed in advance
with attention given to the particular placing of each
film. 'Walkabout' was placed at 9.25 p.m. After 9 p.m.
we regard it as reasonable to expect parents to take a
bigger share of the responsibilities for their children's
viewing and we try to provide them in advance with enough
factual information on which to base a judgment.

Thank you for writing to us with your views.

Yours sincerely,

Sheila Cundy (Mrs)

Programme Correspondence Section

What happened in the early seventies was that a level of violent and/or sexual content which might have passed just about
unnoticed in the shadowy world of specialist art cinema suddenly crossed over into the high-street-Odeon mainstream.
Between 1951 and 1970, the British Board of Film Censors had
given an X certificate to films licensed for cinema viewing by
audiences of sixteen years and over. From 1970 onwards, the age
limit on an X-certificate film was raised to eighteen – a change
which Mary Whitehouse would presumably have approved of,
had it not ushered in an era of increasingly extreme content
being shown to audiences whose average age was maintained
(by such technical expedients as buying a ticket for a different film and then hiding in the toilets, or getting the teenager
with the deepest voice to buy the tickets) pretty much where it
always had been.

It wasn't just the 'X' logo that was updated at this point – from
the kind of font you'd normally see used for a beer brewed by

Belgian monks, to something much starker and more intimidating – the films themselves seemed to follow the same trajectory. A process of brutalisation widely seen to have picked up pace in *Bonnie and Clyde*'s closing hail of bullets in 1967, and accelerated again through *Dirty Harry* and *Straw Dogs*, kicked into a new gear altogether with *The Exorcist* and *A Clockwork Orange*.

The extent of the alarm these films generated on their initial cinema releases is hard to grasp for those who have had their sensitivities blunted by many years of trailers for *Saw VI*. But you didn't have to be a member of NVALA to be alarmed by the levels of sexualised violence in them, nor did you have to subscribe to any half-baked theories about *The Exorcist* and *A Clockwork Orange* being cinema's belated Altamont – a ritualised coming to the surface of the sixties' darker undercurrents. All you had to do was buy a ticket and take your seat.

The sense of shock that emerges in this (lengthy, but remorselessly entertaining) report by two NVALA members from their trip to see *The Exorcist* (they watched it so Mary didn't have to) is nicely offset by the occasional moment of disgruntlement. It would be easy to mock the frequent admissions of complete incomprehension – 'No doubt, this was one of the many points that escaped me . . . Had the priest no money with which to help his mother?' – but perhaps the honesty they showcase is preferable to the vogue among twenty-first-century film critics for fact-checking on the Internet Movie Database.

Two NVALA members' report on The Exorcist

THE EXORCIST (X)
The main characters were a twelve-year-old girl called Reagan (who was actually twelve when filming began); the mother and two priests — one elderly and the other young.
    The first part of the story was extremely uneventful. It opened in Northern Iraq where an excavation was in progress amongst some ruins. The language being spoken at this point

was Arabic meaning that sub-titles kept appearing on the screen. During the excavation, the chief archaeologist (who was, as I learnt later, the older priest to be seen later on) came across a small carved head with a devilish face (small enough to fit into his hand). He also discovered a small coin-like charm with similar markings on it. These discoveries appeared to upset him greatly and, after discussing their significance with a colleague at his headquarters, he returned to the site. I thought, at this point, that some larger lurid statue was about to be uncovered. Not to be! Although he did some more digging, amid a slight build up of tension, nothing appeared. At the end of the scene, he was seen standing upon a hillside in a rushing wind and a devilish statue or shape was silhouetted against the sky near him.

The scene then moved to Georgetown, U.S.A., to the home of a middle-class family. I was baffled, at first, why the discovery of a satanic statue in Iraq should have had a bearing upon this household; and I was even more surprised when they later were seen to have the discovery in their possession. No doubt, this was one of the many points that escaped me.

The events for the next quarter of an hour were both monotonous and irritating. The only link between the 'evil force' and the family in this part of the film was when Reagan's mother heard a snorting noise coming from the lift during the night. On finding that her daughter was safely asleep, she returned to bed.

It was around this point that the young priest — destined to die during the final exorcism — appeared. It was very hard to decide what his circumstances were. He was seen visiting his aged Italian mother in a poor part of a city. I was at a loss to decide — both then and now — why his mother was in such poor circumstances and why she died later in a mental hospital (which was depicted in a somewhat sensational manner). Had the priest no money with which to help his mother? If so, why not? After all, he still appeared to be practising as a priest despite the vague insinuations that he had lost his faith.

The next scene of any relevance took place in Reagan's home where she now possessed an ouija board. Now, if one intention of the film was to show the danger of dabbling with ouija boards, then it failed miserably. I only knew that there was supposed to be a connection between the girl's interest in the ouija board and her later possession by the devil because I read so both

Mary with typewriter and telephone – her weapons of mass instruction.

All photos courtesy of the Mary Whitehouse archive

One of Mary's lesser known petitions – this one demanding the continuation of the Queen's Christmas Broadcast – is delivered to Buckingham Palace. Thank goodness it was successful.

A devout-looking delegation of Scottish clergymen present their Petition for Public Decency.

Nothing finishes off a bundle of signatures quite like a red white and blue ribbon.

Never mind Frost/Nixon, Frost/Whitehouse was the only real game in town.

As part of her long-term plan to enhance NVALA's institutional credibility, Mary established a template later employed by men's magazines such as *GQ* and *Loaded*. She set up an utterly bogus awards ceremony and gave prizes to celebrities so they would turn up to be photographed with her – or even (in the case of Cliff Richard) plant a firm kiss on her left cheek. The psycho-sexual implications of the NVALA award statuette are too murky to go into here. Let's just say 'Paging Dr Freud . . .' and leave it at that.

Mick Jagger blatantly checks Mary out on *Frost on Saturday*.

On the dodgems at David Frost's New Year's Eve party: the look of innocent enjoyment on Peter Cook's face suggests he has no idea who is looming up from the rear. No pantomime villain's approach ever merited a lustier cry of 'Behind you!'

With Hughie Green and some dancing girls in a publicity photo prior to her appearance on *Opportunity Knocks*. Alert readers will observe that Mary is the only person with her feet on the ground.

In televised conversation with Joan Bakewell: it is not necessary to be a body language expert to perceive the atmosphere here as 'frosty'. Mary once sent Joan an admiring letter after a particular TV appearance congratulating her on 'the way you have kept yourself in the background'.

Out on the streets with Lord Longford and the Festival of Light.

At home with her *Radio Times*, Mary is a beacon of eternal vigilance.

before and after I saw the film! When Reagan's mother questioned her about the ouija board, the girl agreed to show her how it worked. There was one slight element of the supernatural before the demonstration began. Shortly after, whilst Reagan was lying in bed, her mother came in to talk to her. The conversation was most trivial and it occurred to me that it was possible that it was being ad-libbed without a proper script (a feature, so I understand, adopted in some films nowadays); and if this was indeed so, then it sounded most unnatural.

I have related the first part of the film at some length to indicate the initial monotony that I felt.

After this point, things began to change. Reagan's mother began to show a propensity for using bad language. This was first noticeable during her exasperation at being unable to get in touch with someone on the telephone. She began to abuse the operator: the word 'shit' entered her vocabulary (which included other such words as the film progressed); the name of Jesus Christ began to be used as an expletive and continued, from time to time, to be so used.

Reagan began complaining that her bed was shaking and the snorting noise was heard again from the loft. Her mother decided to go into the loft to investigate (taking, rather absurdly, a candle as opposed to a torch). After a search, she found nothing there except for a man (whose identity and reason for being there neither of us could establish) who blew out the candle after having made a sudden appearance. Strangely enough, the girl's mother seemed to know who it was. Shortly after this incident, a priest in a nearby Catholic church discovered — to his horror — that a statue of the Virgin Mary had been desecrated.

Sometime later, a party was being held at the family home. During the evening, Reagan came downstairs and stood at the doorway of the room where the party was in full swing. She said that she was going to die and, while standing there dressed in her night-dress, she urinated on the doorway carpet. It was impossible to see — both then and now — why the inclusion of such a scene was deemed necessary.

After this incident, while Reagan was lying in bed, the bed shaking continued. Her mother tried to stop it when it happened and, feeling that her daughter was unwell, she sent for the doctor. Reagan had not, at this point, changed into the devil-child, though she did scream that something was attacking her on the bed (during the shaking scenes). When the doctor came, he gave her an injection, during which she shouted: 'You vulgar bastard!'

The girl was then taken to the hospital to be X-rayed. Once again, the whole procedure was sensational and unreal: every piece of equipment — be it the X-ray machine or the screen containing the photographs — seemed to make far more noise than would actually happen. Her examination showed that she was physically alright.

On returning home, things began to change. Once she was in her bedroom, the noise continued and Reagan began to become possessed by the devil. Her throat swelled up and her voice changed to a low growl. Shortly after this change, the doctors entered her bedroom and — whilst kneeling on the bed — Reagan pushed the lower part of her stomach towards them and, in the devil-voice said 'Fuck me.'

After yet another visit to the hospital, the girl was returned home and a psychiatrist was summoned. He questioned her, during hypnosis, and he ordered the person inside her to reveal himself. This resulted in the girl appearing to give the psychiatrist a forceful blow which knocked him to the ground.

After a visit to the hospital (where Reagan's mother was advised to summon an exorcist) the young priest — seen earlier in the film — was sent for. Before he arrived, Reagan underwent a further transformation in her bedroom into the complete devil-child. I will not dwell upon the details of this transformation except to say that from then on her teeth were discoloured; she had an unpleasant grin; she had scratches upon her body — though not in the profusion that I had anticipated from press reports; her face was pale; she was still dressed in her nightdress; in some scenes she was bound to the bed and her eyes had been made up to make them look evil.

After the complete transformation, her mother came into the bedroom (because, I recall, of the noise). As she entered, Reagan was lying on the bed apparently jabbing herself between the legs with a crucifix — which someone had placed in her room — and though the incident was not shown in close detail, it was perfectly clear what was happening. On seeing her mother, the girl raised herself up — displaying a considerable amount of blood on the lower part of her night-dress, — and, grinning, she muttered in the superimposed devil-voice a blasphemous invitation to her mother (referring to what she had just been doing): 'Let Jesus f*** you' (which I refuse to reprint in full). After uttering this, she proceeded to attack her mother; the wardrobe started moving across the room and her mother was soon seen lying on the floor with a considerable amount of blood on her face, I did not catch the subsequent devil-voice dialogue.

The young priest then arrived for a preliminary investigation and, during his presence in the bedroom, Reagan emitted some green vomit over him which hit him on the chest and lower shoulder. During his questioning, he taped her replies which, on examining them later, he decided were being spoken backwards.

Feeling unable to conduct the exorcism himself, he sent for the older priest (seen at the opening of the film) who was referred to as being experienced at exorcisms. As the two of them, after due preparation, entered Reagan's bedroom — which was now freezing cold — she greeted them with a mouthful of extremely foul language beginning: 'Stick your cock up your arse . . .' Although I recall the substance of the rest of a lengthy and extremely foul sentence, I cannot quote it accurately. During the scene, I noted that the word 'fucking' was used and the phrase 'cocks in hell'.

The two priests then began the exorcism service and they were shown to be remarkably incapable at being able to do anything. During the scene, the bed shook; the girl emitted more green vomit, which left her night-dress unpleasantly stained; she displayed a thick, blue pointed tongue and she laughed — in the devil-voice — at their inability to do anything. The use of the phrase 'fuck him' added to the depravity. There were other incidents during this scene: books flying about; the priests being thrown backwards on to the floor; the girl revolving her head upon her shoulders and her levitating and remaining there for some time.

Later on, she began to talk in Italian — her voice sounding like that of the younger priest's dead mother. The older priest warned his colleague not to be deceived by the trick. Then, after a fairly lengthy attempt at exorcism, the two priests decided to rest for a while. The younger priest left the room at this point — to remove (I think) the green vomit from his vestments. On his return, he found that the older priest was lying dead on the floor. He first started to pound him on the chest with his fists and he then turned in anger upon the devil-child. He started to wrestle with her on the floor and, during this scene, he offered to take the devil into his own body. This brought about a change in him. He hurled himself (or was hurled) through the open bed-room window and was next seen to be lying in a considerable pool of blood at the bottom of a long flight of stone stairs outside the house.

Reagan, now back to normal, was crying in her bedroom. The end of the film which, mercifully, soon came, showed the family packing up and leaving the house. As they were leaving, the girl's mother was quietly assured by another priest that her daughter would not remember what had happened.

COMMENTS

(1) The film did not show the supreme power of Christ over the powers of darkness: the only reason that the devil was exorcized was because the younger priest agreed to take it into his own body which is quite unscriptural.

(2) As has already been indicated, the ouija board (despite what the film's intention may have been) appeared to be a rather harmless toy of little significance to the rest of the story.

(3) As is well known, the film is a distortion of a real incident.

(4) Neither of us was expecting the language to be as foul as it was. Moreover, although one is aware that the foul language was superimposed over the child, neither this fact nor the strong possibility that other trick effects were used elsewhere in the film exonerates those who have involved her in a depraved and extremely morally harmful role. It is clear that a dangerous precedent has been established by this film with respect to what children may be seen to do and heard, apparently, to say and for this reason alone, it is to be deeply deplored. As for the crucifix scene, its utter blasphemy is self-evident.

(5) This film is liable to have delayed shock effect upon one — and I speak from personal experience. By delayed, in my case, it was five days later. It is unreal, therefore, for it to be assumed that anyone who leaves the cinema after seeing it apparently undisturbed has not been affected.

Thus, this film is not only dangerous, but it is also likely to spread confusion. I am not surprised that some members of its audiences have needed counselling afterwards especially because of the unscriptural manner in which the exorcism was eventually performed.

For those fortunate enough to have gone to see *The Exorcist* in the Birmingham area, such help was close at hand, courtesy of the following well-intentioned leaflet.

Extract of leaflet distributed outside cinemas in the Birmingham area

<u>Fear</u>
Fear is contagious, and no fear more so than the awesome dread of disembodied evil.

1974
And, if we become gripped by this type of fear, our minds are opened wide to the psychological suggestion that we too are at risk of invasion by similar powers of evil. We are not immune simply because this is 1974 and we are in Birmingham, we are not immune because our reason tells us such things cannot happen — and we are very vulnerable indeed if we half believe they might.

THE PEOPLE WHO GIVE OUT THIS LEAFLET have not come here because they think they are better than anybody else. They are just aware of the great danger of evil and how it can affect us all. They believe, too, that there is an answer to the challenge of life in Jesus Christ and they want to share this with you. It is because His love and power are real that they have come to see something special about life and they hate to see it smeared by evil and twisted ideas.
    If after seeing the film you need spiritual help, or counsel or just want to talk it over with someone, then please telephone one of the following numbers:-

[16 phone numbers in Harborne, Edgbaston, Moseley and Sutton Coldfield followed]

But what of those exposed to the awesome dread of disembodied evil elsewhere in the country – who could they turn to? Happily, there was an increasing amount of choice. By 1974, a range of new organisations had sprung up to join with

NVALA in the battle to save Britain's collective soul.

As with so many movements dedicated to spiritual uplift, the exact origins of the Nationwide Festival of Light are the subject of intense and sometimes acrimonious debate. It is generally agreed that one of two key preconditions for the advent of the NFOL was the return from India of the evangelical Christian missionaries Peter and Janet Hill (who came back to the UK in 1971 and found the newly free and easy climate of their homeland very much not to their liking).

The other was a telephone conversation between Mary Whitehouse and Malcolm Muggeridge, in which the reformed satirist and *Punch*-editor-turned-Christian-polemicist – often irreverently dubbed 'Saint Mugg' – was so horrified to hear of the riotously disrespectful reception Whitehouse had received in the course of a recent Leicester University speaking engagement that he proposed some kind of grand occasion to set the young people of Britain back on the right road. Whether the form which this event ultimately took – the lighting of bonfires and torches around the country with live performances at a Hyde Park concert by Christian artists including Cliff Richard and Dana – would be the right one to pull the nation's youth back from a decadent abyss, only time would tell.

What can now be pointed out with certainty is an interesting variation in Whitehouse's three autobiographical accounts of the relevant telephonic exchange. In the one written shortly after the actual event, 1971's *Who Does She Think She Is?*, she talks only of Muggeridge proposing a plan to 'mobilise the cohorts' as a way 'to demonstrate our faith and belief'.

By 1982's *A Most Dangerous Woman?* and 1993's *Quite Contrary*, her recall has improved considerably. Malcolm Muggeridge is now credited (rather in the manner in which biopics of great men and women show them delivering their best-known speeches in an improbably unprepared and spontaneous manner) with the following far more grandiloquent and historically significant utterance: 'Mary, what are we going to do for these young people? . . . We must have a great festival of light.'

Whether or not she was directly involved in coining the name of this new grass-roots upsurge, the Whitehouse methodology certainly turned out to be a formative influence on the way the Festival of Light operated. At both the initial NFOL meeting at Westminster Central Hall on 9 September 1971 and the subsequent Trafalgar Square rally on 25 September (at which she spoke), the exploitation of sex and violence by various different branches of the entertainment industry was identified as the single greatest current threat to the nation's moral well-being, and a flurry of monitoring and other initiatives were subsequently set in train, along lines uncannily similar to those laid down by NVALA.

Extract from survey by the Nationwide Festival of Light

Opinions gleaned after discussions with 15–16 year olds in two Comprehensive Schools.

LAST TANGO	Many saw this. Discussed at every possible opportunity. Sexual relations described as dirty. One comment was 'It's surprising what you can do with butter'.
CLOCKWORK ORANGE	Too violent. Pity felt for man to whom violence was being done.
EXORCIST	Really silly. Shock of the unexpected made you think the language was the worst thing.

GENERAL REMARKS

1. Can get into cinema easily (some younger ones were seen to be turned away)
2. Why not be allowed into cinema, if can marry at 16?
3. Violence was enjoyed
4. Any cruelty to children was hated
5. Wide knowledge of slang expressions (teacher had to be initiated)

6. Majority saw late night films on T.V. at home
7. Cult of spotting sexual implications on T.V. advertising
8. Some girls thought above films should be censored.

FROM A SECONDARY SCHOOL TEACHER
As a teacher of girls aged 14—18 I am very concerned about
the effects that films are having on this age group. Many of
these girls come from deeply disturbed backgrounds and go out
a lot in the evenings. Many get into 'X' films two or three
years under age and have seen how difficult it is to enforce
the age limit on them.
   A typical film-going sixth former said to me 'If one remembers
that a film is a film and not to be taken too literally, usually
adverse effects are avoided, but if someone of a vulnerable
age and intelligence and not knowledgeable in a subject is
ready to be influenced and possibly to experiment, the effects
can be drastic. This has happened to several of my friends.'
Of a fifth year group of twenty five girls, twenty three wanted
censorship to continue and to be increased for their own
protection. Many said that the emphasis on sexual perversions
had increased their own problems in the past and there was NO
DESIRE AT ALL FOR LESS CENSORSHIP: QUITE THE REVERSE

   For all the obvious influence of NVALA, there was one clear
contrast between the Festival of Light and Whitehouse's earlier campaigns. Where the latter relied on local mobilisation to
apply pressure at the cultural centre (i.e. by inspiring people to
write individual letters to the BBC or Westminster MPs), the
former instituted a centralised bureaucracy in the hope of co-
ordinating diverse local actions.
   The antiquated planning machinery by which individual town
and city councils retained the capacity to permit or forbid the
screening of particular films created an opening for restrictive
interventions (this regulatory loophole would later be responsible for the cancellation of many of the gigs on the Sex Pistols'
Anarchy tour). Thus it was that Last Tango in Paris came to be
banned in Worthing.

In the course of the struggle to achieve the latter landmark of responsible local governance, the Festival of Light general secretary Steve Stevens (whose Wikipedia designation as a 'missionary aviator' does not fully do justice to his much-decorated war career as a Lancaster bomber pilot) was at one point threatened with prosecution for circulating extracts of uncut dialogue from the film to various Worthing worthies. 'It is dire filth,' observed one councillor. 'How any producer could ever ask a cast to act these lines I don't know.'

Unabashed by his brush with the law, Stevens's campaigning activities would continue well into the current century. He was being pilloried on an atheist website for his involvement in an attempt to launch a UK version of the US 'Day of Purity' virginity festival as recently as 2011, at the not so tender age of ninety-one.

Worthing was not the only south coast resort to stand up and be counted. Hastings Council also decided to ban *A Clockwork Orange* (though the film's influence on behaviour in certain parts of the town centre on Saturday nights can still be observed in the present day). The eloquent testimony of the Hastings councillor John Hodgson – printed below – certainly played its part in that decision.

Extract from the Festival of Light's A Clockwork Orange *press briefing*

```
If you wish to see thugs and bullies glorified, if you wish to
see an old man battered to death and left lying in a pool of
blood, if you would want to see a young girl raped, in detail,
by a gang of four Hell's Angels, or a young wife stripped
and ravished in close-up and colour in front of her captive
husband . . . If you wish to see the police portrayed as vicious
depraved bullies spattering blood from their prisoners all
over the walls of the interview rooms, or the prison service
and probation service portrayed as homosexual and sadistic
maniacs . . . If you wish to see every moral aspect of family
life torn to shreds before your eyes, sex with everybody and
```

anybody as the order of the day, in one scene 20 times in five
minutes (and this is no exaggeration) . . . If you want to see
all these things then I'm very sorry, you've missed a great
picture, but you badly need a psychiatrist.

Ann Whitaker of Bodmin in Cornwall started one of the most
enduring of local initiatives. It would be wrong to make any biblical parallel too explicit, for fear of blasphemous intimations,
but it would certainly be fair to describe Whitaker as an evangelist for the Whitehouse gospel. The fact that she copied Mary
into the correspondence of her Community Standards Association was clear evidence of her respectful attitude.

Letter to clerk of the Cornish county council

21 February, 1973

Dear Sir,
    There is growing consternation at the continual
showing of violent, blasphemous and obscene films in
our cinemas, films which soon afterwards appear on
television. Wherever I go in Cornwall this is the
subject of discussion and concern, young parents and
older people alike voicing their distress and disquiet.
    I am very sorry that 'Clockwork Orange', for instance,
is at this moment being shown in Newquay. This film
provides an education in the techniques of 'mugging' —
and the lessons are being learnt. The assault of a girl
and her rape by four men (described in the national
press a short time ago) was 'classical Clockwork
Orange', as one who has been following the development
of these films commented. When Arthur Bremer was tried
for the attempted murder of Governor George Wallace
it was disclosed that he had written in his diary, 'I
saw Clockwork Orange and thought about getting George
Wallace during the film'. When Bremer was found guilty
he was asked if he had anything to say and responded,
'All I have to say is that I wish you had protected me

from myself'. Mr. David Holbrook, educationalist and
critic, wrote in the 'Western Sunday Independent' on 11
February, 'I recently met a distinguished professional
man who had just been to see the film Clockwork Orange.
This man reported that he was appalled to find rows
of youngsters in the audience.' So much for the
effectiveness of the 'not under 18 yrs' provision!

May I know what are the arrangements of the
General Purposes Committee for the viewing of these
controversial films? I understand, perhaps wrongly, that
only two members of the Committee at a time vet the films
for which licences are sought. In the case of those very
controversial films it would seem right for all members
of the Committee to see the films. We are dealing, here,
with a matter of national importance.

The showing of 'The Devils', 'Straw Dogs', 'Clockwork
Orange', 'Oh! Calcutta' and now 'Last Tango in Paris',
all produce a sense of outrage in people who know that
life has much more to offer than violence, promiscuous
sex, drugs and pornography and who are grieved to
think that these are increasingly being presented to
young people as a way of life, which, apparently, goes
unrebuked and unhampered by the older generation and
those in responsible positions in our society and which,
therefore, presumably offers a possible alternative to a
more stable, responsible and accepted pattern of living
such as has been held up as necessary to the health and
prosperity of our country, at least as a standard, since
as far back as Alfred the Great or beyond.

I am sure that the general public would respect and
react favourably to a much stronger line being taken
by our Local Authorities against the showing of these
depraved films. I do ask you to refuse these films for
cinemas in Cornwall.

Yours faithfully,
Ann Whitaker

Whitaker's letter shows just how strongly concerns about

extreme cinematic content reflected anxiety over the kind of anti-
social action it was thought likely to inspire. Mary Whitehouse
famously – perhaps even notoriously – asserted that the capacity
of, say, A Clockwork Orange to influence the behaviour of some
(albeit not all) of those who saw it did not need to be scientifically proven, as to assume the existence of such a linkage was 'common sense'. For all the mockery to which this view was subject
at the time, no one who has (as I have) witnessed the impact of
an informal screening of the film on a gathering of drunken glue-
punks called the Hackney Hell Crew at a mid-eighties Homerton
squat party can really deny the truth of it.

The extent to which artists should take responsibility for the
possible reactions to their work of disturbed individuals (whether subject to actual psychiatric disorders or merely out of their
minds on Special Brew) is a thorny philosophical issue. In the
case of A Clockwork Orange, tabloid headlines and late-night
telephone death threats (in which no NVALA member was ever
implicated) made up the director Stanley Kubrick's mind for
him, and at his insistence the film was withdrawn from circulation in the UK for almost two decades – re-emerging only after
his death in 1999, and receiving its first full uncut TV broadcast
on Sky Box Office in 2001. It's on ITV all the time, now.

Mary Whitehouse's NVALA and Ann Whitaker's CSA seem to
have collaborated very happily in campaigns over A Clockwork
Orange and other landmarks of cinematic depravity. However,
the increasing eagerness of the Festival of Light (under its ambitious new director Raymond Johnson) to mark out its own territory as an organisation would lead Mary to issue the following
imperious summation of her role in its genesis. Perhaps not surprisingly – Whitehouse kicks to kill – the FOL pulled its head
in a bit after this, and later mutated apologetically into a lower-
profile body called Christian Action Research and Education.

Letter to Festival of Light director Raymond Johnston

29th March, 1977

Dear Raymond,

Very many thanks for your letter — I very much appreciate the tone in which it was written. However, it seems to me that if we are to clear the air completely, there are still some things which need to be said.

I do understand that it is probably quite difficult for you, who have come on the scene comparatively late, to realise fully what has happened since 1963 and indeed, perhaps even in the very early days of FOL.

I am quite sure that the present difficulties have arisen simply because FOL and VALA were, until your appointment, so much involved one with the other. As you will be aware, if you have read Max Caulfield's biography of me, that the first concept of a 'Festival of light' was born in a conversation between Malcolm Muggeridge and myself more than a year before Peter Hill came to Britain. We discussed the idea on a number of occasions and even put out queries about booking the Albert Hall, but both of us were too involved with other matters to be able to organise anything. Then Peter came home, experienced his vision, went to see Eddie, who sent him to me. I shared with him what we had been feeling and arranged, then and there, for him to go and see Malcolm. The rest is history.

I mention this for one reason only — to emphasise that VALA and FOL were totally involved one with the other. Steve and Kay had been members of VALA for years and were working very closely with Roy and Polly Bennett who were our organisers in East London. Since when I have worked in the closest liason with Steve. As you must be aware the Press constantly infers a very close link, often, indeed suggesting that we are the same organisation with two different names. A situation which upon occasion, pleases me no more than I realise it pleases you. However, I suspect — whatever we do — this

will continue though I am always at great pains, these
days, to say it is not so!

So what went wrong? — or perhaps you would say, right!
It is quite clear to me now that at some point — I
imagine when you were appointed — a decision was made
that FOL must carve out its own image and be quite
independent. Raymond, in no way do I quarrel with that
— in many ways, I welcome it. What has been unfortunate
— this at least is how I see it — is that this change
of policy was made without VALA in any way being
informed. My name was taken off the list of the Council
of Reference without anyone even having the courtesy
to tell me; we were left believing that FOL wished
the former policy to continue and, instead of those
responsible for the Festival having both the courage —
though why it needed it, I shall never know! — and the
honesty to tell us what its new policy was we were just
left with a growing sense of estrangement and exclusion,
certainly as far as you were concerned.

There has been no break at all in our teamwork with
Steve. It really is quite wrong to suggest that FOL were
approached in only about 5–10% of our activities. It is
no doubt true that you were for the reasons which I am
sure you now understand. I don't mean that to be in any
way offensive but my contact with Steve has been if not
daily then not much less.

I was really most surprised, Raymond, about how very
little you seem to know of VALA's Modus operandi! The
cosy picture you paint of me just sitting discussing
things with Ernest, and now with John, is so far from
the actual fact of the matter as to be laughable — I had
not expected you to be influenced by those who say 'she
speaks for no-one but herself'! I certainly am spokesman
for VALA but I can — and do — call on a tremendously wide
team of people, in this country and abroad, at a minutes
notice. At times — as in the immediate announcement that
we would launch a Nationwide Petition for Public Decency
— it may look as though I take unilateral action, but the

decision to launch that campaign had already been taken
in committee — the timing was left with me. If I am able
— and I am — to make an immediate statement to the Press,
for example, it is because the thinking and the planning
have already been done.

VALA has been built on teamwork — until David Sturdy
died four years ago, never a day went by but that we
talked on the 'phone two, three, four, even five times
— every development, every major letter, every public
statement was checked with David and Sheila — his wisdom
and perception were one of God's great gifts to us. His
last prayer, only a few minutes before he died, was that
God 'would raise up new men to stand alongside.' And
that, of course, is what has happened. And there were and
are many others with whom I constantly keep in touch and
whose experience and wisdom I cherish and depend upon.

I would certainly be very sorry if you interpreted what
I said in my letter as meaning that I thought you 'were
trying to shoulder me'. If you did interpret that way then
I fear you have not only missed the whole point of it and
go beyond its intention but you have surely introduced a
concept totally out of keeping with the dependance on the
guidance of God which should be at the heart of our work.

So great was the hostility directed at VALA from
certain quarters that one has learned that the only
important thing, day by day, is to seek to try to follow
the leading of the Holy Spirit — on this basis, there
are only people not organisations. I do not have to
be persuaded that FOL and VALA are 'not playing the
same game all the time' — other organisations are not
either, but that has not prevented us having the closest
personal teamwork with them.

However, Raymond, I assure you that I have got the
point at last! I have absolutely no feelings against
you — I accept, with humility, that MW and VALA can be
an embarrassment to FOL and to those who make its work
possible. And I am quite content to accept that and
behave accordingly.

With Kindest Regards
Mary Whitehouse

   The struggle between individual and more corporate forms of
campaigning embodied in the above letter reflects a fundamental
concern of Mary Whitehouse's whole public life – the balance
between what should be private and what should be public. The
reason she was more passionately concerned with TV than with
cinema was that the former was experienced entirely within the
private realm of the home.

   It was only – as in her ultimately successful later campaigns
over 'video nasties' and to censure the IBA for not stopping
Channel 4 showing the film *Scum* – when the flood tide of cinematic ordure lapped at the living-room door that her energies
would be fully engaged. In the mean time, it was a piquant irony
that one of the most imaginative of Whitehouse's attempts to
find a legal application of the concept of 'obscenity' that would
actually work in the courts – her 1974 prosecution of a canni-
bal-themed proto-video nasty called *Blow Out* (not to be confused with Antonioni's *Blow-Up*, though she wasn't a great fan
of that either) using the vagrancy acts – fell foul of the magis-
trate's insistence that the cinema the film had been shown in was
(in legal terms) a private rather than a public space.

   The Web and the iPhone were still not glints in Tim Berners-
Lee and Steve Jobs's eyes, and yet the boundary between public
and private space was already becoming increasingly hard to
define. As a portent of just how intense the struggle to do that
was going to get, the following letter sent to Mary Whitehouse
by a married couple from Oxford could hardly be bettered. Giv-
en the key role played by the evangelical Oxford Group in her
own religious awakening in the 1930s, it is also satisfying to
see evidence of Whitehouse's reciprocal influence on the city of
dreaming spires – especially in the unexpected realm of student
feminist graffiti.

*Letter from two married Oxford undergraduates with enclosure
of statement made in court*

26th March, 1981

Dear Mrs Whitehouse,

  On the evening of Saturday, 13th December, 1980, the
ABC Cinema in Magdalen street, Oxford displayed a poster
for a film. The poster depicted a naked woman at the feet
of a man holding a gun. The film was called 'Violation
of the Bitch' with the sub-title 'she asked for it'.
My husband and I were so outraged by this display that
we sprayed the poster with paint. We were subsequently
charged with Criminal Damage and ordered to pay a total
fine of £65 (that including costs and damages).

  On February 3rd we wrote to our local M.P., our
City Council and the Advertising Standards Authority
protesting about this poster. I enclose a copy of the
statement we made in Court.

  The ASA seems to be taking our complaint seriously,
though slowly. Our M.P. seems to be permanently abroad
and has not answered our letter personally, though his
secretary has acknowledged it with some encouragement.
Our Council is proving very difficult. They seem to pass
our letter from one to another and apart from a very
cool letter from the Council solicitor:

'it is council policy to show any film which has been
granted a certificate by the censor . . . no one else has
complained about this film' (!)

we have not had a proper letter from any one councillor.

  We are particularly disturbed by the attitude of the
police. Every newsagent in Oxford is literally full of
pornography, and I am sure the Police could prosecute
any one of them should they choose to do so. But we
suspect that it is police policy to turn a blind eye
in this area. At the same time there are a dreadful
number of attacks on women in Oxford, a great deal of
harrassment and bullying of women generally, which the

police seem unwilling or powerless to prevent. We feel
that women's bodies and their feelings are treated with
utter contempt.

As you may have gathered, we are totally aware of
the illegality of what we have done, and totally
unrepentant! We have spoken to many people about the
incident, and all say they thought we were right, but
either through laziness or embarrassment hardly anyone
seems prepared to make a fuss.

We should very much appreciate your advice. Can you
give us any 'hints' on how to complain effectively to
(a) the council, (b) the police, (c) the cinema.

Of course, if you felt able to include this particular
obnoxious film in your own campaign we would be very
heartened.

Yours sincerely,

Statement made in court
We felt the public display of this particular poster to be
deeply offensive and provocative.

We had hoped to produce a copy of the poster to show you, as
we thought it would be the best possible justification of what
we have done. Ever since we were charged we have been trying
to get hold of a copy.

First, we tried unsuccessfully at the ABC Cinema involved.

Then we tried the film's distributors, Tigon, who proved
evasive in the extreme — they seem to change Soho addresses,
and telephone numbers regularly. When finally tracked down,
they did promise more than once to send a copy of the poster.
But they have not done so.

Instead, we shall have to describe the poster to you. The
title of the film, 'Violation of the Bitch', was printed across
the top. Beneath it was a picture of an undressed woman lying
at the feet of a man, brandishing a gun. Across the picture
ran the words, 'She asked for it'.

We must stress that this poster was on public display in
Magdalen Street itself. We found it offensive on several
counts: Firstly, the wording is such as provokes and endorses
sexual contempt, abuse, if not attack. Were race involved

rather than sex in the title — and the film called 'Violation of the Coon' — there would, quite rightly, be NO QUESTION of a poster like this appearing.

ANYTHING which asserts that the violation of women is 'asked for' and presents that violation as good entertainment is <u>unacceptable.</u> We are disturbed that this film was ever granted a licence by our city councillors.

There is a frighteningly high rate of attacks on women in Oxford. Indeed, only a few months ago the police declared themselves unable to protect women from these sorts of assaults, and suggested that they kept a curfew.

In this context, the display of this poster is a moral outrage.

It is more than ironical that the violation of a perspex cover of a cinema display is considered a graver offence than the violation of women.

We cannot pretend that we think this is the best way to object to something so offensive, but our immediate reaction was one of deep disgust. We have since written to our MP, the City Council, and the Advertising Standards Authority, who are at present investigating the issue.

I am quite sure that you are aware that under the Obscenity Laws it is virtually impossible to bring a successful private prosecution.

We admit now that it may have been better to complain to the police about it. But even when our misconduct brought the poster display to their attention, they seemed totally uninterested.

I would now like to add that we were very careful to do the absolute minimum of damage. The poster was shown in a perspex-covered frame and we sprayed <u>only</u> the perspex cover, <u>not</u> the frame and <u>not</u> the wall around it. Even then we made quite sure not to obscure anything but the offending poster. Aerosol sprays are considered very emotive things, but to remove cellulose paint from perspex is an easy and cheap operation — it only needs a wad of cotton wool, and some thinners. It is even easier to remove than, say, a sticker.

If only the revolutionaries of earlier eras had been so considerate, how very different the cities of Paris and Moscow might look today.

10th April 1975

Dear Mrs. Whitehouse,

Touché, as they say. You do
your homework extremely well.

Yours sincerely,

Michael Swann

Mrs. Mary Whitehouse,
Triangle Farm House,
Far Forest,
Kidderminster,
Worcs.

Reply from the chairman of the BBC to Mary Whitehouse

10. Swann's Way

The central focus of the romantic comedy genre is the quest for the ideal partner who can be elevated above all possible rivals as 'the One'. The romcom motif which has already been discerned in Mary Whitehouse's relationship with the BBC demands just such a perfect counterpart.

To which of her TV executive sparring partners is it easiest to imagine Mary uttering the immortal words 'You complete me'? Sir Hugh Greene's oft-quoted (for obvious reasons) purchase of a grotesque naked portrait of her entitled *Mary Whitehouse with Five Breasts* by the maverick Wigan expressionist James Lawrence Isherwood (also celebrated for painting *Tommy Steele with Two Heads* and a sadly far from prophetic 1964 work called *The Bald Beatles, 2024*) testifies to a measure of sexual interest on his part, but every indication is that this was not reciprocated.

The passionate love/hate nexus between Mary Whitehouse and the BBC actually found its ultimate expression in her correspondence with Michael Swann, the suave ex-vice-chancellor of Edinburgh University who followed Lord Hill as BBC chairman in 1973. As a portent of the good things to come, here is his first written communication with her.

Letter from Michael Swann

28th December, 1972

Dear Mrs Whitehouse,
  I received a telegram on the day of my appointment as Chairman of Governors of the B.B.C. from Dr Sturdy who is, I believe, your Vice-Chairman. I don't, I am afraid,

know his address but the B.B.C. has given me your
address and perhaps you would be kind enough to pass on
my warmest thanks for his good wishes.

I was intrigued that you should turn up on the
telephone line the other evening. You are certainly
very determined. Anyway I look forward to meeting in
due course, though as I am sure you will appreciate I
am, for the immediate future, very much taken up with
getting to know people in the B.B.C. and their way of
working added to which I am not giving up being Vice-
Chancellor of Edinburgh until the Autumn.

With my best wishes,
Yours sincerely,
Michael Swann

The overture before the grand opera of Whitehouse and
Swann's relationship had been the gradual thawing in the BBC's
attitude towards her which coincided with the chairmanship of
Lord Hill. Within just a few weeks of Hill's appointment, Mary
Whitehouse had made a routine request to be allowed a right of
reply to criticism of NVALA by the maverick BBC controller of
programmes Stuart Hood (a war hero, translator, left-wing activ-
ist and subsequent member of the Workers Revolutionary Party).

Letter to the producer of BBC TV's Talkback

1st November, 1967

Dear Mr. Coleman,
   Mr. Stewart Hood in dismissing the great majority of
people who write in about programmes as 'cranks', is
using a well known technique of self justification, and
one which also has the effect of making people afraid to
speak out in case they should be labelled as 'unstable'.
As Secretary of the National Viewers' and Listeners'
Association I have received over 60,000 letters from
responsible people within the community — people that

Mr. Hood could not possibly call 'cranks' to their faces
— all of whom are disturbed at certain current B.B.C.
policies. It is obvious that Mr. Hood is too personally
involved to be able to view criticism objectively, and
as the representative of over 700,000 viewers I would
appreciate the opportunity of meeting him face to face
on 'Talkback' next week.
  Yours sincerely,
  Mary Whitehouse

To Mary Whitehouse's surprise as much as anyone else's, this
request was agreed to. Although the warm welcome she received
from the producer David Coleman (yes, it was *that* David Coleman) was not echoed by the panel and an aggressively oppositional studio audience, at least she was no longer completely
persona non grata on BBC TV. Any doubts that this change of
heart had come directly from Lord Hill were soon dispelled by
the determined insistence of Sir Hugh Greene's ally Milton Shul-
man that it had been entirely the director general's idea.

Mary's coming in from the cold was by no means an overnight process, though. In August 1968, the BBC's head of talks
and current affairs (radio) J. A. Camacho agreed to meet her
in person, courteously turning down her proposal for a talk on
Woman's Hour about her recent visit to West Germany on the
grounds of her written report's multifarious factual inaccuracies.

Meanwhile, she was conducting an increasingly frustrating
correspondence with the BBC's Secretary, Kenneth Lamb, in
which he repeatedly challenged NVALA's right to be considered
as a representative organisation.

Letter to the Secretary of the BBC

1st October, 1968

Dear Mr. Lamb,
  You ask me to tell you 'in what sense (I) regard (our)

Association as representative of the public as a whole
or organised to represent particular interests'. I would
very much like to reply, first, by asking you whether you
would concede that any organisation could represent 'the
public as a whole'? I doubt if I would.

Nevertheless, in so far as an association can be
representative of a very wide cross section of public
opinion and interests, I believe that this Association
is so. I do not know of any section of our national
life — political, social, industrial, professional,
religious which is not represented amongst our members,
humanists and communists excluded. May I say, in passing,
that since I am well aware that the membership of the
British Humanist Association is under 4000, I am not very
impressed by the suggestion they form a significant section
of our society, except in so far as they are so vocal.

You ask, also, how we are 'organised to represent
particular interests'. Surely the aims of this
Association, as set out on the enclosed leaflets, and as
articulated over and over again in the national press
and elsewhere, make them clear.

You also ask upon what we base our claim that this
Association now represents over 1,000,000 people. Over
half a million people signed our Manifesto; National
VALA now has well over 7000 memberships, hundreds of
which are block memberships on behalf of branches of
organisations of all kinds, and some of which represent
official membership of national associations of a very
varied nature.

In my letter to you I asked whether you would be good
enough to tell me what sort of body you considered
to 'be representative of the public as a whole, or
organised to represent particular interests.' I have
been to some pains to answer the questions raised by you
in your letter to me, so I would be most grateful if you
could answer the questions I raised with you.

Yours sincerely,
Mary Whitehouse

Reply from the Secretary of the BBC

14th October, 1968

Dear Mrs. Whitehouse,

Thank you for your letter of 1st October.

I am glad that we are agreed that it would not be right for there to be any special relationship between your Association and the BBC. That is the basic point I was concerned with.

May I attempt to clarify what I meant by bodies 'organised to represent a particular interest', which I said would be my primary concern? I had in mind such bodies as the B.M.A., the N.F.U., the National Council of Women, and so on, which are acknowledged as having the right to speak for their respective interests, and are organised in a representative way.

I am still puzzled to know in what sense you regard N.V.A.L.A. as being a body of that kind. It might be helpful, perhaps, if I follow up your point that the Association now has over 7,000 memberships. From what you say I take it that most of these are individual and not representative. But you go on to say that some of them 'represent official membership of national organisations of a very varied nature'. If there is a list available of these organisations I should be most grateful if you would let me have a copy.

The other point which arises is the one about being organised in a representative way. In this connection I shall be most interested to hear in due course how your plans for a democratically appointed Central Council are working out.

On the question of bodies 'representative of the public as a whole', I suppose there is only one, and that is Parliament. But what was in the back of my mind is that in this respect the BBC's responsibility is to be sensitive to the reactions of the public as a whole. Our main instrument for this is, of course, Audience Research, and its representative sampling of public opinion about our programmes.

Yours sincerely,
(Kenneth Lamb)
The Secretary

Further reply from Mary Whitehouse

31st December, 1968

Dear Mr Lamb,

I must apologise for the very long delay in replying to your letter of the 14th October. My mother has been, and remains, extremely ill so that opportunities to deal with personal letters have been very inadequate, and as you know I am travelling about a great deal.

Thank you for clarifying in your letter what you meant by bodies 'organised to represent a particular interest', and, of course, I accept what you say about such organisations.

We do not regard VALA as being a body representing a particular interest in the sense that, for instance, the B.M.A. does. We do regard it as a body of persons with a common interest in maintaining high broadcasting standards, out to build a vocal and effective public opinion on all matters relating to broadcasting in so far as they affect the viewer and listener. I would be most grateful if you would explain to me why you do not feel that such an organisation has as much a right to be heard in your consultations as, say, the Women's Institutes, whose only common link is that its members live in the country.

Yours sincerely,
Mary Whitehouse

I make that game, set and match to Whitehouse, with the Women's Institutes sent flying just past the ballboy's nose by her trademark overhead smash. Yet even the replacement of Sir Hugh Greene by Charles Curran still did not finally signal the 'new balls, please' that Mary had hoped for.

Letter to the new director general of the BBC

3rd December, 1970

Dear Mr. Curran,

You may perhaps remember that we discussed the possibility of a meeting at the time of your appointment as Director General of the B.B.C.

You expressed yourself willing to meet me, but we seemed unable to fix a mutually convenient occasion at the time. However, I am writing now to ask whether it would be possible to arrange such a meeting in the near future?

It is of the utmost importance to us that we are given the opportunity of passing on to you personally the great and growing sense of exasperation and one might almost say, fear, regarding certain developments in broadcasting, amongst a very wide cross section of people.

If you are willing to see me I would like to bring with me, if I may, two other people. I look forward to hearing from you.

Yours sincerely,

(Mrs) Mary Whitehouse

Reply from Charles Curran

15th December, 1970

Dear Mrs. Whitehouse,

Thank you for your letter of 3rd December.

I can see no early prospect of receiving a deputation of the kind and for the purpose which you suggest.

I am, of course, well aware of your opinions concerning our programmes.

If, however, some opportunity of our meeting informally were to arise, I should be glad to exchange views on a personal basis.

Yours sincerely

(Charles Curran)

Director-General

Such an informal meeting was in fact arranged – a lunch with the Catholic convert Bishop Basil Butler at the Hertfordshire college of which Butler was principal – but the fact that this encounter was kept secret for more than ten years showed how uneasy Charles Curran felt about it. Two and a half more years passed with Mary Whitehouse still no nearer to seeing the inside of the director general's office. Desperate times (and in NVALA's alarmist cosmology, it was *always* desperate times) called for desperate measures, and Mary embarked on a dance of epistolary seduction so utterly shameless that Salome herself might have thought twice about it.

Letter to Charles Curran

31 May, 1972.

PRIVATE AND CONFIDENTIAL.
Dear Mr. Curran,

  I would very much appreciate the opportunity to have a short talk with you about a private matter which has given me some concern.

  I hope this will be possible, and if so, would like to suggest 21 June as a possible date.

  I have an appointment at 12 noon, but could come to Broadcasting House earlier than that, or in the afternoon between 3 and 3.45 pm.

  Yours sincerely,

  (Mrs) Mary Whitehouse.

Reply from Charles Curran

2nd June, 1972

Dear Mrs. Whitehouse,

  Thank you for your letter of 31st May in which you ask for an opportunity to speak to me about a private matter. I have had to learn from experience that there

are very few things involving the Director-General of
the BBC which can be treated as private and I hope you
will understand if I ask for some further information
from you about the subject which you wish to discuss.

If it relates in any way to the BBC then it can be
confidential, but it cannot be private, and I should need
to know before arranging a meeting in what I might be
involving myself in my official capacity. This is a rule
which I have applied invariably since becoming Director-
General and I have found that it is a wise rule. If it is
personal to me then there can be no reason for not telling
me what it is. If it relates to your dealings with the
BBC then I can see no difficulty in your telling me what
it is. Anything which needs to be kept confidential can be
so protected. If it is personal to you then I think it is
reasonable for me to ask in what way it can concern me.

I have an entirely open mind about whether to make an
appointment as you suggest, but I must know to what I am
committing myself. If the matter is, as you say, private
or personal then it might be better for us to meet in
private circumstances. Broadcasting House is not in that
sense private, as I am sure you will understand.

I should be most anxious to know what it is that has
given you concern and I hope therefore that you will
feel able to tell me.

Yours sincerely,
(Charles Curran)
Director-General

Every resourceful suitor knows the value of a deceptively
harmless pretext, but what kind of lure would Mary choose?

Letter to Charles Curran

7 June, 1972

Dear Mr. Curran,
I do understand your difficulties in accepting my

suggestion that we should meet in a private capacity.

I just wanted the opportunity to correct an impression
which may have been given to you by something which
has happened in connection with the Church of England
Commission on Broadcasting.

It is a small matter, but important to me, that no
unnecessary difficulties should be created. I would
certainly not wish you to give your time especially to
meet me other than at the BBC.

So long as the matter could be considered confidential
and not private in the terms you set out, I would be
grateful for the opportunity to meet you for a few
minutes.

Yours sincerely,

(Mrs) Mary Whitehouse

'Something which has happened in connection with the
Church of England Commission on Broadcasting'! How could
Charles Curran hope to resist the awesome power of White-
house's ruse?

Reply from Charles Curran

9th June, 1972

Dear Mrs. Whitehouse,

Thank you for your further letter of 7th June. You are
clearly much concerned about something which happened
over the Church of England Commission on Broadcasting
and of which I know nothing so far.

I shall be happy to see you on the terms of
confidentiality which I described. Perhaps you could come
to Broadcasting House at 3.00 p.m. on Wednesday, 21st
June.

Yours sincerely,

Charles Curran

Come into my parlour, said the spider to the fly.

Now she finally had the director general's ear (and he had the knighthood that seemed to go with the territory) there was no limit to the number of important issues they would be able to discuss together.

Letter to Sir Charles Curran

21 March, 1974

Dear Sir Charles Curran,

I am writing to tell you that an increasing number of people are complaining to us about the effect on their eyes of the montages of rapidly changing images which is, increasingly, becoming a feature of modern television.

Those who suffer from migraine appear to be particularly sensitive to the effect of this technique. The speed with which election results were flashed on and off the screen during the 'Election Special' programme was found to have a deleterious effect upon some viewers, causing headaches and a sense of pain behind the eyes.

I wonder if you would consider discussing this matter with your medical advisors? I assure you it is causing genuine discomfort, and I would be most interested to have your comments.

Yours sincerely,

(Mrs) Mary Whitehouse

Reply from Sir Charles Curran

4th April, 1974

Dear Mrs. Whitehouse,

Thank you for your letter of 21st March, 1974, already acknowledged by my secretary.

I have consulted my medical advisers who have confirmed with two leading ophthalmic surgeons that rapidly

changing images on the television screen do not cause
pain behind the eyes in the normal healthy individual.

   The cause of migraine is multiple and the tension of
the election situation is just as likely to precipitate
an attack in those who may be predisposed to the
condition.

   It has to be accepted that the speed at which images
can be absorbed by the older age groups diminishes but,
in the end, the decision on the rate of image changes
must rest on editorial judgement. I have no reason to
think that such judgements will be in conflict with the
medical advice I have referred to above.

   Yours sincerely

   (Charles Curran)

   Director-General

   The scene is now set, then, for Michael Swann's suitably
graceful entrance. With Mary Whitehouse having beguiled her
way into, if not the affections, at least the hearing of Sir Charles
Curran, the opportunity now arose for her to pursue something
a little more meaningful. Curran was business, but Swann could
be pleasure. Sir Charles was the dress rehearsal, Michael (soon
to be Sir Michael) was the main performance.

   While Sir Hugh Greene's successor didn't always seem to
know exactly what was hitting him where Mary Whitehouse
was concerned, the BBC's new chairman was fully aware of the
dance in which he was engaged from the outset. Viewed in romcom terms, his formal meeting with Mary Whitehouse at Broadcasting House on 9 January 1974 was a mutually satisfactory
first date. Not only was Mary allowed to bring her own second (Thames Valley NVALA branch president John Standring –
Swann was accompanied by the BBC's Secretary), she was even
allowed to suggest corrections to the minutes.

   Later in that same year, the relationship moved to the next
level, as Mary Whitehouse was invited to attend Swann's lecture

to the Royal Society of Arts commemorating the end of his first twelve months at the BBC. If this stage of their interaction was to be represented cinematically, a montage sequence of a day trip to Paris would probably be necessitated – with the compatible couple perhaps eating a coffee eclair from both ends to meet in the middle, or stopping on the climb up Montmartre to pet an adorable French bulldog.

Extract from Mary Whitehouse's diary

Very lively questions and a reception for a few invited guests afterwards. Richard, [Mary's son] Ros [his wife] and I were invited and Sir Michael came over to me and asked if he 'was forgiven'. I laughed and said I'd just been asked by P.A. what I thought of what he'd said about us. I told the reporter that I didn't accept at all that we 'were extreme' – that Sir Michael had only been at the BBC a short time and that I didn't think he knew enough about our work, 'You never did!' he exclaimed. 'Certainly I did' I replied laughing. Then he told me that his colleagues at the BBC were very angry with him – for giving me 'so much publicity' – and certainly Curran had a face like a thunder cloud – not a bit pleased either to see the Chairman laughing away with us on the opposite side of the room!

Ros was at Edinburgh University when Swann was there, so he was very interested to meet her – asked her how she coped with a mother-in-law like me! She told him she was 100% behind me – lovely.

It wasn't just the fact that she was invited to hear the chairman of the BBC speak that gladdened Mary Whitehouse's heart, there was also cause for cautious optimism in what he had to say. The following passage from a characteristically elegant piece of Swann positioning of roughly the same period (it moves smoothly, but there's a lot of work going on under the surface) incorporates NVALA's strictures into its ideological equilibrium with an ease that would have been unthinkable ten years before. This quotation was carefully cut out and preserved in the archive, like the photo of a much-admired first-team wide receiver from a high-school yearbook.

Extract from address by Sir Michael Swann to the Headmasters' Association Annual Conference at Cambridge on Friday 26 March 1976

By the 1960's, partly because of competition, partly as a reaction from the old-style image, partly because of a deliberate policy by the then Director General, Hugh Greene, and partly because of a huge influx of young producers, the BBC's social stance had altered, at least in Television, out of all recognition. As Malcolm Muggeridge, characteristically, and exaggeratedly wrote at the time: 'Auntie, as we all know, has taken to drink, never goes to divine worship any more, gives noisy parties for disreputable friends and hangers on, and endlessly uses four-letter words . . .'

It is always a risky business bringing history up to date; still more so to attribute causes. But a change of mood in society, and a change of emphasis in Management has indeed brought about a change in the Corporation. It has become, whatever you may think, more careful about sex, violence and bad language. And though there are still, and rightly, plenty of programmes which from a progressive standpoint shock the right wing, there are, I suspect, more programmes than there used to be which shock the progressives. And all this is as it should be. Most people, after all, regardless of their politics, are not very progressive, and if we forget that fact, we are sooner or later in trouble.

Sir Michael Swann knew just the right balance of reassurance and admonishment to strike when it came to keeping Mary Whitehouse vaguely onside without giving her too much ground. He dealt patiently with her endless slightly hysterical letters about (Sydney Newman's longest-lived dramatic brainchild) *Doctor Who*, while never for a moment allowing himself to get caught up in her infectious anxiety.

'On the subject of nightmares,' she wrote to him, 'perhaps I can recount the substance of a recent telephone call: it was from the mother of a little boy of six who had been terrified by the headless creature in the *Brain of Morbius* and he woke up screaming every night and she could not get him off to sleep again.' The chairman calmed her fears by insisting that the BBC 'do look carefully at such scenes, particularly when they show humans apparently being injured by monsters'. In the case of the 'strangulation – by hand, by claw, by obscene vegetable matter' that so shocked her in *The Seeds of Doom*, he was sanguine about a story which (and here Swann's powers of understatement come diplomatically into play) 'seems to me to have some of the characteristics of John Wyndham's "The Day of the Triffids"'.

When (in a letter dated 25th January, 1976) Whitehouse accused the producer Philip Hinchcliffe and his team of creating 'Some of the sickest and most horrific material ever seen on children's television', having 'an obsession with manic atrocities, and [having] become inoculated by the very excesses of their own imagination', Swann calmly pronounced himself 'yet to be persuaded . . . that Dr. Who's recent adventures are essentially different from his earlier exploits. The point, surely, is that Dr. Who always escapes his enemies, and if there is something frightening in a programme it will have resolved itself by the end'.

Even tiny cut-out pictures of the Doctor and his noble-savage assistant Leela included in the *Radio Times* to populate a 'Blue Peter Dr Who Toy Theatre' ('Invent your own adventures and amaze and amuse your friends . . . you don't have to be good at drawing') did not escape Mary Whitehouse's consternated gaze. Leela poured the rough-hewn charm of Eliza Doolittle into the kind of outfits later made popular by *Xena: Warrior Princess*, but neither this nor even the allegation that the character was named after the Palestinian hijacker Leila Khaled was Mary's main source of concern. What bothered Whitehouse about this tiny paper fantasy figure was that she – in the manner of tiny paper fantasy figures from time immemorial – was carrying a knife.

Letter from Michael Swann

28th June, 1977

Dear Mrs. Whitehouse,

Thank you for your letter of 20th June about a 'Radio Times' illustration for 'Dr. Who'.

Yes, it does look a rather lethal knife. The point about 'Leela', however, as the children know very much better than mere adults like ourselves, is that she is a primitive who is gradually being civilised by the gallant Doctor and persuaded that violence is not the way to achieve one's ends. A moral tale — even if the illustration does show 'Leela' in her unredeemed state.

Yours sincerely,

Michael Swann

Like Mr Darcy to Mary Whitehouse's Elizabeth Bennet (or Mr Knightley to her Emma, come to that – 'Badly done, Mary, badly done'), Swann could still be quite strict when the occasion demanded.

Letter to the chairman of the BBC

20th May, 1975

Dear Sir Michael,

On 4 May BBC1 transmitted a programme about a pop artist called CLAES OLDENBURG.

One scene which lasted several minutes featured an over developed female in nothing save an oil skin covering of one leg leaving the pubic hair exposed. There was much talk about phallic symbols and at one point the artist was heard to say 'That's almost as big as my balls'.

There really seems no limit to the offence which the BBC is prepared to give. You once took me to task for talking about 'a collapse of standards' — I wonder how else one can describe this programme?

Yours sincerely,

(Mrs) Mary Whitehouse

Hon. Gen. Secretary

Reply from Sir Michael Swann

4th June, 1975

Dear Mrs. Whitehouse,

Thank you for your letter of 20th May and your comments about the programme 'Claes Oldenburg' transmitted in 'Omnibus' on 4th May.

I have looked into the two specific scenes your Association found offensive.

We must refute the view that there was any talk about phallic symbols. The artist did not say 'that's almost as big as my balls'. He did say 'that's almost as big as my ball'. Oldenburg at the time was referring to a marble ball on top of a column and his reference to the ball was a comment on its size in relation to the ball in his sculpture — a baseball mitt — which features throughout the programme. The idea that a baseball mitt holding a ball should serve as the theme for a piece of sculpture may be unexpected but is a fact.

The other scene to which you refer may have caused offence to a very few people. The fact that artists do paint, or in this case sketch, the nude female body is accepted and shown on television. Whether this particular model was 'over developed' is, I should have thought, hardly relevant. That one leg of the model was clad in a plastic material resembling a vacuum cleaner was relevant to Oldenburg's theories about the relationship of the human body and objects — an important aspect of his work in the 50's and 60's.

'Pop art' is not everyone's idea (or mine) of what
painting or sculpture should be, but, although its
appeal may be limited, it is now recognised as an
important element in contemporary art. This film showed
the kind of work that is being done by an eminent artist
and the reasons for doing it.
   Yours sincerely,
   Michael Swann

As in any long-term relationship, there was inevitably the
occasional misunderstanding, like this early squabble over a
scheduled (or was it just provisional?) appearance on Radio 4's
PM programme to discuss the tenth anniversary of NVALA.

Letter from Sir Michael Swann

6th March, 1974

Dear Mrs. Whitehouse,
   I am sorry there should have been a misunderstanding
about the possibility of your appearing on the 'P.M.'
programme, but I can assure you that the reasons for not
proceeding with the interview were entirely editorial,
and were related to the pressure of the election events.
   On the points of detail which you raise, the
arrangements for the interview were never intended to
be more than provisional, and I am sorry if this was
not made clear — certainly the programme staff thought
it was. Mr. Boyle's recollection of the words he used
differs from yours, but on the question of referring to
his superiors, I should perhaps explain that during the
election the editors of <u>all</u> our daily current affairs
programmes had to clear <u>all</u> their plans in advance.
Obviously we were primarily concerned with double-
checking on items concerning the election and the
national crisis, but inevitably this affected the total
contents of the programmes.
   In the event, the decision was taken on the day that

an interview with you about National V.A.L.A., while
quite possibly of interest on a quieter news day,
would not compete with all the pressing news about the
election. I do not expect you necessarily to agree with
that judgement, but I can assure you this was all that
was involved — a straight editorial judgement based on
news values, and nothing more sinister.

Yours sincerely,

Michael Swann

P.S. In case you think it was the D.G. or I who
decided you were not news-worthy enough, it was not.
The decision was made, I discover, about midway between
Andrew Boyle and me.

At other times, it was Mary who broke the spell by thought-
lessly falling back on the strategies of a more oppositional era.

Letter from Sir Michael Swann

3rd July, 1975

Dear Mrs. Whitehouse,

Thank you for your letter of 1st July. You have, no
doubt, your own reasons for indicating to the national
Press, in advance of the arrival of your letter, the
fact of its despatch; but I must say, in the absence of
any explanation of those reasons, I find it deplorable.
It must lead me and others to believe that you attach
more importance to the letter than to the substance of
any reply.

If the National Council on Alcoholism wishes to raise
any issues in its latest report with the BBC, we shall
be happy to consider the points which they make. In
the meantime, I hope you will not expect me to comment
on your own, rather ill-defined charge that 'Too often,
both in series and drama productions, characters appear
incapable of making decisions without a swig of whisky,
social exchange has to be lubricated by drinks and moral

courage would appear dependent on the "stiffener"'.
I entirely accept that the problem of alcoholism
is deeply disturbing, but it is not to be solved by
superficialities.
   Yours sincerely,
   Michael Swann

   As a general rule, though, differences between the chairman
of the BBC and the hon. gen. sec. of NVALA could now be
ironed out in a civilised atmosphere of mutual respect (well,
relative to the Greene years, anyway), as this only mildly con-
descending clarification from Sir Michael Swann confirms.
Readers will again need to make their own minds up as to
whether Mary Whitehouse's diagnosis of the sexuality of John
Inman's character in *Are You Being Served?* really was all that
overstated.

Letter from Sir Michael Swann

18th February, 1975

Dear Mrs. Whitehouse,
   Thank you for your letter of 6th February about
the 'Guardian's report of my interview with William
Hardcastle in the BBC-2 programme 'In Vision'. Since
I became involved in public life I have found, as
you probably have, that no matter how carefully one
expresses reservations, they tend to get lost in
newspaper reports.
   For the record, this is what I actually said:

'Mrs. Whitehouse and particularly some of her followers
overstate their case so absurdly from time to time that
I think it's rather difficult to think straight about
it, but, you know, Mrs. Whitehouse does stand for a
considerable strand of opinion in society and I think
it's perhaps arguable that five, ten years ago the BBC
dismissed this too readily. But to be honest I don't

think that I've done anything very much about that, I
rather think it's a bit of a shift in society.'

You will see that I was by no means dismissing your
point of view out of hand. In fact, I was trying to be
fair, and I think that what I said (save for the word
'absurdly') was both fair and accurate. For example,
very shortly after I became Chairman, you wrote to me
in advance of an edition of 'Horizon' to tell me that
the announcement of a programme in 'Radio Times' led
one to suspect that it might well prove to be a piece
of propaganda in favour of free contraception, abortion
on demand etc. Knowing what I know of 'Horizon' — which
has a long record of serious and balanced achievements
to its credit   I believe that you were overstating your
case in that instance.

Another example of overstatement came very shortly after
the one I have just quoted, when you described 'Are You
Being Served?' as a programme with an unmistakable homosexual character.

It seems to me that the few examples which I
have quoted offer, on any reasonable view of the
circumstances, compelling examples of what I meant when
I talked about overstatement. I am willing to concede
that I myself was guilty of overstatement in using the
word 'absurdly'.

It only remains to deal with the point you make about
your supporters. It has long been your practice to
include in your letters to the BBC some reference to
the representation which you have received from members
of your Association. In passing them on to the BBC you
rarely, if ever, dissociate yourself from the views and
fears expressed, however extreme and however unjustified.

Yours Sincerely,
Michael Swann

Sir Michael Swann had obviously made it clear that Mary
Whitehouse's improved standing at Broadcasting House was

not necessarily going to translate itself into the thing she really wanted – which was the opportunity to state her case on television – because when the time came to make her big move in that department, she directed it towards someone else.

Letter to the Controller of BBC1, Bryan Cowgill

22 September, 1975

<u>Private and Confidential</u>
Dear Mr Cowgill,

I was very sorry not to have the opportunity of speaking to you at Cambridge to thank you personally for what you said and for the encouragement you gave to those who are so concerned about the use of bad language on TV.

I wonder also if I might raise another matter with you? Sir Charles Curran said, in his address, that every view point has a right to be heard. But the simple truth of the matter is that during twelve years of campaigning I have been on BBC-TV for a total of just about 1 hour, and 30 minutes of this was taken up with an early 'Talkback' programme in which I was exposed to a very great deal of unsympathetic interpretation.

I know, from what several BBC producers have told me over the years, that I was 'blacklisted' by Sir Hugh Greene. I know that a very different attitude pertains towards me personally these days – but this never gets as far as me being invited to appear on programmes.

This is not a personal matter. I believe that the viewpoint I hold is rational and representative of many viewers, and that the issues raised are of fundamental importance to broadcasting. We are concerned also with wide issues, but even here I am 'persona non grata'.

I have never raised this issue before but I have the confidence to do so with you, hoping that you may see fit in some way to end the censorship which has undoubtedly existed.

I am marking this letter 'private and confidential' and
any reply which you may see fit to send will be treated
in the same way.
  May I wish you all success in your work?
  Yours sincerely,
  (Mrs) Mary Whitehouse

Reply from the Controller of BBC1

29th September, 1975

Dear Mrs. Whitehouse,
  Thank you for your letter of 22nd September.
  There is, of course, no censorship of the views
which you express and I think you would agree that
you have been fairly widely quoted and reported in
BBC programmes. I am not, however, in a position to
create programme opportunities for any particular
viewpoint and, even if I were, it would be quite wrong
for me to do so, still more for me to do so on behalf
of a particular individual. I am sure that producers
responsible for programmes covering the area of your
special concerns are aware of your willingness to appear
and that, if and when suitable opportunities arise, they
will be in touch with you.
  Incidentally, I am not quite sure why you marked your
letter 'Private and Confidential'. It is not unreasonable
for anyone to seek broadcasting opportunities — I can
assure you I receive a great many such letters every
week.
  Yours sincerely,
  (Bryan Cowgill)
  Controller, BBC-1

  Far from being crushed – as any normal human being would've
been – by the contemptuous iron fist wrapped in the velvet glove
of that last sentence, Mary Whitehouse came back fighting, as
she always did.

Reply to the Controller of BBC1

2nd October, 1975

Dear Mr. Cowgill,

  Thank you very much for your letter of the 29th
September. I was not at all asking for special programme
opportunities to be created for me: I was hoping that
you might have done something — possibly indirectly
— to make clear that I was 'an acceptable person' to
appear in BBC programmes. I cannot at all agree that
I 'have been fairly widely quoted and reported in BBC
programmes' — unless you are referring to the many
occasions that I have been the subject of a comic
reference or sketch of some kind.

  As I said in my earlier letter, my total time on
BBC television in the course of twelve years has been
between one and one-and-a-half hours. I know that this
embargo on my appearance exists as BBC producers who
have moved over to ITV have told me so. I also know that
any producer who wishes to use me in a programme has to
'check at the top'.

  I am very well aware, of course, that this attitude
originated with Sir Hugh Greene and although the general
attitude of the BBC to the work of this Association is
now very different to what it was in his time, there is
still a great unwillingness to give any publicity to our
views or personalities. However, I realise that there
is absolutely nothing I can do to change the situation.
Whether things do change, only time will tell. I hope
so.

  Yours sincerely,
  Mary Whitehouse

  The thing about Mary Whitehouse was, it didn't matter how
well you handled her, she was never going to go away. It's not
quite clear what prompted the sudden withdrawal of her cherished direct access to Sir Michael Swann – though his growing

frustration with her inability to resist trying to play chairman
and director general off against each other may well have been a
factor. Like all the most devastating 'Dear John' letters, this one
seemed to arrive out of the blue. It began – in appropriately 'he
said, she said' fashion – with Swann's response to Mary's complaint about the somewhat stringent letter from Richard Eyre
displayed at the start of an earlier chapter in this book.

Letter from Sir Michael Swann

14th December, 1979

Dear Mrs. Whitehouse,

Thank you for your letter of 27th November.

I agree that Richard Eyre's reply to your complaint
was not felicitously worded. However I can understand
that, as the Producer of 'Play for Today', he
instinctively wished to defend his work. I am sorry that
in doing so he was betrayed into a certain tartness. It
is a not unnatural response on the part of a creative
person who may well have spent months working on a
production, but it is one that we discourage.

I am glad you find BBC replies are normally courteous,
but producers and heads of output departments are
frequently preoccupied with their next production and
engaging in correspondence with individual members of
the public or pressure groups is not really part of
their duties. When they do it well we applaud them; when
they do it not so well we understand, but disapprove. A
producer capable of operating as a one-man secretariat in
addition to making good programmes deserves to go far.

I would suggest once again that you should address
your letters to The Secretary, who is the person best
placed to deal with them. You can take it that any which
it is necessary that the Director General or I should
see will reach us.

Yours sincerely,

Michael Swann

Proud battler that she was, Mary could not help but let her true feelings show.

Reply from Mary Whitehouse

18th December, 1979

Dear Sir Michael,
  My heart was filled with dismay when I received your last letter (14th December) in which you suggest that all correspondence regarding programmes should be addressed to the Secretary of the BBC.
  Sixteen years ago, when this campaign began, all correspondence between ourselves and the BBC — no matter to whom we wrote — was dealt with by then Secretary of the BBC Mr., now Sir Charles Curran. In the intervening years we have, I like to think, built up many personal contacts, one could well say relationships, even friendships, with people who work, in one capacity or another, for the Corporation. Are you seriously suggesting, I wonder — still with a good deal of disbelief — that we go back to square one? And that members/representatives of the public should not write direct to those employed in a public service and who have the privilege of entering our homes?
  You say that Richard Eyre 'instinctively wished to defend his work'. I can only say that there are many things that all of us would 'instinctively' wish to do but part of the business of being mature and civilised is, I know you fully realise, that we don't give way to 'instinct'.
  Furthermore in many industries and professions creative people spend not months but many years on some production but in the last resort their efforts have to face public scrutiny and criticism — and they have no secretariat to act as a protective shield.
  Am I to take it that your last paragraph, being translated, means that you are asking me to write to

the Secretary rather than yourself? That I really do find
hard to believe.

May I, in spite of all that, wish you a very Happy
Christmas.

Yours sincerely,

Mary Whitehouse

There's a dignity about that closing sentence which is the
most eloquent argument Whitehouse could have possibly made
for the benefits of not 'giving way to "instinct"'. It didn't change
the fundamental situation, though. A golden age of direct access
was now over – but why? The following courteous yet still
implicitly devastating response from BBC Secretary J. F. 'Johnny' Wilkinson (written a full thirty days later . . . and how this 'I
am sure the Chairman would wish . . .' must have stung!) gave
some clues.

Reply from the Secretary of the BBC

17th January, 1980

Dear Mrs. Whitehouse,

Thank you for your letter of 18th December, already
acknowledged. I am sure the Chairman would wish me to
reciprocate your good wishes.

I am sorry that your 'heart should be filled with
dismay' at the prospect of corresponding with me rather
than with Sir Michael Swann. You yourself mention that
this was the practice formerly followed and there are
very good reasons for our decision to return to it. It
need not be invariable or inflexible, but I shall be the
central point of communication.

First, although you refer to your 'relationships even
friendships' with people throughout the BBC, you have in
fact twice written recently to the Chairman to complain
that letters direct to programme departments were
answered inadequately. I hope the new arrangements will

ensure that you have no further grounds for complaint of
this kind.

Second, you say that 'members/representatives of the
public' should have the right 'to write direct to those
employed in a public service'. Indeed they have. In
fact, however, you have regularly claimed not to be an
ordinary member of the public but to be speaking on
behalf of your organisation, or indeed of 'the silent
majority', which you usually assume shares your own
views. That being so it surely makes sense for us to
reply as an organisation.

Third, you have, as you know, not in practice written
solely to one person (whether the producer, Director-
General or Chairman) about a programme but have
frequently sent copies to all three. Collating such
copies, and ensuring that BBC time is not wasted in
sending three separate replies, albeit in very similar
terms, to the same complaint is obviously unsatisfactory
from our point of view.

Fourth, the answer to the question you ask in your
penultimate paragraph is 'Yes', as I think Sir Michael
Swann's last letter made clear. However, as he has
already assured you, I shall ensure that he and the
Director-General are kept informed of correspondence
from you, as necessary. You perhaps do not appreciate
that as Secretary to the Corporation I have indeed a
formal responsibility to this effect and letters not
addressed to them personally are always drawn to their
attention when appropriate.

Yours sincerely,

(J.F. Wilkinson)

The Secretary, BBC

All good things must come to an end, but anyone who has
allowed a painful break-up to go on that little bit too long will
understand why Mary Whitehouse couldn't let it lie. The ideal
soundtrack to accompany your reading of the ensuing selec-

tion of painful moments of rejection would probably be Barbra Streisand singing 'The Way We Were'. These poignant vignettes were not edited together by me, but had been masochistically compiled on tear-stained NVALA foolscap – presumably for inclusion in yet another anguished letter demanding a return to the old way of doing things.

The MW/MS/JFW post-break-up triangle of recrimination

7th February 1980
MW to JFW
'Thank you for your letter of 29th January in response to mine to John Grist. May I now enquire whether the "Look. East" team have now been made aware of the matter I raised in my letter of 13th December?'

18th February 1980
JFW to MW
'The answer to your question about "Look East" is, "Yes" . . . You may take it when you write to me that I shall ensure that the proper people are consulted about your complaint and where necessary informed of the terms of any reply.'

16th April 1980
JFW to MW
'Thank you for your letter of 20th March, addressed to the Head of Light Entertainment Group, Television, and copies to the Director-General and Controller, BBC1. As I have previously indicated, I shall be replying to all your letters to the BBC.'

24th April 1980
MS to MW
'Let me repeat the assurance from Johnny Wilkinson that he shows both myself and the Director General all letters of consequence.'

9th May 1980
JFW to MW
'I am replying on behalf of the BBC to your letter of
15th April to the Controller BBC2, of which you sent a
copy to the Director General.
'To save time may I ask you once again to address your
letters to me. As has already been made clear to you,
they will always be shown to the appropriate member of
the BBC, and, when necessary, brought to the attention
of the Chairman and the Director General.'

6th June 1980
MW to MS
'I trust that you will feel these considerations are
worthy of a personal reply.'

4th July 1980
JFW to MW
'The Chairman has asked me to reply to your letter to
him of 6th June. I am replying at the same time to the
copies of your letter addressed to the members of the
Board of Governors.'

17th July 1980
MW to MS
'On 4th July Mr. J.F. Wilkinson replied to my letter to
you of 6th June.
   'I am in no position to know whether you read our
letter and whether you approved his reply . . .
   'We would appreciate an assurance that you have in
fact read this letter.'

23rd July 1980
MS to MW
'It saddens me that you join the brigade of people who
think that I don't read my letters and am unaware of
what the Corporation may reply on my behalf. You are
wrong on both counts.'

25th July 1980
MW to MS
'You did suggest that I should address my letters to
The Secretary, and you will no doubt be aware that I
did not take kindly to this suggestion. However, it was
on account of it that the doubt existed in my mind as
to whether or not you had seen both my letter and Mr.
Wilkinson's reply.'

30th July 1980
MS to MW
'I know you were annoyed about funnelling correspondence
through Johnny Wilkinson, but the fact of the matter is
that both the Director General and I get letters at the
rate sometimes of hundreds a week, and to find similar
letters coming to each of us, not to mention other
people, really causes a lot of confusion and difficulty.
May I say that you are not the only person who gets
what one might call co-ordinating treatment from the
Secretary to the Board.'

18th August 1980
JFW to MW
'Thank you for your letter of 5th August, addressed to
the Director General. I have been asked to reply on his
behalf.'

PORNOGRAPHY..

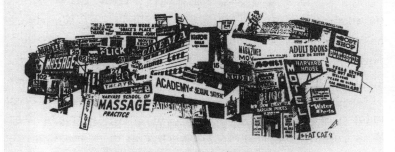

a matter of taste ?

Published by:

THE NATIONAL VIEWERS' & LISTENERS' ASSOCIATION

Ardleigh, Colchester, Essex, CO7 7RH.

Tel. Colchester 230123

Front page of NVALA briefing pamphlet

11. Mary vs. the Pornographers

Of all the areas of public concern in which Mary Whitehouse has subsequently been adjudged to have been ahead of the times, pornography looms the largest. The most X-rated dreams of the louchest hippie libertine might have come true with the advent of the internet, but the universal accessibility of porn has caused many to see Whitehouse's warnings in a newly prophetic light. Wildly unfashionable at the time she first made it, her (implicitly Marxist, but let's not open that can of worms at this juncture) critique of the sixties and seventies counterculture's determination to equate pornography with sexual liberation rather than the oppression of women has subsequently come to be echoed by all sorts of people who would not previously have expected to find themselves agreeing with her.

Although the debating chamber of the Cambridge Union is not an arena which should generally be given too much credence as a bellwether of shifts in intellectual opinion, Mary White-house's regular appearances there offer the perfect controlled environment in which to observe an increasing willingness to be persuaded by her arguments on this issue. In a riotous 1971 debate with *Oz* magazine's Richard Neville, his 'Schoolkids issue' defence lawyer John Mortimer, and British Pregnancy Advisory Service co-founder Martin Cole (dubbed 'Sex King Cole' by the tabloids for his explicit approach to sex education), Mary Whitehouse's emphasis on the primacy of the profit motive in pornography was inevitably going to be quite an isolated position (although she did have Lord Longford along for back-up).

In 1979 (a pivotal year for Whitehouse, and not just because of her painful break-up with Sir Michael Swann) radical feminists greeted her anti-porn statements with cries of 'Right on, Mary.' Seven years later, the balance of power really seemed to have shifted. Alongside her on the platform opposing the motion 'This house believes pornography to be a lesser evil than censorship' was a former president of the Union for whom the description 'the coming man' might have been designed.

Peter Bazalgette – the former *That's Life* researcher whose illustrious great-great-grandfather had designed and built London's sewer system and who would himself bring Britain the revolution in showbiz social engineering that was *Big Brother* – played to the gallery by describing having Mary as 'a bedfellow' as 'a very enjoyable experience'. Yet the acceptance of the validity of her position which underpinned his crowd-pleasing assertion that 'A debate on censorship without Mary Whitehouse would be like Lady Chatterley without her lover or Portnoy without his complaint' transcended the familiar innuendo.

What type of person was still willing to take up the pro-pornography cudgels at the Cambridge Union by 1986? The British Library's recording of the debate reveals the biggest name on the anti-censorship side as John Stonehouse – a one-time sparring partner of Mary's as Labour Postmaster General, who had gone on to achieve notoriety by faking his own death on a Miami beach in November 1974 in the hope of starting a new life with his secretary in Australia (after emerging from the ensuing short prison term, he was subsequently revealed to have been an agent of the Czech government while in office).

None of this somewhat incriminating backstory is even alluded to by his chivalrous opponents. Stonehouse's best shot – 'If she supports censorship, one day someone might censor her' – is effortlessly batted away by Whitehouse's 'I was officially banned by the BBC for eleven years.' The debate is so one-sided it's effectively a rout, and the audience of expensively educated movers- and shakers-in-waiting leaves with Mary's anti-porn battle cry – 'You can't begin to equate this with freedom, this is exploitation of the worst possible kind' – ringing in their ears.

How did Mary Whitehouse's position on pornography develop? Of course, the inevitable letter to the *Nationwide* presenter Michael Barratt played a part.

Letter to Michael Barratt

10th November, 1969

Dear Mr. Barratt,

I have received a number of letters as a result of a programme, in the 'Nationwide' series, screened on October 28th. I understand that in this you interviewed a young man making jig-saw puzzles which have been described to me as verging on the pornographic. Perhaps I can quote from one of these letters:

'I do not shelter my children unduly from life, and hope they will grow up to appreciate art, but what chance is there of this when it is made ridiculous and obscene by the B.B.C? I can find no excuse for the promotion of material of this kind which was indeed nothing more or less than a 'plug' for a specific product. There are so many more worthwhile products on the market which might well be brought to the public's attention if the B.B.C. is indeed to become involved with advertising of this kind.'

I would like to take this opportunity of expressing concern, on behalf of national VALA, that features of this kind should be included in early evening viewing such as 'Nationwide'. One is tempted to go further and question the value of the publicising of such dubious and 'cheap' material at any time of the evening. If you would care to give me your comments on this matter I would gladly forward them to our correspondents.

Yours sincerely,
(Mrs) Mary Whitehouse.
Copy to Lord Hill.

The P-word was one that came quite easily to Mary White-house, so her admission that the jigsaw in question only 'verged on' pornographic suggests several possibilities with regard to its subject – perhaps a frisky heifer in a field, or a Victorian seaside scene with a suppressed undercurrent of sensuality? Yet for all the levity which this topic has often tended to induce, the letters Whitehouse received often contained the kind of heavyweight emotional content that resists such frivolous responses.

Statements received from husband and wife NVALA correspondents

<u>Summary of a letter from Mrs. N. 2nd March, 1967</u>
Last year I was in Hospital with a coronary thrombosis due to violent emotional disturbance over a long period. I am in the distressing position of having witnessed my husband in action with so-called 'Art Studies' (pornography). It was far worse than just 'looking' at pictures. No wife is going to be able to satisfy her husband sexually, once he has indulged in these books or other forms of depravity.

After my return from hospital I still became emotional on seeing unpleasant articles of this type in newspapers etc; and my husband would try and remove certain pages before I could see them. Because of the detrimental effect they could have on my condition I consulted our doctor and he suggested I should see a psychiatrist. I also discussed with him my theory that child murders were the result of immorality and especially pornographic books and so-called 'Art Studies'.

On Monday Feb 20th he saw in the afternoon on television a woman on the beach wearing a topless bathing suit. This was followed by the showing of the words, 'Pet of the Month'. The camera then moved up the screen to reveal a semi-nude pin-up. The caption and picture are believed to have come out of the magazine 'Penthouse'. The programme was educational

for schools and entitled 'Twentieth Century Focus, The Other
Sex.' It was re-televised on Tuesday and Thursday at 10.25
a.m. and on Wednesday at 2.30 p.m. My husband came home and
said, 'You said this would happen and I did not believe it.
I thought you were mad. I really thought you had gone round
the bend'.

My husband had such a jolt over what he had seen that he
went right to the House of Commons to lobby Sir Cyril Black,
but he was not available. He then went to the County Education
Office only to be told that they had no jurisdiction over the
B.B.C. although they appreciated his feelings on the matter.
The government evidently had no control, and so it appears
that the B.B.C. is all-powerful.

Since then we have spoken to many people about this incident.
The attitude of most of the <u>men</u> is, 'Why should we, the
majority, be deprived of what we want? If you don't want to see
these things on television you can always switch off.' One of
these was the father of an eight year old girl who had already
been approached on two occasions by men indecently exposed.
This man must have seen the look of terror in his wife's eyes
like a trapped animal many times, but he is determined to
ignore this if it means giving up his 'pleasure'. Another man,
who condoned these television programmes thought nothing of
coming home at 3 a.m. and then expecting his wife to make love
to him at that hour, and then complained that he was being
'rationed'.

The women, I feel, are being blackmailed into silence because
of the attitude of their husbands regarding women like me who
voice their objections!

(My view that wrestling, often seen on television, was also
an indecent form of entertainment was recently borne out by
my niece aged 10 who innocently remarked 'It always makes me
want to go to the toilet.')

I must say that the present attitude of my husband, plus
the fact that he is prepared to give any help of which he is
capable in combatting the present trend has wiped out many
long years of terrible bitterness and a future of complete
meaninglessness. I now have nothing but the highest regard for
his moral strength and courage in that he is prepared to take
the line he is now taking at a cost only to himself.

Copy of a letter from Mr. N. 2nd March, 1967
For years I have 'enjoyed' these filthy magazines. They had almost ruined my marriage and I truly wonder if they didn't contribute to almost killing my wife. This filth is like a drug. The more you get, the more you want. The more you want, the more you hate yourself for wanting — and then you get again and hate yourself for getting. One moment it seems a desirable private dream. Then later it is empty — and so is life, and you are so awfully alone in your own made private Hell. It sets up a fearful combination of guilt and self-reproach, coupled with a soul-destroying feeling of emptiness and dissatisfaction. Believe you me, I know what I am talking about:

Since the war, this class of publication has become easier to obtain, to the point of being almost impossible to avoid in most ordinary newsagents, in the last few years being strategically placed so as to create 'impulse buying' as it is called in the retail trade. Then along comes the same theme on television, not so blatant as yet, in fact it started in very subtle and cunning ways, gradually feeling its way from one step to another. I particularly felt this when I was in a mood of some resistance to this curse. Then I used to feel trapped and unable to get away from it wherever I have turned. I mention this to endorse the terrible seductive forces, television in particular, which have confronted me and others in my position. When the BBC say they do not have 'commercials' it is false — They do, and in a clever way they are advertising this sort of thing every day.

Regarding the schools broadcast on television, my wife referred to. The two offending pictures which were shown on the T.V. screen, if shown to any person classified by law as a minor by a member of the adult public would constitute an unlawful and immoral act under the laws of this country, but they can be shown by the B.B.C. to school-children.

When mentioning this to sympathetic listeners I got the retort, 'Shocking: isn't it? A sign of the times we live in'. Or 'Oh dear: But what can we do?' This may seem a far cry from Nazi Germany, but I suddenly realised that this was probably how decent and well-meaning Germans may have spoken during the thirties.

As particular as the psychosexual circumstances of the above case may seem (especially the bit about wrestling), it was by no means an isolated incident. Mary Whitehouse's postbag bulged with evidence of the emotional damage wreaked by porn. From the sanctity of the bedroom to the contemplative haven of the railway station news-stand, she saw its dehumanising impact as an invasive threat comparable to the one Sir Winston Churchill had rallied the nation to withstand in the Second World War.

He had promised to lead the fight against the Nazis 'on the beaches . . . on the . . . landing grounds . . . in the fields . . . in the streets . . . [and] in the hills', and Mary's war on porn was built on an only slightly less expansive four-pronged strategy. The first was the classic combination of grass-roots campaigning and high-level establishment lobbying at which she had always excelled; the second involved a shrewdly tight focus on the PR concerns of major newsagents; the third was her ongoing courtroom struggle to make what she contemptuously termed 'Roy Jenkins' obscenity laws' work for her; the fourth was a guerrilla parliamentary campaign to tighten up that regulatory apparatus and make it more fit for her purpose.

In response to the release of the *Oz* magazine editors Richard Neville, Felix Dennis and Jim Anderson after their obscenity conviction was overturned on appeal, NVALA launched its Nationwide Petition for Public Decency. This public plea for a strengthening of the obscenity laws accumulated 1,350,000 signatures between its launch in January 1972 and the time it was presented to Edward Heath in April 1973 – a serious tally in pre-internet times (when a signature really meant a signature). Whitehouse's ABUSE anti-child-porn petition racked up a quarter of a million more than that in just three months, in the process paving the way for one of her greatest triumphs – the passing of the 1978 Protection of Children Act.

As in 1939–45, the danger to Britain's moral survival came from Europe. Mary Whitehouse travelled all around the world in the course of her campaigning life – meeting and inspiring like-minded individuals and organisations in the USA, South Africa and particularly Australia (which even had its own Festival of Light). No foreign visit made more of an impression on her than the one she made to Denmark in 1970 at the behest of ITV's *World in Action*.

The reported decrease in sex-crime figures in that country since the removal of a number of sexual offences from the statute book had made Denmark something of a cause célèbre in the permissiveness debate (although, as Whitehouse and her allies did not hesitate to point out, if you cut down the number of things that are illegal, it is probable that the number of offences will decline in parallel). While the programme producer's attempts to get her to visit a 'sex fair' on camera failed miserably, in the process of buying an English-language paper from a stall in a rare moment of leisure, *Who Does She Think She Is?* recalls that Whitehouse 'casually opened the first of a pile of books with a most amusing pen and ink cartoon on the cover', and found herself instantly plunged into a world of hardcore porn depravity.

Her initial anguish gave way first to a determination to 'give the whole beastly business to God', and thence to a renewed sense of mission. 'How could I deal with the threat of pornography if I didn't know what it really was? Well, I knew now, and was ready to use my knowledge.'

One of the uses to which she put that knowledge was the following imperious warning to Sir Edward Heath of the moral pitfalls associated with his cherished move towards greater European integration.

Letter to the Prime Minister

29th August, 1971

Dear Mr. Heath,

You may perhaps be aware that I have just spent
several days in Rome with a group of Europeans deeply
concerned about moral pollution. We were privileged to
have a private Audience with the Pope who expressed his
great interest in and sympathy with our work.

While in Rome I had the opportunity to talk at great
length with Dr. Siegfried Ernst and Professor Dr.
Georg Siegmund the eminent anthropologist and scientific
author. They expressed the very great concern they feel
about the German Government's apparent intention to
repeal the pornography laws in the very near future.
They assured me that, in this event, the whole of
Western Europe, and the underdeveloped countries, would
be subject to a flood of pornography which would make the
Danish porn export appear but a drop in the ocean.

Dr. Ernst and his colleagues begged me to do
everything in my power to alert the British Government
and people to the dangers we face should the German
obscenity laws be repealed. While it is quite clear
that no foreign country has a right to interfere with
the internal policies of another state it is equally
true that we in Britain have every right to protect our
society against moral pollution from whatever source it
comes.

We stand on the threshold of entry into the Common
Market. The first essential for its success is the
establishment and maintenance of respect and trust
between the member countries. If Britain is flooded by
the effluent of a highly organised German porn industry
then the whole basis of co-operation between our two
countries could become soured and bitter.

Since I know how deeply you care that the European
Community should flourish and grow on a sane and healthy
basis may I beg you to take an early opportunity to

express to the German Government our feelings in this
matter?
  Yours sincerely,
  Mary Whitehouse

Beyond her established methodology of generating mass petitions at the same time as badgering the great and the good on an
individual (or c.c.ed) basis, the second strand of Whitehouse's
anti-porn endeavour was a pioneering application of the power
of the consumer. As early as 1963 – before CUTV was even born
– she had written a letter to Charles Forte questioning the character of publications available at Trust House Forte service stations. Twenty-one years later – and mindful of the awful shock
she'd received from that Danish bookstall – she was still at it.

Letter to the chairman of John Menzies Holdings, Ltd

24th May, 1984

Dear John Menzies,
  I was on Crewe station yesterday and approached your
stall on the Platform. Right at the very front of the
stall was a pile of Volume 16 Number 5 of KNAVE.
  The magazine is, in any case, one of the worst of the
pornographic magazines on sale. For it to be placed,
not on the top shelves as is the normal practice but at
a level where almost any child could see and pick it
up is surely the height of unresponsibility. May I add
that I am, in any case, surprised that a company of your
standing should profit from such material.
  I am sending a copy of this letter to each member of
your Board of Directors and I await your reply with
interest and concern.
  Yours faithfully,
  Mary Whitehouse

Reply from John M. Menzies, Esq.

28th May, 1984

Dear Mrs Whitehouse,

 Thank you for your letter concerning our bookstall at Crewe Station. I have passed your letter to our Retail Division for their comments. Our policy is to keep magazines like 'Knave' on the top shelves or at the back of the bookstall and in any case, it is not to sell these magazines to children.

 Yours sincerely,

 John M. Menzies

Further reply from John Menzies' Retail Outlet Director

31st May, 1984

Dear Mrs Whitehouse,

 I would refer to your letter of 24th May addressed to our Chairman.

 I note the points you make and can assure you that as a company we do take a responsible attitude to the display and selling of this type of magazine.

 We do have a strict policy on the sale of adult magazines which is known to all our managers. I enclose a copy of the section of the policy relating to display.

 It would appear that these instructions have not been followed at our Crewe Bookstall and this will be remedied immediately together with a reminder to all our outlet managers.

 I would thank you for bringing this to our attention.

 Yours sincerely

 R. Black

 The Festival of Light took Mary's anti-porn message of 'voluntary self-restraint and moral concern' to smaller retail outlets as well.

Festival of Light leaflet

<u>An Appeal To All Newsagents</u>
Your customers see the local newsagent's shop as the place where
all the family goes. Mothers and teenagers, school children
and toddlers call for magazines, sweets and sundries, as well
as the menfolk for their paper. They enjoy seeing the show of
colour and variety on the racks and shelves, especially well-
produced glossy magazines prominently displayed. But among
these they often see pornographic publications — books which
'could at the very least be said to represent an outrage to
fundamental human decency', to quote Charles Grimwood in the
<u>NATIONAL NEWSAGENT</u> (15.3.74.). Mothers with children must
run the gauntlet of these displays.

It is highly embarrassing to speak over the counter on this
subject, and no one wants to create bad feeling. So this
leaflet comes as a personal request for you to do something to
help us and our children.

In these magazines, and in some books too, women are made
out to be mere objects for lust, their dignity debased by word
and picture. The use of living persons for the making of these
photographs is exploitation. Love and caring are left out of
sexual relationships. Marriage, the family and the security
of the young are ignored.

<u>DANGEROUS EFFECTS</u>
Pornographic publications do teach. They must be partly
responsible for the fact that in 1974 there were 130,000
petitions for divorce and 520,000 single parent 'families'.
Over 1,000,000 children are deprived of a real home. Through
the teaching of pornographic magazines books and films the
natural sex drive of young people, as well as adults can be
awakened and diverted into modes of behaviour which attack the
roots of married life.

In the end health of mind and body can be affected, leading
to assaults upon women and worse.

After the conviction of a multiple rapist at Cambridge in
1975, Chief Constable, Mr. Frederick Drayton Porter, said:

'The fact that the Cambridge rapist was addicted to pornography
showed the danger of allowing sales to go unchecked. Let those

who think that censorship interferes with the liberty of
the individual reflect upon these crimes and ask themselves
would they express these views if the victims were their own
relatives or friends.'

Until the rapist was caught every woman and girl in Cambridge
must have felt at risk. So his freedom to read what he liked
and his subsequent actions were actually denying freedom from
fear to thousands in that neighbourhood.

PORNOGRAPHY AND THE LAW

Successful [obscenity] prosecutions have been taking place
across the land with both heavy fines and imprisonments. For
example:— Snaresbrook, London in 1976 — 12 months imprisonment;
Sheffield in 1976 — a fine of £660, with a suspended prison
sentence, etc.

There have also been numerous confiscations of stock in
recent months through warrants issued by magistrates on
police applications in places such as at Tyneside, Woodstock,
Kidderminster, Nuneaton etc. A list of some of the confiscated
titles is given below:—

Adam And Eve	How To Enrich	Pentact Unisex
Adult Digest	In Depth	Penthouse
Best Of Forum	Very Best From In	Profile
Best From New	Depth	Relate
Direction	Intro	(New) Relate
Caprice	Janus	Search
Carnival	Janus Special	(New) Search
Cinema X	Knave	Sensuous Symposium
Climax	Late Night Extra	Slant
Club International	Love In	Special Search Soho
Curious	Lolita	Special Affair
Double Take	Mayfair	Variant
Exciting Cinema	Men Only	Variant Special
Experience	New Chance	Vibrations
Very Best Of	New Direction	Viva
Experience	Best Of New Direction	Witchcraft
Erotic Dreams	New Exclusive	X Films
Fiesta	Open	
Forum	Parade	
Heat	Probe	
Hot Line	Probe Spring Spread	

The battle of the news-stands was well and truly joined, as the following characteristically combat-ready memo from NFOL's Steve Stevens (a man, lest we forget, who had actually watched the Dambusters take off) makes clear. The identification of a suspected porn mailing address had inspired one local campaigner to direct action, and as befitted the earthy nature of the conflict zone, neither side was afraid to get its hands dirty. The somewhat mystifying last paragraph of Stevens's communication leads us into one of the most bizarre of the many bizarre chapters in the Mary Whitehouse story.

Memo from NFOL secretary Steve Stevens

23rd October, 1974

At a meeting last night I was given the following information by one of the men who was in my meeting.
  There is a shop for customers in Upton Lane, Forest Gate and all the mail comes to that address. The local person who is incensed about this shop put a petrol bomb to it recently but only the front was burnt down! It is estimated that between 2000–10,000 items go out through the post daily. Our informant said that he is told that they pay between £10–£20 per book. We understand from someone in the Post Office that some of the books are as thick as telephone directories and the informant considers it to be 'hard porn'.
  I was also informed, but am not sure if this is accurate or not, that the girl who is changing her name by deed poll to Mary Whitehouse is writing a book which will come out under her name and is due to be out in two months time.
  Steve Stevens

The reassurance that 'imitation is the sincerest form of flattery' does not always sit well with the person who is actually being imitated. This has rarely been truer than in the case of

Mary Whitehouse and (to employ her official title) 'magazine editor Sexy Doreen Millington'.

At the suggestion of her boss – the then East London porn entrepreneur (later founder of the *Sunday Sport*, and now co-owner of West Ham United Football Club) David Sullivan – his editor Doreen Millington announced her intention to change her name by deed poll to 'Mary Whitehouse' in the autumn of 1974. In a bid to simultaneously capitalise on the allure of the Whitehouse name as a rallying cry for the anti-censorship community, and cock a snook at his most prominent ideological adversary (the practice of snook-cocking being widespread within his particular field of endeavour) Sullivan had decided to launch a pornographic magazine called *Whitehouse International*.

'We are also looking for another girl who really does have that name to pose in the nude for us,' the twenty-five-year-old Sullivan had assured the *News of the World*, shortly before the launch of the magazine. On page 24 of the first issue of *Saucy* – another new Sullivan title (business was booming!) – a sharp-eyed NVALA informant noted a full-page ad for the inaugural issue of *Whitehouse International*: 'MARY – See her as the world has never seen her! It cost us a small fortune to get her to pose nude – but everybody has a price! Shocking? Obscene? We ask you to be the judge.'

Happily for Mary's blood pressure (and her health was an issue at this stage, as she had recently suffered a serious bout of malaria contracted while on a rare holiday in the Gambia), by the time *Whitehouse International* actually hit the news-stands, the threat of legal intervention from Mary's solicitors had ensured a certain amount of backtracking.

Letter from NVALA supporter

21st February, 1975

Dear Mrs. Whitehouse,

  Re: Whitehouse International

  I trust you received my letter of the 8th January and
I wondered whether you had had time to consider matters.

  The third edition has now been published — I do not
know whether you have seen it. It is the usual 'girly'
publication but a disclaimer is now published to the
effect that the 'Mary Whitehouse' referred to in the
stories published is in no way linked with you.

  I must confess that I find it a little naive for a
Publisher to have gone out of his way to change the name
of a girl so that she identifies with you and in fact to
make it obvious that the whole publication was linked to
you and then to deny the fact that it was ever intended
to mean you.

  It is obvious that Sullivan must have taken some
advice about the matter and put in the disclaimer in an
effort to avoid the explicit innuendo.

As if taking her name in vain was not enough of a backhanded
tribute, David Sullivan also did Mary Whitehouse the dubious
honour of emulating her campaign strategies. In the wake of the
fines and custodial sentences handed out by a Sheffield court to the
publishers of *Sexy Laughs* magazine, a circular letter from Doreen
Millington not only asked loyal readers to write to them in prison
– 'Let them know that they are not forgotten. Make them feel
alive!' – but also to make their views known to the *Sunday Times*
about the extent to which 'ordinary men and women are fed up
having "pornographers" treated as hardened criminals', and even
to contact the Home Secretary Roy Jenkins, who (and this was
one statement guaranteed to solicit a rueful nod of assent from
Whitehouse) 'is known to be sympathetic to our cause'.

Sullivan's willingness to play Mary Whitehouse at her own game did not stop with these heartfelt requests for epistolary intervention from a constituency previously assumed to have favoured pictures over words. If anti-porn campaigners could have their own ponderously named campaigning organisations, why shouldn't he have one too? Missing an obvious trick – the name Festival of Darkness had not, after all, been trademarked – his right-hand woman announced an important campaigning initiative.

Extracts from the CFP Manifesto

THE SOCIETY FOR THE CAMPAIGN FOR FREEDOM IN PUBLISHING
By Doreen Millington

As a direct result of our campaign to legalise pornography we have received hundreds of letters from 'Private Readers' and 'Club' members suggesting we form a society to press forward our aims – namely, FREEDOM IN PUBLISHING. If you believe in Freedom in publishing then join today.

THE AIMS:
The aim of the Society is to allow the individual complete freedom of choice in the purchasing of books and magazines without the fear of harrassment of antiquated laws. To this end the society will take up the fight of individual newsagents and publishers – taking the fight to authorities via protests, marches, and petitions. By organising into areas and groups we will fight for our aims on both a regional and national basis – including the picketing of police stations.

If we have the choice to choose our government, then they in turn should listen to the majority of the electorate with regards to what we wish to buy and read. The permissive society is here to stay, so what is wrong with books and magazines that give advice on a subject which is showing today to be a very prominent feature, it appears in our daily and Sunday newspapers, and very little is said about it. Sex is not an ugly word, without it one would not be in existence today, and pornography is what some people see in anything they see or read.

So many concepts can be placed on pornography, but it should be left to the individual to choose whether they read it or

not. This is what democracy is all about. So many of our
readers fought for this in the 1939-45 war, and we should be
left free to choose what we read, in the same way as we could
switch off the television if we did not wish to view a certain
programme. Censorship is on the way out. BUT only by insisting
on the rights of the individual will these antiquated laws
be changed. The purpose of the Society is to hold regular
meetings with the object of promoting the aims of the Society.

If you support the aims of the society WRITE TO THE ORGANISERS/
SECRETARIES for your areas. If we do not have an organiser for
your area write direct to Doreen (The National Organiser). If
you would be interested in becoming a regional organiser, or
be prepared to allow your home to be used for meetings etc.
write direct to Doreen. There is no fee to join the Society
and the Society is a complete non-profit making organisation.

Addresses of four regional secretaries followed – based in
South London, the Midlands, Wales and North Wales (which
suggested that the imprisonment of publishers of 'sexy books'
was an injustice that was felt with particular keenness in the
principality). Strangely, not much more was heard from the CFP
– the whereabouts of its archive, for example, are unknown – but
Doreen Millington's surname at least would echo down through
the decades. Introduced to an excited public as Doreen's 'bisex-
ual nymphomaniac sister', Sullivan's next protégé Mary Millington (whose real name was Mary Maxted) would go on to
become arguably Britain's best-known porn star – starring with
Alfie Bass and Irene Handl in the record-breaking sex comedy
Come Play with Me, with other less salubrious career highlights
including a rumoured one night stand with Harold Wilson –
until she committed suicide at the age of thirty-three, the day
after being caught shoplifting.

The adversaries Mary Whitehouse faced in her endless courtroom battles of the 1970s were no less formidable on their own
turf than the ferociously streetwise Sullivan. It seemed that every time she managed to either browbeat the reluctant DPP Sir

Norman Skelhorn into pressing charges himself, or drag some hapless filth-peddler into the dock under her own steam via one of her numerous private prosecutions, she would look across the courtroom to see one or both of the dynamic liberal QC duo Sir John Mortimer and Geoffrey Robertson (both about as down with the underground as barristers could be at this point) smiling urbanely back at her.

After he had helped secure an acquittal in the obscenity trial of the *Deep Throat* star's fake porn memoir *Inside Linda Lovelace* in January 1976, *The Times* wrote of the 'particular gift for amusing irrelevance' with which Mortimer reassured juries that the material under consideration was far too harmless and silly for those who peddled it to require legal sanction. History does not relate if the subsequent emergence of Lovelace's actual 'true story' (two gruelling memoirs – 1980's *Ordeal* and 1986's *Out of Bondage* – detailing the levels of coercion involved in the making of *Deep Throat*, and her testimony to the 1986 US Attorney General's Commission on Pornography asserting that anyone who watches that film is 'watching me being raped') caused him to reconsider that position.

Either way, the topic was never addressed in an episode of Mortimer's much-loved ITV legal drama *Rumpole of the Bailey* (at least not to my knowledge, and I watched it every week). Back in real life, the effect of Mortimer's persuasive dockside manner on juries was devastating, especially in tandem with expert witnesses such as Dr Brian Richards – a 'leading authority in the field of sexual medicine', who, Whitehouse's *A Most Dangerous Woman?* recalls in horror, once described a picture of a woman tied up in chains with a sword pointing at her genitals as being 'for the public good because it produces a masturbatory situation'.

Small wonder that Whitehouse found herself digging deep into NVALA coffers to pay the travel expenses of her own in-house expert (Dr John Court, associate professor of psychology at Flinders University, Adelaide, and a supporter of the Australian Festival of Light), but even with Dr Court by her side, it was still an unequal struggle. With an informal alliance of the great and the good queuing up to suggest that any changes in the obscenity laws should be in the direction of liberalisation or even total repeal – from Lord Goodman's Arts Council working party on censorship in 1968 (which she first accepted but then refused a request to appear before, on the grounds that its overwhelmingly progressive make-up made its findings a foregone conclusion) to the eminent philosopher Bernard Williams's 1979 report on Obscenity and Film Censorship (to which Mary's book *Whatever Happened to Sex?* was submitted as testimony) – Whitehouse knew Westminster was going to be her most important battlefield.

The successful passage of the Bexleyheath MP Cyril Townsend's private members bill as 1978's Protection of Children Act was a rare moment of unalloyed triumph amid the frustrations of legislative trench warfare. Its seemingly uncontentious (to twenty-first-century eyes at least) provision of a legal barrier to the sexual exploitation of minors was helped past a slightly reluctant Callaghan government by a tabloid 'Kiddie Porn' storm which Whitehouse was instrumental in orchestrating. The following letter to the Peterborough MP Brian Mawhinney – in which Mary offers him the fruits of her considerable experience with failed private members' bills – gives a more representative picture of the attritional nature of this particular political conflict.

Letter to Dr Brian Mawhinney MP

29th October 1979

Dear Dr. Mawhinney,

    I am writing to ask whether there is any way we can help you with your Indecent Displays Bill? We have comprehensive files covering both the previous two attempts in 1974 and

1979. I do not wish to overburden you with paper but I could go through them and pick out particularly significant material if you feel this would be of help.

I wonder what you feel about the amount of Parliamentary support you have? We could stimulate a letter writing campaign to M.P.s through local papers if this would help.

I wonder, furthermore, whether there is any pressure for your Bill to be held back so that indecent display may be covered by comprehensive legislation following Williams?

Perhaps you know that I have met both Leon Britten and Lord Belstead during the vacation. I discussed with them, amongst other things, the question of the inclusion of television in indecent display legislation, as you and I spoke about. It appears that there is considerable Home Office resistance to this, and of course, we do understand that the television screen unless on display in shop windows is not technically public display. I got the impression, incidentally, that the Civil Servants in the Home Office are very entrenched in their resistance to any legal controls over broadcasting and deeply imbued with the previous Government's policies in this regard!

Nevertheless so gross is some of the material seen and heard on television I enclose examples that we would be most grateful if, at least, the matter could be debated.

I am often in London and am at your disposal if we can help in any way.

With all good wishes,

Yours sincerely,

Mary Whitehouse

In the end, Mary withdrew NVALA's support from the Indecent Displays Bill (which had by that point been taken over by Mawhinney's fellow Tory Tim Sainsbury) at the last minute in protest at its sponsor's refusal to extend its strictures to television (a move that would have resulted in the measure's inevitable defeat). Although this tactic caused consternation among the bill's parliamentary supporters – the word one of them used in a letter to her was 'Horror' – Whitehouse's concern that the Indecent Displays (Control) Act (as it became law in 1981) might actually lead to a proliferation of sex shops received a warmer reception from another newly influential quarter: James Anderton, the outspokenly authoritarian Mancunian police chief who Happy Mondays would later immortalise as 'God's Cop'.

The chief constable of Greater Manchester wrote to her on 7 May 1981, adding the substance of detail to some of Mary's misgivings about the bill. Were its loopholes not closed, he argued, there was a real danger that Britain might be 'deluged with porn'. This warning was not heeded, and while opinions will vary as to the ultimate accuracy of Anderton's apocalyptic forecast, the machinery of sex-shop commerce certainly moved much more smoothly after the bill was passed than it had done before. Mary Whitehouse had been given good reason to hope that the advent of Margaret Thatcher's Conservative government would be the beginning of a new era. This it did ultimately prove to be, although not quite in the way that she had imagined. In the mean time, the letters testifying to pornography's non-therapeutic effects continued to flood in.

Letter with signed statement from a minister of the United Reformed Church

18th October, 1983

Dear Mary Whitehouse

  The enclosed statement proves that pornographic magazines can cause a respectable married man to commit a crime.

  This was a foolish act, yet frequently enacted throughout the country. In my particular case, the newpapers might well have a field day. This may be an opportunity to use the situation to attack the sale of pornographic magazines in newsagents.

I am prepared to stand alongside all those who are occasionally foolish and weak, accepting at times I am foolish and weak.

Newsagents must accept the fact these magazines are harmful, and are sold purely to the motive of profit.

Can you help?

Statement

I am 56 years of age, sometimes I am absent minded and do things I cannot always explain, as family and friends would testify. Maybe some of it may be due to the fact I have a very high blood pressure, and take tablets prescribed by my doctor. On Monday 9th October I went into town to return a piece of guttering I had bought in error. On my way back to the car I decided to enter the newsagents, just to look around, whilst there I saw some pornographic magazines and I wondered what the latest trend was, as I only see them lying around at work or in shops, I never buy them as I do not believe in financing the pornographers.

I saw a woman in the shop, and suddenly a church acquaintance appeared outside the shop; and for some unaccountable reason I put the magazine under my coat and walked out of the shop. I did not want the magazine, because most of them are not worth looking at.

I did not have much time to make any decision when I was challenged, physically grabbed on the arm, and taken back in the shop by three or four people, who continued to threaten me with violence. I offered to pay for the magazine out of the money I had on me, but the girl was already calling for the police before I entered the shop and no attempt by me to explain was accepted.

Shopkeepers are prepared to sell these magazines, not taking into account the effect they might have on others, even causing people to commit crime. In my particular case there was little concern for my welfare or the harm publicity of a case like this might do.

I was publicly arrested, taken to the Police Station, questioned and finger printed.

Whether I am guilty of theft is for the magistrates to decide.

BISHOPTHORPE
YORK
YO2 1QE

Personal.   15. VII. 77

Dear Mary,

Just a personal note to say how
pleased I was at the verdict in the
blasphemy trial. Whatever the merits of the
case, it did say 'halt' to the 'demoralising'
powers which has been at work in this country
for so long. The tide begins to turn – and
we have cause to be grateful to you.

As ever,

Stuart

Letter received from the Archbishop of York in the aftermath of the *Gay News*
blasphemy trial

12. Mary vs. the Blasphemers

The very highest level of Mary Whitehouse's multi-storey demon-ology – some way above porn barons, and almost out of sight of Joan Bakewell and irresponsible advocates of water fluoridation – was reserved for blasphemers. Like the P-word, the B-word came to Mary readily enough to beguile the unwary into think-ing that she had no clear conception of what she meant by it. The following somewhat ritualised complaint about the great Irish comedian Dave Allen rather invites the short shrift it gets from the ever-courteous Colin Shaw.

Letter addressed to 'The Producer of Show of The Week'

25 March, 1975

Dear Producer,
  We have received a number of complaints about 'The Dave Allen Show' (6 March) which was felt to be blasphemous.
  In this particular programme Dave Allen was portrayed as a priest and there were dancing figures, presumably representing evil spirits. You are no doubt aware of the episode in which Dave Allen snatched the cross from the wall and sprayed these figures with water from the font.
  Mr Allen is a very accomplished artist, and it is greatly to be regretted that he has to sink to blasphemy to 'entertain' the viewers.
  Yours sincerely,
  (Mrs) Mary Whitehouse
  Hon Gen Secretary

Reply from the Secretary of the BBC

16th April, 1975

Dear Mrs. Whitehouse,

I am writing to acknowledge and thank you for your
letter of 25th March, which you addressed to the
Producer of 'Show of the Week'.

We also have received some letters of complaint
about Dave Allen, in addition to a number of letters
in praise of his recent series. Mr. Allen, as you say,
is an accomplished artist, but he is also a believing
and practising Catholic with an awareness of what
does and does not constitute blasphemy. In replying
to correspondents who have raised this question, Sir
Charles Curran has said that as a fellow Catholic he
is as sensitive as any other to what might be taken
as offensive to his faith. He does, however, greatly
enjoy Dave Allen's jokes about religion and religious
practices and he has said so in public. It is a well-
known tradition that the best jokes about religion are
told in monasteries and convents. Dave Allen has been
doing no more than telling them outside these precincts
for the enjoyment of all.

It is not clear on what grounds your correspondents
have said that any of the jokes are blasphemous. The
scene you describe in your letter would certainly not
seem to deserve this description, but if you have
received any detailed arguments in support of this view,
we should of course be glad to consider them.

Yours sincerely,
(Colin Shaw)
The Chief Secretary

The director general's considered response to one of Mary
Whitehouse's innumerable complaints about *Till Death Us Do
Part* supplies a fascinating insight into the extent to which the
BBC's attitudes to different religions were shaped (at least in the

Corporation's own mind) by a stereotypically British sense of fair play.

Reply from Sir Charles Curran

15th Jan, 1973

Dear Mrs. Whitehouse,

I was glad to learn from your second letter that you came to share our view of the Christmas edition of 'Till Death' and felt it to be without those qualities suggested by some of the criticisms levelled at it in advance. I was glad too that you should find yourself in sympathy with at least some of the aspects of Mr. Speight's work which have encouraged us in our continuing use of his talents. It was not, incidentally, my impression that the Stations of the Cross were shown in a setting of 'titters, sniggers and foolish levity'. Their appearance at the start of the programme was, in my view, played quite straightforwardly.

There is, I believe, a considerable difference between the ridiculing or satirising of the beliefs of, say, the Sikh minority and the ridiculing of Christian beliefs. In the former case, the vast mass of the audience does not share the common background of understanding which exists in the latter case. The Sikhs are, quite genuinely, a small minority in the country. As such, they should be protected. I do not feel that Christian beliefs need the same degree of protection. Their position is secure enough to withstand the kind of assault launched by Mr. Speight and, occasionally, other people, which is intended to expose foolishness and credulousness among some of those who claim to be believers without being at all well instructed in the creed to which they profess allegiance.

Yours Sincerely,

(Charles Curran)

While Mary Whitehouse's chunterings about the '103 blood-
ies' she claimed to have counted in one episode of *Till Death Us
Do Part* found her at her most wilfully pedantic, her complaints
following the first screening of 'The Bird Fancier' on 20 January
1972 (often referred to, for reasons that will become obvious,
as 'the Virgin Birth Episode') brought her the rare prize of an
actual apology from the BBC. In setting out to prove that 'no
one's reputation was safe' from the port- and gin-fuelled gossip
of his wife and Old Gran, Alf Garnett reported them suggesting 'that Mary couldn't be a virgin – cos she was in child by
[he looks reverently upwards] Him'. Alf's son-in-law Mike later
earned himself the familiar sobriquet 'blasphemous Scouse git'
for suggesting that the mother of Jesus might be 'on the pill'.

Lord Hill's diplomatic concession that Johnny Speight had
crossed a line ('May I say straight away that we do not seek
to defend the inclusion, in a recent edition in the latest series
of "Till Death Us Do Part", of one short passage – the one in
which references were made to the Virgin Mary?') was not the
end of the matter as far as Mary Whitehouse was concerned.
Her attempt to persuade the Director of Public Prosecutions to
charge the BBC with blasphemy was respectfully rebuffed, after
consultation with the Attorney General, on the grounds that the
chances of success were 'not sufficient to warrant instituting proceedings', but the twist in the tail of this disappointing response
was an assurance that although there had been no prosecution
under this particular statute for many years, the offence of blasphemy was 'not obsolete'. All that would be required to allow it
to be successfully invoked would be an attack on the Christian
faith involving 'such an element of vilification, ridicule or irrev-
erence as would be likely to . . . lead to a breach of the peace or
to deprave public morality generally'.

The renegade Danish performance artist Jens Jørgen Thors-
en's 1976 proposal to come to Britain to make a film about 'the

sex life of Christ' seemed to be the perfect provocation. The fact that he had already been banned from doing this in the permissive hotbeds of Denmark and Sweden (and later achieved the same distinction in France and Italy, after petrol bombs were thrown at the Danish ambassador's residence in Rome) was some indication of the nature of the script, which Mary rapidly had translated from the original Danish.

The Danish government's surprising willingness to step into action against Thorsen had been at least partly motivated by the fact that protests about the planned film came from Muslims as well as Christians. Given subsequent clashes between that country's expansive notion of freedom of speech and some of the more authoritarian versions of Islam, this was one of those ironies of such overwhelming intensity that it ultimately turns out to be something more like an explanation.

Such was the strength of feeling in the UK that even the Archbishop of Canterbury, Dr Donald Coggan – whose reluctance to get involved in such matters was a source of perennial frustration to Whitehouse – proclaimed himself willing to consider recourse to the blasphemy laws to prevent Thorsen's film being shown, were it ever to be made. As it happened, the need for such drastic steps was obviated by the achievement of a degree of consensus that Mary Whitehouse had often claimed for her campaigns, but not always actually achieved.

Michael Hastings – described by Whitehouse in *A Most Dangerous Woman?* as 'a West Indian and a member of our executive committee, who was only 18 at the time' – had been one of a number of citizens moved to express his concerns about the film in a letter to the Queen. Her Majesty in turn 'graciously gave permission' for her unusually forthright expression of opposition to this 'obnoxious' film to be made public, and 'Michael was mightily surprised and delighted to find his photograph transmitted alongside one of the Queen in the first item of television news that night.'

Hastings – later Lord Hastings of Scarisbrick, and at the time of writing vice-president of UNICEF – was not the only solid citizen to be driven to action by Whitehouse's anti-Thorsen campaign. A schoolteacher from Enfield organised a prayer vigil outside the Home Office, which the new Home Secretary Merlyn Rees credited with finally convincing him that the Dane's admission to the UK would not be 'conducive to the public good'. Rees's parliamentary announcement of the resulting banning order was, Whitehouse reported with great satisfaction, 'greeted with cheers on both sides of the house', and when he finally turned up at Heathrow in early 1977, the 'squat, bearded Dane' was placed firmly on the first plane back to Copenhagen.

Mary Whitehouse's next anti-blasphemy initiative would constitute her most notable single intervention in the cultural life of the nation. Such historical significance as is accorded to the year of 1977 has traditionally been divided up between punk rock and Queen Elizabeth II's Silver Jubilee, but the wider importance of Mary Whitehouse's private prosecution of *Gay News* – culminating in a guilty verdict at the Old Bailey in July of that year – is very hard to overstate.

Someone who was determined to give it a go might say this event marked 'the turning of a tide that had flowed steadily one way since the publication of Darwin's *Origin of Species*' or even 'the beginnings of a resurgence of faith over reason'. The fact that the latter process ultimately moved in a very different direction from the one its initiator wanted was no fault of Mary Whitehouse's.

Her private prosecution of *Gay News*'s editor Denis Lemon for publishing James Kirkup's poem 'The Love That Dares to Speak Its Name' relied upon a reactivation of the long-thought-dormant common law offence of 'blasphemous libel'. However, the character of the ensuing debate was defined by the pressing contemporary issue of gay people's right to freedom of expression.

When addressing Mary Whitehouse's feelings about homosexuality (which will have a chapter all to themselves starting on page 341) the phrase 'can of worms' is not adequate for the job in hand. In fact, 'barrel of cobras' doesn't even cover it, and in the context of Whitehouse's profound and very public antipathy towards what she disdainfully termed 'Gay Lib', it is hardly surprising that many people chose not to believe her insistence that 'This poem came to me unsolicited in the post – I read it and reacted to it before I knew which paper it had been published in.'

Yet while the fact that the defendant was the editor of a campaigning gay newspaper was hugely relevant to the atmosphere of the trial – and to many people's responses to the prosecution on both sides of the ideological divide it opened up – it was not really relevant to the accusation of blasphemy itself. Even the most cursory glance at 'The Love That Dares to Speak Its Name' – now instantly available to all who wish to read it via the magic of the internet – confirms that Mary Whitehouse would have been just as certain to launch a private prosecution of its publisher in the (admittedly unlikely) event of it having appeared in *Angling Times* or the *Catholic Herald*.

In *A Most Dangerous Woman?* she recalls experiencing the poem as 'a kind of re-crucifixion, only this time with twentieth century weapons', and if an ecstatic account of a necrophiliac sexual assault on the crucified body of Christ does not constitute blasphemy, it is hard to be sure exactly what would. What so mobilised forces on both sides of the secular/religious divide was a shared understanding of the broader significance of this legal battle – that the way it went would decide if the concept of blasphemy actually had any meaning in the late twentieth century, and by extension whether the designation of Britain as 'a Christian country' had any lingering validity.

Given the unprecedented expression of national anti-blasphemer solidarity generated by the Thorsen case (which was concluding in triumph just as 'The Love That Dares to Speak Its Name' dropped through her letter box), Mary Whitehouse had every reason to expect the same coalition of the pious to fall obediently in line behind her in the run-up to the *Gay News* trial. Denis Lemon, however, was nothing like a Dane.

The vision reading the poem gave her – of Jesus Christ 'utterly defiled and at the mercy of those who hate the sound of his voice' – left Whitehouse with no alternative but to take action. 'If I did not do something to end this sacrilege', she explained, in a letter written in May 1977 to the archbishops of York and Canterbury, 'then I would carry the shame of this abdication for the rest of my life.'

Not everyone who called themselves a Christian, it transpired, felt as she did. In the same communication, Whitehouse pronounced herself 'dumbfounded' by the Church leaders' refusal to give her resolute invocation of the blasphemy law their official blessing.

A 'puzzled' Donald Coggan wrote back, insisting that his and Cardinal Hume's individual decisions to decline the request of Whitehouse's lawyer Graham Ross-Cornes that they might appear as witnesses for the prosecution was a purely tactical one, based on the feeling that the jury, 'who may in the main, or perhaps all[!] be non-believers', might be alienated by the testimony of '"professional" church leaders'. The exact nature of his pragmatic considerations was between Coggan and his conscience, but whether for the reason he had stated, or because (as Mary believed) internal tensions within the Church of England over the issue of homosexuality made him reluctant to take an active part in a prosecution that might be seen to have an anti-gay subtext, Whitehouse went into battle alone.

Isolated as she was, one tactical masterstroke laid the foundation of her ultimate success. The decision not to go after the eminent poet responsible for 'The Love That Dares to Speak Its Name', but only the newspaper that disseminated it, neutralised at a stroke a large portion of the free speech argument that *Gay News*'s formidable defence team of Mortimer and Robertson (the libertarian Batman and Robin) would otherwise have been able to mobilise. It meant that Whitehouse was not seeking to legally enforce the view that the poem shouldn't have been written, only that Denis Lemon was wrong to publish it.

Although they initially assumed that 'the poem was the product of a tortured mind', Whitehouse and her lawyers were surprised to discover that James Kirkup was now a distinguished academic and fellow of the Royal Society of Literature. On finding out that the poem was an early work, not written for publication, and the poet himself 'considered it lacked maturity', they shrewdly decided to concentrate their fire on a target that might be easier to hit.

The perception that her overriding objective was to limit other people's opportunities for creative self-expression is perhaps the greatest of all the distortions to which Mary Whitehouse's life and work have been subject. The goal she really wanted to achieve was to win something akin to a fair hearing for a Christian message which she felt was being drowned out by decadent secularism. To this end, while not fully subscribing to the PR man's mantra that 'all publicity is good publicity', she was always on the lookout for an opportunity to turn a negative into a positive.

'Thorsen's projected film made Jesus Christ headline news in Britain day after day!' she exulted in *A Most Dangerous Woman?* And the diary entries she wrote during the *Gay News* trial offset the 'dreadful sense of despair' induced by Geoffrey Robertson's 'truly remarkable performance' against the glad news that the terrifyingly eloquent defence lawyer had 'talked about God's love for sinners'.

Whitehouse marvelled at 'the sight and sound of Geoffrey Robertson, who is a "Protestant sceptic", speaking with such intimate knowledge and perception of the New Testament and its teachings', and rejoiced that he had '"rarely been seen without a copy in his hands for the last six months"'. 'In some strange unbelievable way', she insisted, 'there has been more of the Gospel preached in this court this week . . . than surely ever before,' concluding that 'God must have spoken through Robertson's words, whatever his intent.'

The tsunami of personalised opprobrium that broke over Whitehouse's head in the aftermath of the jury's surprise guilty verdict on 12 July 1977 would test her holy-rolling equanimity to its very limits, but more of that in what she would have disapprovingly termed 'the homosexual chapter'. Meanwhile, as Lemon prepared his appeal against a nine-month suspended prison sentence and fine of £500 (*Gay News* itself was fined a significant but by no means ruinous £1,000), the forces of permissive humanism rallied to the counter-attack.

Within a month of the verdict, a committee had been formed to campaign for the abolition of the law against blasphemy. 'The Love That Dares to Speak Its Name' was provocatively republished in the *Anarchist Worker*, *Socialist Challenge*, *Peace News*, *Liberator* and *Freedom*, and copies of the poem were handed to members of the public, with *New Humanist* editor Nicolas Walter offering – in, of all places, the *Church Times* – to send one to anybody who supplied him with an SAE. In January 1978, William McIlroy – former editor of the National Secular Society's journal *The Freethinker* – published a collective condemnation of the prosecution signed by some 140 well-known names (including twelve peers, ten Members of Parliament, nine professors, four churchmen, some writers and journalists and a concert pianist).

NVALA struck back with its own collective declaration 'To demonstrate that among men and women of distinction, learning and experience, there is a substantial body of opinion in support of legal restraint on blasphemy'. The resulting document saw McIlroy's 140 signatures, and raised him another forty. In an apparently throwaway coda whose true significance would take some time to emerge, it was noted that 'Many of those who have signed believe that the [blasphemy] law might well be extended to cover other religions'.

Sample thirty of the 180 names collected

Masood Archad, Student, Pakistani nationality
Arthur Askey
Lt. Col. & Mrs. George Badley, Salvation Army Officers
   (retired)
Brigadier Lord Ballantrae
Sir Roderick Barclay, Ambassador (retired)
Lady Isobel Barnett, Broadcaster
Sir Cyril Black, J.P., D.L.
Chin Yun Choy, Chinese student
O.W.H. Clark, House of Laity, General Synod of the Church of
   England
R.E.D. Clark, M.A., Ph.D., Editor of Faith and Thought,
   Victorian Institute
Colonel The Lord Clifford of Chudleigh, O.B.E. B.A., D.L.
Canon Frank Colquhoun, Vice-Dean of Norwich
Commissioner W. Stanley Cottrill, Chief of Staff, The
   Salvation Army
Dame Cicely Courtneidge
Robert Dougall, Writer and Broadcaster
Colonel F. Lane Fox, Royal Horse Guards, (retired)
Canon Michael Green, Rector, St. Aldate's Church, Oxford
Miss Joyce Grenfell
Rabbi Ephraim Isaac Groundland, Southport Hebrew Congregation
Ian T. Hall, Executive Director, Gideons International
Lord Halsbury
Miss Irene Handl, Actress and author
John T. Hansford, M.A., B.Sc, Headmaster, King Edward's
   School, Witley
Ralph Harris, Author and Economist

Miss Sheila Haughton, B.Sc, Headmistress, Clarendon School,
  Bedford
Professor J.N. Hawthorne, University of Nottingham
Dickie Henderson, O.B.E., Entertainer
Philip S. Henman, F.C.I.T., Former High Sheriff of Surrey
Dr. Kenneth A. Kitchen, Reader in Egyptian and Coptic,
  University of Liverpool
The Earl of Longford, former Leader of the House of Lords

Any alliance of Lord Longford, Arthur Askey, Joyce Grenfell, Irene Handl (Mary Millington's co-star in *Come Play with Me*) and 'Masood Archad, Student, Pakistani nationality' could not help but represent a significant new body of opinion. In further testimony to the applicability of Newton's third law – to every action there is an equal and opposite reaction – in July 1978 Mary received a communication through the post from an organisation called the United Order of Blasphemers.

Extract from UOB newsletter

Although the meeting at which it was decided to re-form the United Order of Blasphemers took place as far back as January, it was agreed that no public announcement would be made until 4 July. There were two reasons for this. First, it was decided at the start that we should break the laws relating to blasphemy before the authorities or Christian informers were aware of our existence. Secondly, it was felt appropriate to make the announcement on the first anniversary of the opening of the 'Gay News' trial.

Internal newsletters have been circulated among members only, but in future certain issues of the Newsletter will be circulated to the public and the media. Members will be aware that the Order is divided into seven divisions. These are London (north of the Thames), London (south of the Thames), Southern Counties, Western Counties and South Wales, the Midlands, Merseyside, North Wales, Northern Counties (with Scotland until the Scottish divisional organisation is established). There are 33 groups (excluding schools see page 2), each with a group leader who maintains contact with the divisional organiser.

There are three important sub-committees: FINANCE (raising funds through donations, loans, etc., and operating a special bank account); EDUCATION (promoting our work in Schools and Colleges, selecting material for, and arranging publication of Study Papers); PUBLICATIONS (responsible for the selection, editing, production and distribution of pamphlets and leaflets).

The National Committee consists of representatives of all divisions, Publication, Education and Finance sub-committees. In addition there is the Hon Secretary and three others who have been invited to serve because of their specialist knowledge.

THE FIRST NATIONAL MEETING of the UOB will be held in Birmingham during the weekend of November 18th.—19th. A detailed programme will be sent with the next internal Newsletter, but here is a provisional agenda:

Saturday, 10 a.m. A SUMMARY OF OUR ACHIEVEMENTS — Reports by the Hon Secretary and divisional organisers. Saturday, 2.30 p.m. Discussion on the Hon Secretary's and divisional organisers' reports. Saturday, 3.30 p.m. WORK IN SCHOOLS AND COLLEGES. Sunday, 10 a.m. Discussion on 'Work in Schools and Colleges' Sunday, 2.30 p.m. LOOKING TO THE FUTURE.

There will be a buffet social on Saturday. The programme will include readings of 'blasphemous' poetry and prose (by a professional actor) and two school groups have promised to perform sketches. Tickets will be £1.50 each.

Offers of accommodation for delegates on Friday and Saturday nights would be much appreciated. Arrangements for the weekend's activities are in the hands of the Midlands divisional organiser.

THERE ARE NOW 33 UOB GROUPS (excluding schools and colleges) in different parts of the country. We aim for 40 groups by the New Year. Meetings are arranged in Lancaster, Birkenhead, Oxford, Cambridge, Wimbledon, Hampstead, Tunbridge Wells and Canterbury. The groups are successfully raising money for our publishing work and some are making their own arrangements for distribution of 'blasphemous' literature.

WE THANK THE CONVENOR OF THE EDUCATION COMMITTEE for the following Report:

The Education Committee has held six meetings, including a joint meeting with the Publications Committee. Every division, except Northern Counties, is represented on the Education Committee and there are school/college groups in all the divisional areas.

There are now 23 school and college groups, and individual members of the UOB in educational establishments without groups are doing excellent work.

A lively discussion ensued at the May meeting as to how UOB members should treat RI lessons and morning assembly. It was agreed that our members could not be expected to join in hymns and prayers, but it was strongly recommended that they should NOT boycott RI lessons. It was felt that we could do more damage to Christianity by asking carefully-worded questions, and presenting the anti-Christian case, than by avoiding attendance at RI lessons.

The disco organised by a London school group raised £31 for UOB funds. Our grateful thanks to all concerned.

There will be a short meeting of members from school and college groups immediately after the National Meeting in Birmingham.

WE THANK THE HON. TREASURER for the following report: Although the Finance Committee has met only twice, the three members meet regularly on a social basis and at National Committee meetings. We held an emergency meeting to discuss the possibility of purchasing a small printing press which will shortly be available for the bargain price of £900. It was generally agreed that the expenditure of this sum would make serious inroads into the general fund, but the advantage of having our own printing machine was so obvious it was decided that an attempt should be made to ask a number of friends for loans. At the time of writing we have succeeded in raising £690, and we are deeply grateful to all who responded to our appeal.

Does the resolutely – maybe even wilfully – sub-NVALA tone of this communication remind you of anyone else? Basically, it was the Society for the Campaign for Freedom in Publishing all over again, only with a less explicit topless dimension and more disruption of religious instruction lessons.

Whether the United Order of Blasphemers actually existed in the form outlined in this newsletter, or was merely a detailed flight of satirical fancy designed to induce alarm in a particular recipient, there should still have been quiet satisfaction to be taken in the evident admiration of Mary's adversaries for her organisational methods, and their lack of long-term success in emulating them (unless the annual UOB disco is still a fixture of the school calendar). In this case, however, there were more urgent concerns Having received guidance from the DPP that 'if this department received firm evidence of distribution of the pocm following the Court of Appeal's judgment, then consideration would be given to whether any action would be taken', Whitehouse saw to it that the UOB newsletter was forwarded to the DPP.

One prominent NVALA member took still more direct action. 'I wrote to [*New Humanist* editor] Nicolas Walter, using a pen name . . . and the address of a house I bought for my mother-in-law,' he advised Mary in a letter. His main aim was to take issue with Walter's claim in the British Humanist Association newsletter that 'the principal effect of Mary Whitehouse's prosecution of *Gay News* has been to increase the circulation of the offending poem . . . far beyond its original readership . . .'

While a widening of the poem's readership had indubitably been one consequence of the blasphemy prosecution, whether it was 'the principal effect' is a rather different matter. Whatever one's view of the rights and wrongs of this case, the one incontrovertible fact of it – and we have the discreet concurrence of James Kirkup himself on this point – is that 'The Love That Dares to Speak Its Name' was, and is, a truly awful poem. For those who'd prefer to dip no more than a toe into its semen-heavy waters, hopefully the line 'foxy Judas, a great kisser' will convey something of its adolescent determination to shock.

In this context, Walter's heroically specious attempt to present the poem to the *Church Times* as 'a poetical expression of the

sexual interpretation of the Atonement' left him lagging some
way behind Mary Whitehouse in the aesthetic acuity stakes. A
truer reflection of his feelings was probably to be found in the
November 1977 issue of *The Freethinker*: 'My own objection
to the poem', he wrote, 'is that it drags sex down to the level of
religion, spoiling a healthy activity with unhealthy ideas, in the
manner of the Bible and the wedding service.'

The notion – as shocking to Walter and his secular cohorts
as anything they could say to Whitehouse – that there are many
people to whom certain things actually are, and always will be,
sacred would stage something of a revival in Britain in the years
after the *Gay News* conviction. 'It is quite beside the point that
you did not <u>intend</u> to blaspheme with a parody of the Creed,' a
NVALA correspondent lectured the BBC's Secretary in the aftermath of a near-the-knuckle *Not the Nine O'Clock News* sketch
in 1979. 'A drunken motorist may not intend to kill a pedes-
trian, but does exactly that.'

The Bishop of Wakefield's earlier insistence that 'blasphemy
does irreparable harm for which an apology is not enough' was
the kind of unabashedly fervent statement that would become
increasingly widely heard as the twentieth century hurried
towards its conclusion, although largely in the context of another faith. One sign of how much things were changing was that
Mary Whitehouse found herself in the unaccustomed position
of writing to thank the BBC for the fairness of their treatment
of her, in the aftermath of a two-part *Everyman* documentary
about the *Gay News* court case screened in March of 1978.

Letter to the director general of the BBC

23rd March, 1978

Dear Mr Trethowan,

  I would like to place on record both my personal
appreciation and that of this Association of the two

'EVERYMAN' programmes dealing with the recent blasphemy case.

I feel sure you will well understand the difficulties and pressures under which those programmes were produced and having worked as closely as I have with Daniel Wolf over these last months I have nothing but the highest praise both of his integrity and his qualities as a producer. Both he, and Peter France, as well as the other members of the crews concerned were very kind to me personally at a time of some strain, and some ill health.

I have heard nothing but the highest praise of both the programmes and I would like you to know how very grateful I am.

Yours sincerely,
Mary Whitehouse

After Denis Lemon's appeal was dismissed in February 1978, his struggle to clear his name moved to the House of Lords, where a hefty quorum of nine judges ultimately found in Mary Whitehouse's favour, with Lord Scarman delivering the following historically significant judgment, emphatically typed out in capitals in the archive, so that is how it should be presented here.

Extract from Lord Scarman's judgment

I DO NOT SUBSCRIBE TO THE VIEW THAT THE COMMON LAW OFFENCE OF BLASPHEMOUS LIBEL SERVES NO USEFUL PURPOSE IN THE MODERN LAW. ON THE CONTRARY, I THINK THERE IS A CASE FOR LEGISLATION EXTENDING IT TO PROTECT THE RELIGIOUS BELIEFS AND FEELINGS OF NON-CHRISTIANS. THE OFFENCE BELONGS TO A GROUP OF CRIMINAL OFFENCES DESIGNED TO SAFEGUARD THE INTERNAL TRANQUILLITY OF THE KINGDOM. IN AN INCREASINGLY PLURAL SOCIETY SUCH AS THAT OF MODERN BRITAIN IT IS NECESSARY NOT ONLY TO RESPECT THE DIFFERING RELIGIOUS BELIEFS, FEELINGS, AND PRACTICES OF ALL BUT ALSO TO PROTECT THEM FROM SCURRILITY, VILIFICATION, RIDICULE, AND CONTEMPT . . .

I WILL NOT LEND MY VOICE TO A REVIEW OF THE LAW
RELATING TO BLASPHEMOUS LIBEL WHICH WOULD RENDER IT
A DEAD LETTER, OR DIMINISH ITS EFFICACY TO PROTECT
RELIGIOUS FEELING FROM OUTRAGE AND INSULT. MY CRITICISM
OF THE COMMON LAW OFFENCE OF BLASPHEMY IS NOT THAT IT
EXISTS BUT THAT IT IS NOT SUFFICIENTLY COMPREHENSIVE.
Per Lord Scarman:
Whitehouse v Lemon (1979)

At the end of her account of the *Gay News* trial in *A Most
Dangerous Woman?* Mary Whitehouse expressed the hope 'that
the day when society regards blasphemy as an unexceptional
offence will never come'. Even she could not have expected how
seriously this crime would come to be taken in Britain over the
decades ahead, but by 1989 she would be writing to the new
BBC chairman Duke Hussey to emphasise that a letter of complaint he had received from a 'prominent Muslim leader' about
the TV comedy show *Something for the Weekend* was both 'very
responsible' and 'worthy of sympathetic consideration'.

Christian and Muslim alike had been 'deeply distressed' by a
sketch 'in which Abraham is seen to throw a custard pie in the
face of Isaac to the accompaniment of the singing of Psalm XXI-
II'. Mary Whitehouse felt the addition of an Islamic counter-
point to her chorus of complaint 'might mean it would be more
carefully considered than are those from Christians, particularly
in view of the anger aroused by Salman Rushdie's publication of
his *Satanic Verses*'.

'We have not yet solved the *Satanic Verses* affair', warned her
new Muslim ally, somewhat ominously, under the circumstances, 'and in view of [the] sensitive nature of jokes like this, we
would urge you to ask the authors to be more careful in future.'

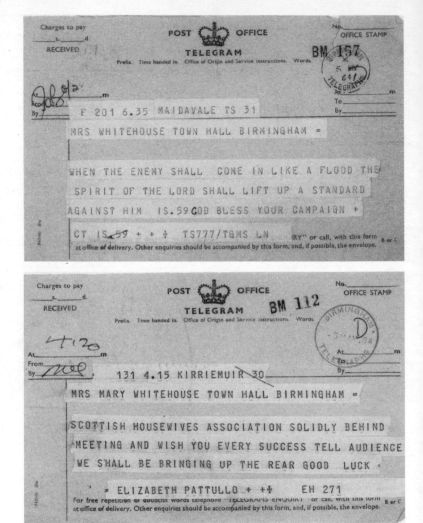

Telegrams received on the day of the Birmingham Town Hall meeting

13: Mary and the Church

'We need to revive the militant Christian spirit of Britain,' proclaimed the original CUTV manifesto, 'and in this everyone must strike their own flint and raise the spark.' Among the messages of support read out on that historic day in Birmingham was the following from the then Archbishop of Canterbury, the Rt. Revd Michael Ramsey: 'I have been hearing from many people about the Women of Britain Campaign. I am sure that it is doing much good by its own impact. I do what I can to help in the same cause whenever opportunity comes.'

The contrast between the language of these two statements – the first clear, urgent and ringing with poetic intensity, the second a mealy-mouthed shrug – would inform Mary Whitehouse's whole relationship with organised religion. In *Quite Contrary*, her last volume of memoirs, she berates 'The unacceptable – culpable – silence of certain leaders and sections of the Church', and 'its abdication in the face of the intellectual/humanistic control of the media'.

In a next few lines which are remarkable (even in Whitehouse's frequently splenetic canon) for their bitterness, she asks '"Where were you when they crucified my Lord?" Busy counting the collection and signing the latest petition in favour of easier divorce or abortion?'

While not as central to the Mary Whitehouse story as her interaction with the BBC, her relationship with the Church of England was every bit as freighted with painful nuance. The resulting tensions were a constant background hum throughout her three and a half decades in public life – like the presence of the barflies Norm and Cliff in the sitcom *Cheers*, or John Cale's viola in the Velvet Underground song 'All Tomorrow's Parties'.

In the early 1960s, Britain's established Church was struggling to redefine its role in the same rapidly changing social landscape that Mary Whitehouse found so alarming. Needless to say, that wing of the C. of E. which opted to embrace those changes rather than resist them – specifically the 'South Bank theologians', such as the Bishop of Woolwich Dr John Robinson, whose unabashedly liberal thinking flourished under the patronage of the formidable Mervyn Stockwood, the socialist Bishop of Southwark – was fighting it out with Lenny Bruce and Che Guevara at the top of Whitehouse's lightly perfumed shitlist.

The vision of the Anglican Church that Mary Whitehouse could feel at home with was, inevitably, a more traditional one. It was the kind of faith hinted at in the following (very sweet) pre-Town Hall meeting letter from the nearby Bishop of Hereford – a far more fulsome expression of support, incidentally, than the one the Archbishop of Canterbury managed – wherein the advent of the new churchwardens' wands was the most radical innovation on the agenda, and rampant individualism went no further than an expression of ecclesiastical-furnishing-related ennui.

Letter from the Bishop of Hereford

4th May, 1964

Dear Mrs. Whitehouse,

Thank you for your letter. I am so glad about your Mother's birthday. I shall be thinking of you all, especially if I see the new Churchwardens' wands. I am glad to have something designed locally. I get so tired of those boring brasses from ecclesiastical furnishing shops.

Will you give my very best wishes to the meeting in the Town Hall, Birmingham? I think the keen response

which has been given to your magnificent Campaign shows
how many people care for the Christian ideals to-day in
spite of all publicity in the contrary direction. I pray
for God's blessing on the meeting and for the guidance
of you and your helpers in all that you undertake.
Yours Faithfully,
Mark Hereford

The Bishop of Hereford was one of a number of high-ranking
clergymen who – in Mary's eyes at least – flattered to deceive in
terms of their willingness to join her crusade, expressing initial
support for first CUTV and then NVALA, only to pull out on
further acquaintance with some of the more extreme elements
among her support.

Letter from the Catholic Vicar General

4th March, 1965

Dear Mrs. Whitehouse,
Thank you for your letter of March 1st. I very much
regret that I shall be unable to attend the first meeting
of the Working Committee on March 16th as I already have
an engagement for that afternoon.
I have been intending to write to you after the
meeting on February 25th. I was somewhat disturbed at
many of the views expressed, particularly the suggestion
for a campaign of civil disobedience with regard to
radio and television licences. I support most of what
the Reverend Kenneth Greet had to say and I feel that we
should proceed with great prudence; otherwise we shall
merely get the image of a group of Mrs. Grundies!
With all good wishes,
I am,
Yours sincerely in Xto,
Vicar General
Monsignor Patrick Casey

For all their doctrinal disagreements, churchmen of different hues had a disconcerting tendency to pull together when their ecumenical equanimity was threatened by outside intervention from people who actually believed in something. Monsignor Casey's willingness to fall in behind the criticisms of the rogue Methodist Kenneth Greet – whose sneak attack on her movement was one of the most traumatic formative incidents in the early years of Whitehouse's campaign – would certainly have left a mark. Luckily, the shining sword of NVALA was forged in adversity, as the following lusty counter-blow to the armour of the perfidious Greet demonstrates.

Letter from NVALA vice-president to the Methodist Recorder

17th August, 1965.

Sir,
  Mr. Greet does a disservice to the cause of truth, love and unity by his self-justification and distortion.
  I was present at the meeting called by Mrs. Whitehouse which Mr. Greet describes. It is true that some emotionally charged people said some foolish things, but these did not represent Mrs. Whitehouse's views, the Clean-up T.V. Campaign, nor the Viewers' and Listeners' Association, which was inaugurated at the time. I should have thought that a Minister of the Gospel would have seen the value of a spontaneous movement to replace what is dirty and degrading by clean and wholesome material. He is clearly out of touch with life if he thinks that the Churches can afford to disparage a spontaneous lay attempt to do what the churches ought to have been doing all along. He could at any rate have tried to be helpful.
  Mr. Greet protests his patience and courtesy, he was in fact sarcastic and uncooperative. Having dissociated himself from the stupid remarks made by irresponsible people he could well have played a useful role.
  It is high time that all who want television and

broadcasting to be a constructive influence in the
nation's life, endeavoured committedly to plan and work
to this end.

Signed E.E. Claxton
Vice-President
Viewers' and Listeners' Association

It has already been pointed out that NVALA had to be as
wary as any other newly formed institution of attempts to co-
opt it by longer-established rivals, and Mary Whitehouse would
defend her own turf with the heart – and claws – of a lioness.

1965 NVALA memo to the British Council of Churches

We have noted with great interest the resolution put forward
the Rev. Kenneth Greet, at the Methodist Conference in which
he calls on the British Council of Churches to set up a
Committee to deal with television criticism.

May we make certain comments on this matter? First, we would
like to establish our great pleasure that the Churches see the
need for such a Committee and are prepared to take practical
steps in the matter. We believe that it is of the utmost
importance that these steps are considered against the light
of what is already happening. A spontaneous movement, with now
well over 400,000 supporters of all denominations has sprung
up all over the country. In correspondence which has passed
between us and the heads of the Anglican and Catholic church,
much satisfaction has been expressed that this movement has
originated from lay people, and a concern that it should remain
so has been expressed. Much has already been achieved, not only
in the field of vision where Mr. Sydney Newman's memorandum
recently called on [TV] producers reminding them of the need for
good sense in the treatment of sex, religion and minorities, but
also, and even more important, it has been a rallying point for
people who have wished to take Christian initiative.

May we, with respect, suggest that the following possibilities
are considered.

a) would such a Committee appear in the eyes of ordinary
people as taking over the work of the Campaign?

b) would this have the effect of taking the initiative out of the hands of 'ordinary people'?

NVALA's self-image as the mouthpiece of 'ordinary people' – as opposed to the lackadaisical career churchmen who had let the nation's morals go to pot (in every sense) – was the key to Mary Whitehouse's relationship with organised religion. She did not just capitalise on the perceived failures of the Anglican, Catholic and Methodist hierarchies, she actually depended upon them, in much the same way as (to use an example from a rather different sphere) the NME Awards relies for its continued existence on a widespread belief that the Brit Awards (the music industry's official showcase) is pitifully out of touch.

A letter written to the *Guardian* by a NVALA supporter perfectly captures the appeal of her non-aligned status. In response to an Anglican priest's somewhat snooty assertion that Whitehouse had 'never been the representative of any church in this country when going about her various actions', the theologically clued-up correspondent notes that 'God frequently raises up very ordinary people from the backwaters of a nation's life (e.g. a shepherd – Amos, a fisherman – Peter) to challenge the apathy, apostasy and immorality to be found within that nation and often its official religious leaders'.

An established Church that was vigorously contesting every moral point would have precluded the necessity for NVALA's existence. Once it is accepted – as I think it should be – that Mary Whitehouse's campaigning activities were an expression of her own creativity as much as of deeply held religious convictions, it can be appreciated that her continued significance as a public figure was entirely dependent on the vacillations of liberal theologians, in much the same way that Jeremy Clarkson owes a profound debt of gratitude to the framers of health and safety legislation, or Richard Littlejohn sucks at the nipple of 'political correctness'.

Mary Whitehouse's need to define herself against organised religion as well as alongside it did not stretch to gratuitously alienating the supreme head of the Catholic Church, though. It would be impertinent to suggest that the air must have turned blue when she opened the following letter from an agitated NVALA colleague, but it is certainly possible that a fly on the wall at Triangle Farm House might have been party to some unusually direct language.

Letter from NVALA treasurer

3rd September, 1966

Dear Mary,

I enclose the Banker's order which came to hand this morning.

You will no doubt remember telling me that the Knights of St. Columba had withdrawn their support of our campaign. I got in touch with a local schoolmaster who is a friend of mine — Captain St.John Hougewerf, Forest School, Timperley, and he is doing what he can to put things right.

This morning he asked me to send a telegram to the Pope — I did not like the idea but he said it was imperative, so I telegraphed as follows:

His Holiness The Pope, Vatican City, Rome. Most Holy father in the name of 500,000 members of the Viewers' and Listeners' Association and supporters of our British Clean-up Television Campaign, as well as hundreds of thousands of other supporters and associates of ours, we wish to thank you and Archbishop Beck from the bottom of our hearts for your great act of Christian charity in fostering our common cause in the fight against immorality.

Cobden Turner, J.P.
Treasurer of the Viewers' and Listeners' Association

While a trusty lieutenant in financial matters, Cobden Turner's willingness to go along with Captain St. John Hougewerf's impetuous plan on the spur of the moment suggested that a measure of respectful executive supervision might be a good idea in the future. In the mean time, Mary Whitehouse had a crisis to deal with.

Copy of telegram sent to the Pope by Mary Whitehouse

```
Telegram sent to His Holiness The Pope. 5th Sept 66.
From Mrs Mary Whitehouse
Secretary National Viewers Listeners Association
His Holiness The Pope.Vatican City.Rome.
Have learnt with consternation of unauthorised telegram
sent to Your Holiness in name of Clean Up T.V. Campaign.
Explanatory letter follows.
```

This makeshift tourniquet had staunched the bleeding. Now she had to remove the bullet.

Copy of letter sent to the Pope by Mary Whitehouse

```
15th September, 1966

Your Holiness,
  I understand that on September 3rd a telegram was sent
to Your Holiness on behalf of the 550,000 supporters
of the British 'Clean Up T.V. Campaign' and National
Viewers and Listeners Association, thanking Your
Holiness for your support for our work.
  I wish to express my deep regret that this unauthorised
telegram should have been sent.
  While believing wholeheartedly that Your Holiness would
look with sympathy and understanding on any move to combat
immorality, I would not presume, nor would my committee,
to claim Your Holiness' specific support for our work. Your
Holiness will, no doubt be interested to hear that many
```

thousands of Catholics in Britain support this work, which
aim to establish responsible, Christian broadcasting.

Alderman C.S. Scheill, Secretary of The Catholic Teacher's
Federation publicly asserted, on November 5th 1965, that
the C.T.F. was affiliating with the Clean Up T.V. Campaign
'With the interests of the children of God at heart.'

Since this campaign has been brought to Your Holiness'
attention I have readily agreed to a suggestion put
to me by a Catholic supporter that he should forward
to Your Holiness some material which may satisfy any
question regarding our work which may have been brought
to Your Holiness' attention.

I humbly trust that Your Holiness will forgive any embarrassment that the original telegram may have caused you,

I remain,

Your Holiness' Child,

Mary Whitehouse

'I remain Your Holiness' child' may well be the accepted
form of sign-off in concluding a letter to the pontiff, but to one
unschooled in papal etiquette it does seem a form of words liable
to induce alarm in the head of an institution as prone to scandal
as the Catholic Church. Although the initial surgery had passed
off without incident, Mary Whitehouse knew that the removal
of the bullet from NVALA's self-inflicted foot wound would not
necessarily stop it going gangrenous. She sought guidance on
how best to deal with the potential PR disaster of the papal telegram from one of the number of fringe ecclesiastical authority
figures upon whom she could unobtrusively call for advice.

Letter from the Bishop of Sinda

September 14th, 1966

Dear Mrs. Whitehouse,

Thank you for letting me have the copies of the
telegrams.

In the first place, I am quite sure that it would be
most unwise to give any news of this unfortunate breach
of normal protocol to the Press, this could do only harm
to the cause of VALA.

Secondly, the whole matter should be referred to the
Apostolic Delegate, Apostolic Delegation, 54 Parkside,
London. S.W. 19. All communications of this kind are
normally dealt with through the Delegation and certainly
any enquiry about the first telegram and VALA would be
through this channel.

I should think it advisable to send copies too, to
Archbishop Beck since his name was mentioned.

With all good wishes.

Yours sincerely,

Bishop of Sinda

Mary Whitehouse wisely took the bishop's advice, and broke
the habit of a lifetime by issuing no press release. In fact, such
was the level of reticence about Cobden Turner's misjudgement
that prevailed at NVALA high command that I am proud to
claim this as the first public account of the papal telegram.

The need for discretion came to the fore again in Whitehouse's
slow-burning but richly entertaining correspondence with the
Church of England's information officer the Revd (now Canon)
Michael Saward – not so much from her side as from his.

Letter from Revd Michael Saward

PRIVATE AND CONFIDENTIAL
6th November, 1968

Dear Mrs. Whitehouse,

It was most kind of you to write and suggest that we
might meet and I should be very happy to do this. I am
free on December 4th from 10.30 onwards and would be
glad to have the opportunity of talking to you then.

If it is convenient to you I should be very happy for

you to come to my office or, alternatively, if you are
staying in central London I could meet you at your hotel
or some other suitable place. Perhaps you could let me
know which arrangement you would prefer.

I know you will understand that my job has a somewhat
tricky side to it in relation to the broadcasting
authorities and I have to exercise a diplomacy which
does not come altogether naturally to me and for
that reason I should be grateful if our meeting and
discussion could be in confidence. I doubt if I need to
spell out what I mean by this.

Yours sincerely,
Michael Saward

Again, there was no press release. Within less than two years,
Revd Saward was sufficiently confident that Mary Whitehouse
could be relied upon not to compromise his relationships with the
broadcasting authorities by making details of their association
public that he could entrust her with damning details about the
production of the ATV religious affairs show which Lew Grade
defends so eloquently in a letter printed earlier on in this book.

Revd Saward's assurance that 'the more public stir you can
create, the more it will help those of us who have to work rather
more behind the scenes' smacks of the cunning colonial official,
deftly encouraging an indigenous terrorist group for his own
political ends.

Letter from Revd Michael Saward

PRIVATE & CONFIDENTIAL
8th April, 1970.

Dear Mary,

Thank you for your letter and for sending me both the
leaflet concerning your Annual Convention (which I shall
do my best to attend), and also the newspaper cutting of
A.T.V.'s 'Beyond Belief'.

I saw the first of this new series while away in
Bristol last Sunday and would like you to know, in the
strictest confidence, that the Religious Advisers were
placed in the most impossible position by not being
allowed to see the scripts until some forty-eight hours
before the actual recording. This is a disgraceful state
of affairs, and while I have no personal objection to
religious programmes being humourous, I do think that
this one was not particularly funny or any real use to
the Christian faith. I hope that you will therefore
accept my assurance that this matter is not going to be
overlooked, and I believe that the more public stir you
can create, the more it will help those of us who have
to work rather more behind the scenes.

The one great encouragement to me at the moment is to
know that opinion in the Anglican hierarchy is definitely
hardening in relation to the present type of religious
broadcast, and I believe that this trend will continue
in reaction to the so-called 'open-ended' approach.

All good wishes,
Yours sincerely,
Michael Saward

When attendance at the 1970 NVALA congress brought him
face to face with the organisation's warriors in full cry, Revd
Saward did not let his enjoyment of an excellent lunch stand in
the way of some fairly trenchant criticism.

Letter from Revd Michael Saward

20th May, 1970

Dear Mary,
   It was most kind of you to invite me to your
Convention and to throw in an excellent lunch — I
thought you were in good form! Thank you so much.
   I should be less than honest if I said that I found
myself in sympathy with all the day's business — in

general, I felt it was a more militant occasion than
last year with your Chairman, Mr. Keating, and Mr. Clegg
leading the hounds! To confuse the metaphors, Mary,
I just hope you can ride your tiger without personal
injury and that your angels don't don jackboots.
  My warm regards,
  Yours sincerely,
  Michael Saward

Although invariably brave and dignified in the face of verbal
abuse, Mary Whitehouse did not generally take direct criticism
well. So the frank yet conciliatory tone of the following exem-
plary exchange is a testament to the extent of the understanding
she and Revd Saward had developed.

Letter from Revd Michael Saward

CONFIDENTIAL
June 25, 1970

Dear Mary,
  Thank you for your long and interesting letter. I am
so sorry that you won't be able to be present at the
[Church of England General Synod] Assembly debate. I
will do my best to get you a copy of the transcript. The
'Proceedings' are not published for about four months
so it may have to be a photostat of the typescript but I
assume that will be O.K. with you. It may take a month,
I'm afraid.
  I am glad you wrote frankly about my misgivings and I
smiled over your riposte about my two horses. Fifteen
all! I don't think it is in any way secret that I take
up a position which draws the fire of both sides and
my intense desire for fairness makes me suspicious
of irrational or emotive statements from either. I am
as sick as you are of the squeals of the frustrated
trendies who want anarchy and chaos but I am equally
disturbed by the cries for 'discipline' when they come

from those who seem to want to oppose 'restrictiveness'
to 'permissiveness'.

I can only tell you, as I told you before on the
phone, that my reaction was building up all day and my
reference to Mosley was not intended to be insulting so
much as to show the real anxiety which gripped me at
various points during the day. I still think that the
Convention would carry more weight if it could be seen
to be composed of a wider spread in terms of age and
outlook and less numerically dominated by women fifty and
over (and I don't wish to be offensive in saying that).

Another matter which causes us all problems is the
relationship between taste and morality. The great
danger seems to me to be either equating the two or
divorcing them. I suspect that some of your more vocal
members lean towards the former position. It is a
middle-class habit which I am trying to shed.

You and I both walk tight-ropes (no mean feat when
coupled with riding tigers and driving horses) and
I feel sure that we will sometimes disagree and find
our ropes crossing or diverging. The important thing
is surely for us both to recognise that as Christ's
servants our ultimate aim is to relate our desire for
his glory to be manifested with the problem of a fallen
world in which none of us is right all the time. Clip me
round the ear if you think it's necessary and I will try
to learn to live with it. I'll try not to reverse the
procedure too much!

Warmest good wishes.

Yours sincerely,

Michael Saward

P.S. I have been meditating on the following from
Christopher Booker's 'The Neophiliacs', p. 68:

'Throughout history right-wing fantasies have tended to be
concerned more with the rightness of power and the wrongness
of sex while left-wing phantasies have been concerned more
with the wrongness of power and the rightness of sex.'

Reply to Revd Michael Saward

2nd July, 1970

Dear Michael,

Your letter tempts me! Particularly your p.s. — I also am reading Christopher Booker's 'The Neophiliacs' and am finding it absolutely fascinating. I agree entirely with what he says on the matter of 'right wing fantasies' and 'left wing fantasies' — but we do not happen to be either! We would fight the one as strongly as we now fight the other.

You must forgive me for saying that if the Convention seemed to be 'dominated by women of 50 and over', so surely is the Church. Such a fact does nothing to invalidate either the Church or National VALA — by their very temperament women are perhaps more deeply concerned than men with the issues raised. Anyway we felt it was a great step forward to have so many young speakers at the morning session.

On the question of taste and morality there is surely a close relationship since bad taste can be very much a symptom of immorality. Thank you very much indeed for your generous reception of my previous letter. We have very much in common, since each of us in our own sphere are committed to the struggle not between right and left but between right and wrong.

I do hope that the Debate goes well — I am greatly disappointed that I shall not be there. I am so grateful for our fellowship and am entirely at one with you when you say that the important thing is surely for both of us to recognise that as Christ's servants our ultimate aim is to relate our desire for His Glory to be manifested in a fallen world.

With warmest greetings,

Yours ever,

Mary Whitehouse

They weren't quite in Michael Swann territory, but the tantalising possibility that Mary Whitehouse and the established Church might one day be able to find a mutually congenial accommodation had at least been raised. With the retirement of her trepidatious nemesis Donald Coggan and his replacement by Dr Robert Runcie at the end of the 1970s, the prospect of détente finally loomed in the cold war between NVALA and the historic see of Canterbury.

Runcie's politically astute appearance at 1979's NVALA Awards presentation (to present that not overly coveted gong to Thora Hird for *Songs of Praise* – a show on which Mary Whitehouse's long-yearned-for debut was still astonishingly twelve long years away!) appeared to have sealed the deal. This – like Swann's Royal Society of Arts lecture – was one of those magical nights that made the years of brickbats and stink-bombs worthwhile.

The archbishop, Mary Whitehouse recalls fondly in *Quite Contrary*, was 'full of fun', and her account of the evening then turns to her diary to ensure 100 per cent accuracy. After the 'very appreciative' *Songs of Praise* producer asked Mary to name her favourite hymn, 'I turned to Ernest to ask him which it should be. "'Fill thou my life, O lord My god' – our wedding hymn", he said, whereupon the archbishop gave a note and Bill Cotton and the rest of us all joined in. What a lovely way to finish the day!'

Except the day wasn't quite over yet. The Controller of BBC1 Bill Cotton gave Mary a kiss on the way out (the sly old devil), prompting her to observe to Ernest – and the following might be fairly assumed to be the ultimate expression of satisfaction in the Whitehouse lexicon – 'Hugh Greene would have had an apoplectic fit!'

The following acrimonious exchange between Whitehouse and a Devon clergyman who had the temerity to question some

of the assumptions behind NVALA's awkwardly named 'Stoporn
Now' Campaign (a scorched-earth response to the Williams
Report on Obscenity and Film Censorship) paints a rather more
representative picture of Mary Whitehouse's relationship with
the Church of England.

Letter to the editor of the North Devon Journal-Herald

18th September, 1980

Dear Sir,

It always seems to me very sad when Christians are
seen to be in conflict rather than working together for
the common good. And these were my feelings when I read
your report 'Five Clergy say why they won't sign the
anti-porn petition'. The only people who will benefit
from such controversy will be the pornographers!

The five clergy say that they found supporting
literature of the 'Stoporn' campaign 'not just
misleading but in fact downright inaccurate as indeed is
the wording of the Petition'. I would like to challenge
these gentlemen to state, through the column of your
newspaper, precisely in which respects (a) the Petition
and (b) the literature is 'misleading' and 'inaccurate'.

I find their recommendation that people should 'Write
expressing their general support' of the Williams
Committee while, laudably, asking that printed obscenity
should also come under restriction, very puzzling. It
rather makes me suspect that they have taken the Report
on its face value — always a very dangerous thing to do
when so much is at stake!

Let me give an example of what I am talking about.
The whole of the recommendations of the Williams Report
are based on the Committee's conclusion that 'there
does not appear to be any strong evidence that exposure
to sexually explicit material triggers off anti-social
sexual behaviour'.

But how did it come to such a conclusion? The

Committee devoted 19 pages of its report to an attack
upon the work of Professor John Court whose research
into the link between pornography and serious sex crime
is most highly regarded by academics all over the world.
Dr. Court submitted 120 pages of evidence and graphs.
The Committee in its 19 page attack dealt with only 25
lines of that submission.

   Speaking in the House of Lords in July Dr. Court said:

'The dishonesty of the Report's recommendations lies in
their claim to be supported by evidence. My case is that
the evidence has been reviewed selectively, evaluated
with bias, ignored when convenient and critiqued
tendentiously. I make this claim only because I am
aware of the kinds of evidence which were presented,
but I repeat the serious problem raised by the evidence
presented to the Committee being unavailable for others
to make their own assessment. In these circumstances,
before requiring "proof beyond reasonable doubt", we
need "the truth, the whole truth and nothing but the
truth".'

We would welcome the help of your readers in the fight
against this insidious evil and invite them to write to
me for copies of the Petition and supporting literature
(S.A.E. please). I am grateful for the courtesy of your
column.

   Yours sincerely,
   Mary Whitehouse

   So irritated is Mary by the Revd Oliver's lengthy, meticulously
argued demolition of her position that she accidentally on purpose replies to plain old 'Mr Oliver'. Then again, the start of his
letter seems to be missing a 'Dear'.

Reply from Revd John Oliver

9th October, 1980

Mrs Whitehouse,

I have seen your letter to the 'North Devon Journal-
Herald', published in the edition of October 2nd, and
although I do not think it useful to continue the
public debate (my views and those of my colleagues were
clearly put in the report which appeared on September
18th), I feel that I should answer the questions you
raise.

First, however, I do wish to emphasise that we are
in broad agreement that pornography is an evil, that
it is being used cynically for the sake of profit
by a large number of unscrupulous people, and that
it ought to be controlled. Our disagreement is over
the best way to proceed, and in particular over the
value of the Williams Report. I much regret that you
have seen fit to attack the Report, which seems to
me to be a most praiseworthy attempt, by a group of
highly competent, sensitive and responsible people, to
solve a vast and difficult problem which has defeated
many previous efforts to find a means of effective
legislative control. I am immensely impressed by the
clarity, perception and compassion of the Report, and
find that its arguments and recommendations compare very
favourably with the shrill tone, muddled reasoning and
impractical demands made in the VALA petition and its
supporting literature. The major recommendation of the
Report which deeply concerns us is over the exclusion
of the printed word, and we have encouraged our
parishioners to write to their local M.P. expressing
doubts about the wisdom of excluding the printed
word from any form of prohibition or restriction. I
wish that you also had been prepared to take a more
favourable view of the Williams Report, and instead
of attacking it had concentrated on the matter of the
printed word. I recognize the arguments which led the

Committee to their conclusion over this matter are
weighty ones, but on balance I am still concerned that
the printed word could, freed from any restriction, be
very damaging to certain kinds of people.

To turn to your specific questions, you ask why we
criticise your petition and the supporting green sheet
as inaccurate and misleading. We do so on these grounds:

The green sheet purports to sum up or describe the
recommendations of the Report, but in fact travesties
them in highly emotive language.

a) your implication that there are likely, if the
Williams recommendations are implemented, to be more
outlets than at present for pornography, whereas the
whole point of the Williams recommendations is to
restrict the display and availability of offensive
material; the corner shops would indeed be cleaned up,
contrary to your claim in para. 6 of the green sheet.
What do you mean by indecent if not that which 'deals
with or relates to violence, cruelty or horror, or
sexual, faecal or urinary functions or genital Organs.'?
b) the question of postal delivery; recommendation 12
of the Report (p.161) would very severely restrict the
sending of restricted material through the post.
c) the question of the relation between pornography and
crime; paras. 1.9 and 1.10, and the whole of chapter
6, deal very carefully with the evidence. para. 6.4
in particular shows that the Committee members were
conscious of just how carefully the evidence must be
treated in order to avoid complacency or the possibility
of overlooking a connexion between pornography and
crime, and I am entirely convinced by the argument of
paras. 10 and 6.11. You complain in your letter to
the 'Journal-Herald' that the evidence supplied by Dr
Court in particular was largely ignored or unreasonably
rejected by the Williams Committee. I cannot see how the
extensive treatment of his evidence (paras. 6.22–43)
can reasonably be regarded as inadequate or unfair. I do
not, of course, know what other evidence Dr Court may

have submitted which the Committee may have decided to
ignore, but they clearly did deal very carefully with
some of Dr Court's evidence, and their verdict that his
case is 'not proven', together with their exposure of
serious weaknesses in his evidence, seems to me to be
entirely convincing. I therefore believe that your green
paper is dishonest and mischievous. I also think that
your petition is unreasonable and likely to be counter-
productive as it demands the impossible – a ban on all
pornography – and takes absolutely no account of the
difficulties of translating desirable moral objectives
into practical legislation, difficulties which are dealt
with at length and in a refreshingly realistic manner by
the Committee.

Apart from these weaknesses in your material, I find
it extraordinary, and regrettable, that a responsible
body such as VALA should issue shoddy documents that
are riddled with mistakes of grammar, spelling and
punctuation, as VALA itself is likely to be brought into
disrepute as an incompetent organisation. The Church
has been associated too often in the past with muddled
thinking and amateurism, and I do not wish to see
Christian witness in this matter undermined or ridiculed
because of its association with the VALA material.

These are harsh criticisms, but I believe that they
are entirely justified by the facts. In general I am
of course in sympathy with your ideals and objectives;
I hope that you will see that these criticisms are
intended to be helpful, and have been made in the hope
that future campaigns by VALA will be more carefully
researched and better presented; they may then have
greater success. I might say the M.P. for North Devon,
Mr Tony Speller, has declared himself in agreement with
my views on this matter, and has expressed considerable
doubt over the value of petitions.

Yours sincerely,
Rev'd John Oliver

Reply to the Revd John Oliver

October 12th, 1980

Dear Mr Oliver,

I am in receipt of your letter of 9th October in
response to mine in the 'North Devon Journal and Herald'
of October 2nd.

I can fully understand that anyone such as yourself
who does not have access to the kind of worldwide
research available to this Association could be
'immensely impressed by the clarity, perception and
compassion' of the Williams Report.

I think the best thing I can do is send you a copy of
the address given by Dr. Court who is, incidentally,
Associate Professor of Psychology at Flinders University,
Adelaide, and a consultant psychologist. In paragraph
(c) you talk about the 'extensive treatment' of his
evidence. In fact as I said in my letter to the paper the
19 pages which the Report devoted to a 'critique' of his
work concentrated on only 25 lines of 120 pages of the
evidence he submitted. You may care also to take note of
the fact that the state of South Australia was completely
omitted from the reports on the rest of the Australian
states. Legislation very similar to that recommended by
the Report was passed in 1970 with disastrous results
(see graph in John Court's pamphlet p.3).

Your points (a) and (b) take no account whatever of
the fact that the concept of 'indecency' would cease
to exist in the courts. This means that material now
generally regarded is indecent (as distinct from the
pornographic material categorised as 'restricted') would
be freely distributed by post and every other means.

The fact that the Petition was printed without being
proofed accounts for the mis-spelling of bestiality and
the following grammatical errors. This was unfortunate,
but we are grateful for the understanding of people who
realise that such things rarely happen and when they do
are prepared to put first things first. You are in fact

the only one who has written in such lengthy, emotive terms.

I am sending a copy of this letter to Mr. Speller and to each of your colleagues.

Yours sincerely,

Mary Whitehouse

Could anything be done to heal the breach between Mary Whitehouse and Britain's established Church? Robert Runcie's well-received confession on the night of the *Songs of Praise* award ceremony that he 'now had a good many reservations about "the permissive sixties"' might offer some hope of a rapprochement. Either way, such a juicy admission was not going to be allowed to wither long on the vine, and before the year was out, the call of NVALA had come.

Letter to the Archbishop of Canterbury

5th December, 1980

Dear Dr Runcie,

You were kind enough to say that there might be occasions when we could work together and I was very grateful indeed for that.

I wondered, therefore, whether you might feel moved to take some action over an episode in 'Not The Nine O'clock News' (BBC2) on 24th November. I enclose a transcript of what was said.

Many people who do not, and I suspect would not, watch the programme, rang here the following Friday because throughout the day (28th November) the words of this particular sketch were 'trailed' on Radio 4 in preparation for the highly regarded 'Pick of the Week'. An act of great insensitivity at best.

We have already written to Mr. George Howard, Chairman of the Governors of the BBC about this sketch and another which took the story of the Royal Train

further than any newspaper had done, using 'the' four
letter word in the process. I tell you that simply
to illustrate that the sketch on the Creed was simply
typical of a without doubt often very funny programme
which does not hesitate to cause pain if it so desires.

Of course I fully understand that, if you decide to
take any action, it will be in no way connected with the
fact that I have drawn this to your attention.

With all good wishes and warm personal regards.

Yours most sincerely,

Mary Whitehouse

'Let us all say the Apostles' Creed as contained in the
New Revised Version of the New Revised Version of the
Book of Common Prayer — or Meditation — it's the same
thing really: —

'I believe in God — I believe in God the Father
Almighty — it stands to reason there has to be some
sort of greater power — you know — like an electricity
sort of thing, and in Jesus Christ who was obviously a
fantastic bloke, and it's been proved historically he
actually did exist around that time — actually. He was
conceived by the Holy Ghost, born of the Virgin Mary —
no, don't laugh, it could happen, after all they can do
it in a test tube these days... And on the third day he
rose again from the dead, a sort of reincarnation if you
like — did you see that programme on BBC2? I believe in
the Holy Ghost, telepathy, flying saucers, black magic,
there must be something in astrology, gay liberation,
the Loch Ness Monster, the Abominable Snowman, the
Surrey Panther, copper bracelets for rheumatism,
meditation, water divining, poltergeists, and the life
everlasting — that is if the bloody Russians don't
invade Poland. Amen.'

'Not The Nine O'Clock News'

24th November 1980

'Pick of the Week' 28th November 1980

Trailed all day.

To anyone with even the most basic understanding of the purpose and practice of satire, this sketch appears not as an attack on the Creed, but rather as a fairly strong defence of its fundamental tenets against exactly the kind of fashionably relativist Anglican shilly-shallying that Mary Whitehouse had spent most of her adult life bemoaning. Whitehouse, however, had no such understanding, and consequently sent a copy to the one man in Britain most likely to have his conscience pricked by it.

A satire needs a victim like a fox needs a chicken, but in this case (as with many involving Mary Whitehouse) it was hard to tell exactly who the joke was on. Either way, Robert Runcie replied with an only implicitly pained admission that he had heard the item in question on *Pick of the Week* himself, and while he had not found it to his liking, he did not feel it would be appropriate for him to make any public declaration on the matter.

Sending that *Not the Nine O'Clock News* sketch to the Archbishop of Canterbury was possibly the most exquisitely ironic piece of postal endeavour Mary Whitehouse ever effected. Well, up there with the time when Cardinal Hume asked her to send him some child pornography to inform his stance on the Protection of Children Act.

'Imagine the headlines', she wrote later in *A Most Dangerous Woman?*: '"Mrs Whitehouse charged with sending obscene material to His Eminence the Cardinal . . . The mind boggled!' Some time later, her initial, prudent refusal gave way to a rather bolder strategy. She 'put a catalogue advertising child pornography and some of the "boys magazines" into an envelope and posted it to the press officer without giving any indication of who had sent it'.

Mary Whitehouse was – perhaps above all other things – a bit of a renegade. Catholicism couldn't contain her. Neither could the C. of E., Methodism, nor even the parliament of nutjob conspiracy theorists that was Moral Re-Armament. In the parlance of the kind of films and TV shows about maverick cops that she routinely eschewed in favour of more suitable viewing such as *Match of the Day* or *Highway*, Mary Whitehouse 'lived by her own rules'.

Without access to the relevant page of her diary, it is impossible to be certain of the reason for her unannounced withdrawal from the formal religious/showbiz occasion whose organisers sent her the following aggrieved communiqué, but on the available evidence a shrewd bookmaker would make 'She found out she was going to have to pay for her own lunch' a short-priced favourite.

Extract of letter from the Catholic Women of the Year Lunch Organising Committee

30th June, 1986

Mrs. Whitehouse,
  We were so sorry you did not attend the luncheon — we of course ordered lunch for you and seated you at the top table.
  I enclose the lunch programme as a souvenir for you. With 42 women nominated we could not possibly supply to all a complimentary lunch £9.50 per head, much as we would like to be able to. I have to say the 250 ladies who came were most disappointed by your absence. We too are most concerned at the disintegration of moral standards in this country and fully supportive of those who try to combat the trend.
  With all good wishes,
  Yours sincerely,
  Chairman

Was Mary Whitehouse right to take the precipitous step of last-minute withdrawal? Only with access to the menu will readers be able to make a fully informed decision.

Menu for the Catholic Women of the Year Lunch, 1986

Florida Cocktail
Steak Kidney & Mushroom Pie
Fresh Garden Vegetables
Blackcurrant Cheesecake
Cheese
Coffee

NATIONAL
VIEWERS'
AND
LISTENERS'
ASSOCIATION

ARDLEIGH, COLCHESTER, ESSEX, CO7 7RH.
Tel: Colchester (0206) 230123
PRESIDENT:
MRS. MARY WHITEHOUSE, C.B.E.
ORGANISING SECRETARY:
Mr. John C. Beyer
CHAIRMAN:
Mr A. J. Hughes,
40 Fitzwalter Road,
Colchester, Essex, CO3 3SX
Tel: Colchester (0206) 45658

HON. TREASURER:
Mr. R. C. Standring,
Still Waters, Pine Walk, East Horsley,
Leatherhead, Surrey, KT24 5AG
Tel: East Horsley (04865) 2573
HON. BRANCH DEVELOPMENT OFFICER:
Mr. John R. Wilson,
18 Corstorphine Bank Terrace,
Edinburgh, EH12 8RX.
Tel: 031-334 1727

Mr. Stuart Young   18th August, 1986
Chairman
The B.B.C.
Broadcasting House,
LONDON W1A 1AA.

Dear Stuart,

I am writing in response to press reports that the 'EastEnders'
cast is to include a homosexual couple living together.

Had this office not been closed for a few days I would have
written earlier.   Now I find that Richard Ingrams (Sunday
Telegraph 17th August, photostat attached) has most neatly
encapsulated our concerns over this development.

I cannot emphasise too strongly our anxiety about the threat to
the young - and others - of any "normalising" of homosexual
practices in your programmes.   It is important that we have
compassion and concern for homosexuals.   It is equally, if not
in your circumstances more important, that concern for the impact
of such material upon young viewers in particular should be
paramount.

The duty, surely, is also laid upon each one of you, as a Governor
of the BBC, to ensure, not least because of the terrible threat
of AIDS, that nothing is transmitted which might lead the young
to believe that being 'gay' is just another acceptable life style.

We are well aware of your understandable reluctance to interfere
directly in programme content.   We would suggest that in this
case, your responsibility is clear.

Yours sincerely,

Mary

Mary Whitehouse
President.

Copy sent to all the Governors.

PATRONS:

SIR CYRIL W. BLACK, J.P., D.L., F.R.C.S.
LADY CHAPMAN
PROFESSOR G. N.M. COLLINS

THE MARQUIS OF DONEGALL
J. AUDREY ELLISON, B.Sc., Secretary Royal Society
   of Health
GEORGE GOYDER, C.B.E.
THE EARL OF HALSBURY, F.R.S.
THE VEN. BERTIE LEWIS, M.A. Archdeacon of Cardigan.

THE EARL OF LONGFORD, K.G., P.C.
AIR CHIEF MARSHALL SIR THEODORE McEVOY,
   C.B.E., K.C.B
LADY PRICHARD
THE RT. REV. M. A. P. WOOD, D.S.C., M.A., R.N.R.,
   Former Bishop of Norwich

Letter to the chairman of the BBC

14. Mary and the New 'Gaiety'

To try and acquit Mary Whitehouse of the charge of homophobia would be a bit like defending Spike Milligan against accusations of racial insensitivity: not merely a pointless activity, but one based on a dangerous underestimation of the pervasiveness of the cultural climate that shaped their individual geniuses.

Whitehouse's evangelical Christian beliefs started her off with the kind of attitude to homosexuality which is still all too prevalent among twenty-first-century African bishops. By the time the rabid reds-in-the-bed conspiracy theories of the MRA (which viewed the 'active encouragement of homosexuality' as 'one of the avowed objectives of Communism in its plans for world takeover') were factored in, gay people – along with communists, atheists, yippies and Johnny Speight – were by their very nature implacable adversaries of all that was decent and godly.

Hers was homophobia in the literal sense – not hatred, but fear – the kind of overwhelming irrational response that others might experience on encountering spiders or clowns. This undated letter from a Northern Irish NVALA sympathiser gives a clear sense of the confusion that Whitehouse's 'visceral' (to use Geoffrey Robertson's characteristically well-chosen word) response to homosexuality induced in some of those who would otherwise have been liable to count themselves amongst her supporters.

Undated (but it must've been before 1982) letter from Northern Irish NVALA supporter

Dear Mrs. Whitehouse,

I spoke to you from Belfast on the telephone the other evening and asked you for the name of the Psychiatrist, whom you referred to on the Television Chat programme on B.B.C. TV., recorded in Belfast earlier in the year.

I didn't give you my name as homosexuals are 'illegal' in Northern Ireland and the telephone not renowned as an instrument of privacy, particularly in this country. What interested me about your psychiatrist was that he considered my misfortune as a curable disease and had successes when treatment was performed in conjunction with the mothers of the young men (!) concerned.

I have never quite belonged to the lobby who sees the new 'gaiety' as 'normal' behaviour, nor have I ever joined any gay organisation. As a musician and creative artist I have chosen to channel my frustrations into altruistic channels — but the feedback is not without its moments of despair. I have often contemplated thoughts of suicide.

Belief in God, who also made my condition (one sometimes looks in vain for evidence of good reason!), is the one thing which sustains me. In Ireland we are still prepared to die for tenets of faith — we have our own notorious jihad! — and 'sexual repression' is part of the culture. It is no sacrifice to either Catholic or Protestant, as 'guilt' is a life-style here.

My peculiar propensities have been with me since childhood, before I could properly walk. At school I already identified with the so-called 'opposite' sex and only reluctantly joined in boys' games. I even had a private girl's name for myself. I think I have managed to suppress all the tell-tale signs over the last 35 years or so, though I dare say some still exist. Other homosexuals tell me that they would know right away! But I wonder.

The only help I have ever sought was from the late Harry Edwards, the faith healer, and through my own constant prayers, in which I ask God's will be done. Am I to deduce from these many years of prayer that it is God's will that I remain as I am!

As a schoolmaster, and musician — I 'took up music' I suppose to compensate — I decided to resign two years back when, for the first time, I found my inclinations beginning to interfere in my work. I had always taught juniors, for whom I had hitherto enjoyed no unnatural attraction. I gave another reason for resigning, and have applied for my first job since then, only last week. I find I must teach!

I shall be staying in London for a week or so after Nov. 3rd. I have given you my London address at the top of this letter. I would be most grateful if you could see your way to writing to me at this address.

I attended a meeting of the National Viewers and Listeners Association in Belfast a few weeks ago, where I thought I might see you — but to no avail. I was impressed by what the speaker had to say and would like to think that, despite my eccentricity from the norm, I have a responsible attitude to life. I have also joined Ronald Higgins' Richmond Fellowship of late and share the current concern of most Christians for the moral problems that beset twentieth century life. We've never been so well informed, yet never so much in the dark . . . my own darkness being no exception.

I do look forward to hearing from you,

There is no way of knowing from the archive whether Mary subsequently called the phone number handwritten on the top of this painstakingly typed-out missive. Given the ease – and apparent obliviousness to the phrase's condemnatory implications – with which the mantra 'hate the sin, but not the sinner' seems to have come to her lips, for the sake of her anguished correspondent, one almost hopes not.

In her diary's effusive paean to the religious subtext of Geof-frey Robertson's summing-up for the defence at the initial *Gay News* blasphemy trial, Whitehouse expressed the joyful certain-ty that 'All the gays, secularists and others who packed that court must have glimpsed something of the wonder and beauty of the Christian faith.' Her clear underlying assumption – that homosexuality was inherently incompatible with Christian faith – was often subject to robust challenge.

Letter from a loyal mother who was not a NVALA supporter

15th July, 1977

Dear Mrs Whitehouse:

On the announcement of the verdict in the 'Gay News' blasphemy trial you are reported to have exclaimed 'Thank God!' In a sense, this is just as much a blasphemy as the reputed blasphemy which has been the subject of the case, since you probably have no conception of the distress which this case has caused a considerable minority of our fellow countrymen and women.

As a practising Christian, I have for long sought to understand and appreciate the position of homosexuals and their peculiar problems in a society which by and large is hostile. In this, I am considerably helped by our well-loved son — himself homosexual. Years ago, he came to his parents with his problem, which he has reasonably resolved, lives a blameless and upright life, and with his companion has created a beautiful home, which it is a joy to visit.

I can understand, therefore, why this case has caused them, and many thousands like them, so much unease. At a time when, legally and socially, and above all Christian-ly, a much more liberal attitude towards homosexuality was becoming evident, I can understand why such people believe that their 'clock has been

put back', and why they regard the 'Gay News' trial
as a witch-hunt. I can readily understand their
interpretation of such remarks as those made by Crown
Counsel to the jury, that 'their verdicts would set
the standard for the last quarter of this century, and
perhaps beyond'.

Whether or not you had due regard to all these
distressing repercussions when you instituted the
case I do not know, but I consider such actions highly
dangerous to a section of the community, and I deeply
regret all the implications placed on so many of our
fellows who try, against many odds, to live honourable
and fulfilled lives.

Yours faithfully,

The extent to which Mary Whitehouse was not alone – either in her assumption that homosexuality and Christianity were incompatible, or in an apparent determination to prove as much by the uncharitable drift of her own actions – is all too clear in the archive. The dispiriting impact of the stratospheric levels of bigotry on display in many of the letters she received is often compounded by a closing signature that begins with the prefix 'Revd'.

While there is no reason to doubt the sincerity of White-house's claim that homophobia was not part of her initial motivation in launching the *Gay News* blasphemy prosecution, the battle lines subsequently drawn around the case were clear to all. It wasn't just – as she liked to claim – a conspiracy on the part of 'the homosexual/intellectual/humanist lobby' to present what she was engaged upon as an anti-gay crusade. Many of her most outwardly respectable supporters saw it that way too, as this official communication from the Free Presbyterian Church of Scotland makes uncomfortably clear.

Letter from the clerk of the Scottish Free Presbyterian Church Synod

20th June, 1978

Dear Mary Whitehouse,

  At its recent meeting, the Synod passed a motion unanimously that a letter of thanks should be sent to you for your unflinching stand against Sodomites in a recent Court case. The Synod appreciates your efforts and were glad that they were crowned with success.

  With kind regards,
  Yours sincerely,
  Clerk of Synod

The militancy generated by Mary Whitehouse's 'unflinching stand against Sodomites' was no less intense on the other side of the barricades. Gay rights campaigners protesting against her speaking tour of Australia in September 1978 circulated a leaflet featuring a mocked-up picture of this sixty-eight-year-old grandmother with a meat cleaver plunged into her back. The caption was 'Let the blood flow'.

At the time of Denis Lemon and *Gay News*'s initial appeal against their joint conviction – in February of the same year – the National *Gay News* Defence Committee had organised a five-thousand-strong march and rally in Trafalgar Square. Although this demonstration was not widely reported in the media at the time (as the case was still *sub judice*), some protesters were widely acknowledged to have chanted 'Whitehouse Kill! Kill! Kill!' Posters were also seen picturing Mary's face alongside that of Adolf Hitler.

From the Rushdie affair onwards, Britain would become grudgingly accustomed to such extremes of language and visual imagery in demonstrations by Islamic fundamentalists – a group whose views on the topic of homosexual equality are all too well known. The more forgiving – yet no less impassioned – testimony of a volunteer Solent Gay Switchboard operator goes a long way to explaining how such depth of feeling was generated in the aftermath of the *Gay News* verdict.

Extract from Southampton gay community newsletter

IN SORROW AND IN ANGER by Paul

A few weeks ago whilst on duty at the Solent Gay Switchboard I answered a call and a child's voice replied: 'Queer, why don't you piss off?'

It was originally my intention to entitle this article 'In Sorrow, Not In Anger,' and so far as the child is concerned it is sorrow and not anger that I feel. But the more I think about that small incident, the more indignant I feel about a society that so poisons and perverts a child's mind that the child will at length pick up a telephone receiver and speak like that to a total stranger whom he (or possibly she) has never even seen.

We who work on the Switchboard are quite accustomed to receiving calls that are silly, abusive and obscene. This is partly because the attitude of an influential section of 'normal' society towards sex is silly and, if not obscene, certainly sick. But the real tragedy is that although we who work on gay switchboards do so to advise and to assist homosexual men and women in need of help, and are sometimes confronted with personal problems as distressing as those dealt with by the Samaritans, yet we have always to be prepared for hostility and oppositions: offensive calls, obstructive attitudes, and the lurking possibility of an anonymous 'test' call made by the police.

I am quite sure that people like Lord Longford, Mr Paisley and Mrs Whitehouse would strongly disapprove of the telephone call recorded at the beginning of this article, but would it ever occur to them to ask themselves to what extent they may be responsible for encouraging attitudes that have such consequences? Who is really responsible for the state of mind of that child or for the virulent hatred of the young man who rang up the Switchboard and who called the woman who answered a fucking lesbian? Certainly not the homosexual population, the 'sick-minded perverts and corrupters of young people.'

Many heterosexuals like to remark that if everyone were homosexual, the human race would come to an end. (The human race would suffer the same fate if the entire male population became Roman Catholic priests, but God in his infinite and unfailing wisdom ensures that only about 5% of us are homosexual and that even fewer are Roman Catholic priests.) In view of the acknowledged importance of sex in perpetuating the human race, it is strange that there are still those who regard it as something shameful, embarrassing or rather awkwardly special.

As a Christian I am saddened to feel obliged to lay the blame for this unhealthy, even sick-minded attitude towards sex fairly and squarely on the Christian Church . . . Even in the Church of England Marriage Service reference is made to satisfying 'man's carnal lusts and appetites, like brute beasts that have no understanding'. It is to the credit of the clergy that many of them now omit this piece of neurotic nonsense. The Church intended to make foul something that is intensely beautiful and indispensable to the continuation of life itself.

During the war certain women evacuees were seen walking through my home village making no attempt to conceal their pregnancy by wearing discreet, loose-fitting clothing. The village headmistress was outraged. 'They are a disgrace to our little village,' she declared to my mother one day. 'Anyone would think they were proud of it!' 'Perhaps they are,' replied my mother who couldn't see anything wrong with having babies. Nor for that matter could the Virgin Mary who, on learning that she was to have a child (admittedly a rather special one), sang the great song known as the Magnificat which is said or sung daily at Evensong.

About 18 months ago a Bournemouth lady distributed very widely copies of a questionnaire on such matters as the age of consent for homosexuals and heterosexuals, rape, and the sexual involvement of young children with adults. What might have been a useful enquiry was ruined by heavily loaded questions which transformed a potentially interesting and instructive questionnaire into a wickedly irresponsible document which by implication linked homosexuality with rape and sex with children.

'We must save our children!' was her exhortation at the end of her introduction to her far from objective questionnaire.

A laudable intention, and I for one would save our children from the sick-minded puritans of our society who have made a literally unholy mess of the Christian church on Earth and who, in their attitude to sex, have made sinful that which is good, hideous that which is beautiful, and hateful that which is the culminating expression of love, trust and mutual respect. We are taught that God is love, so love is infinite and all-powerful, love knoweth no laws and cannot be confined to the puritanical strait-jacket of heterosexual prejudice. Yet too often those who profess the Faith of Love preach judgment, condemnation and hate, and it is certainly not the homosexual community who have done anything to encourage young people to become sneerers and jeerers and queer-bashers, forcing uncounted and uncountable thousands of men and women, teenage boys and girls to live lives of confusion, uncertainty, anxiety and loneliness. In their moments of dramatic eloquence on the subject of the corruption of youth and the destruction of all sense of decency, let the Christian puritans ask themselves who really is responsible for the perverted minds of the queer-bashers and the anonymous switchboard callers with their 2p-worth of pitiful obscenities.

Those of you who have read this far will perhaps be saying: 'This is all very well, but what is the point of writing all this for "Gay Solent" where it certainly won't be seen by the people who really should be reading it?' An entirely reasonable observation which brings me to my final point.

It is my intention to send a copy of this article to three people who will, I hope, read it carefully and thoughtfully, bearing in mind that, notwithstanding the title, it was written in sorrow rather than in anger. And those three people are Lord Longford, the Rev. Ian Paisley and Mrs Mary Whitehouse.

I just thought you'd like to know.

Paul's eloquent anti-homophobia manifesto finishes halfway down a page, and the remaining space is filled up with two considerably more light-hearted items, which have been included here as happy portents of more inclusive times ahead. Nothing says 'impending normalisation' quite like a gay crossword and an annual car treasure hunt.

Further extract from Southampton gay community newsletter

Clues Across
1. Lions come in this.
2. Haughtiness
3. What goes before destruction.
4. A Gay week.

Clues Down
1. Vegetables
2. Bum?
3. They have it!
4. Cheshire Rivers
5. Facility

ANNUAL CAR TREASURE HUNT will be on June 24th (note
change). Meet at Shopping precinct Car Park, Chandlers Ford
at 3 p.m. Bring picnic basket.
Editorial Friendly Hint: Navigators in Ken P.'s car are
advised to take appropriate precautions, to wit: road atlas
of the entire British Isles, sellotape (for front-line
repairs to car), sleeping bag, and supplies for about 8 days.

Contemplating the web of contradictory psychological
impulses that led Mary Whitehouse to set her heart so implac-
ably against the Pauls and Ken P.s of this world, it's hard not to
experience the same sense of bewilderment that someone who is
not a British Telecom engineer feels when confronted with one
of those junction boxes by the road that spew out a metallic spaghetti of multicoloured wires. Yet it doesn't take too much fid-
dling around in the analogue workings of Whitehouse's mindset
before distinct patterns begin to emerge.

Going back to the very beginning of her career in public life,
the first demonstration of Whitehouse's capacity to provoke a
mass response – which was something, it turned out, that she
very much liked to do – had been her anonymous *Sunday Times*
debut 'Mothers & Sons'. 'We know how dangerous is the dic-

tatorship and power of a mother over her son', she wrote ominously, 'and yet this domination creeps in by so many doors.'

In the immediate aftermath of the furore provoked by this article, the *Sunday Times* modestly credited its own bravery in 'ventilating frankly and earnestly the social problem of homosexuality' with the subsequent setting up of a government committee to consider the issue. It was this committee – chaired by J. F. (later Lord) Wolfenden, who had put the opposing point of view to Whitehouse's in the following week's *Sunday Times* – whose recommendations would pave the way for the decriminalisation of homosexuality in Britain.

While it would be a slight exaggeration to claim either that Mary Whitehouse spent the rest of her life struggling valiantly to get the gay genie back in the bottle, or that a mischievous deity had used her as an unwitting double agent in the cause of homosexual equality, some of her mystifyingly intense feelings on the issue must have been generated during this period. There was also the vexing question of a missed opportunity for a BBC radio interview to be ruminated upon.

A few weeks after the publication of 'Mothers & Sons', in December 1953, Mary Whitehouse received the following intriguing and deferential letter, forwarded on to her by her new media contact, the editor of the *Sunday Times*.

Letter on New Statesman *headed notepaper*

3rd February, 1954

Dear Madam,

I am asking the editor of the SUNDAY TIMES to send this letter on to you, because I know neither your name nor your address, and he very properly won't disclose them although he has kindly agreed to re-address my letter.

The B.B.C. have decided to get together a discussion radio programme, or rather a symposium of views, on the

subject of homosexuality, particularly as it affects
parents. Would you help?

What it would entail would merely be talking to me
with a 'tape' recording machine, answering a few of
my questions (I shall be the completely non-expert
reporter), and expressing more or less the views you did
in the excellent SUNDAY TIMES article which impressed
us all so much. You could do it anonymously, of course.
I am to go and see a number of experts — doctors and
psychiatrists, sociologists and lawyers — and get their
views too. And then the whole thing will be 'scissors-
and-pasted' into a forty-five minute programme; in the
first instance it will be a dummy programme — that's to
say it will then be heard and pondered by the pundits,
the Director-General and the programme organisers; and
if it's considered suitable and useful, it will go out in
the Home Service late one evening — say 10.15 to 11 p.m.

Of course, it may never go out. But the B.B.C. feel
that a subject affecting so many parents is one that
it cannot allow to go by default, and I suppose it's
quite a courageous decision even to contemplate such a
programme. Personally I think it can be done, soberly
and factually; and that, anything is better than the
terrified secrecy that surrounds the thing at the moment.

My brief is to treat the subject, or rather get my
'interviewees' to treat it, as a problem of society, not
as a series of clinical studies about individuals, and
I am to keep in mind that 'society' in this sense means
a multitude of conflicting interests, moral taboos, and
occasions for the subjection of feelings that do not
belong to the human idea of civilised behaviour. All
very difficult, but still not impossible?

I therefore write in the hope that you do not live in
the wilds of Invernessshire or the Isle of Man, because
if I am to come and see you (which I would gladly do
with your permission) it's got to be somewhere fairly
accessible to London.

I could almost assume, since you write for the 'Sunday

Times', that you do not read this benighted journal. But
if you do, it may be of some interest if I tell you that
I write here under the pseudonym of C.H. Rolph.
 Yours sincerely
 (C.R. HEWITT)

Mary agonised long and hard about whether it would be
appropriate for her to take part in a radio programme on such
a hot-button topic, and eventually – in the wake of some rather paranoid advice from one of the same London-based MRA
contacts who would rear his discreet head again a decade later
– decided not to. Although there is no copy of Whitehouse's
finished reply in the archive, there are a series of draft sentences
written in pencil on the back of her MRA mentor's letter, polite-
ly and regretfully declining the kind invitation of the profes-
sionally dissatisfied C. R. Hewitt/C. H. Rolph, and at one point
referring to the subject matter of his proposed investigation as
'this excrescence'.

Even in view of some of her subsequent pronouncements,
it's still a shock to find Mary Whitehouse lapsing so easily into
such ugly eugenicist language at the tender age of forty-three. I
think part of the reason her unyielding attitude to homosexuality retained such an enduring power to inflict pain in later life
was that – in all respects other than her actual opinions – Whitehouse had great potential as a gay icon. Max Caulfield's sympathetic but now out-of-print biography is especially good on this
aspect of her appeal: 'she appears to have cheated degeneration
. . . The early part of the day is often spent in a stitch-quilted
housecoat'.

A quarter of a century after 'Mothers & Sons', on Whitehouse's turbulent 1978 tour of Australia, a public meeting in
Darwin was disrupted when the whole three front rows leapt
up and charged towards her, shouting at the top of their voices
and hurling pies topped with a 'revolting mess' of shaving cream

and red dye. 'One hit me in the chest and covered my brand new pink blouse with great lumps of the stuff,' she recalled doughtily in *A Most Dangerous Woman?* Mary was determined not to let herself be silenced: 'Scraping handfuls of the concoction off myself and flinging it on the floor, I shouted above the hubbub "At least it matches my blouse!"'

If you were looking for a lyricist to capture the drama of that moment in song, you'd have no option but to pick Jacques Brel. In another life, Whitehouse's combination of resilience and fragility, quick wit and impeccable personal styling might have given Bet Lynch a run for her money behind the bar of the Rovers Return, or even supplied an extra helping of acidity to Armistead Maupin's *Tales of the City*. In this one, she found a roll of clean butter muslin and used it to soak up the gloopy pink liquid which had drenched her skirt.

That difficult Australian trip was not without its compensations. In between the death threats, the stink-bombs and the round-the-clock police guard, there was time for a trip to the theatre to see another Housewife and Superstar. Dame Edna Everage's adoption of the 'swept-up' style of glasses in her honour had reputedly caused Mary Whitehouse to tone down her own choice of spectacles, but she was not one to bear grudges (at least, not on this issue).

'One does have to hand it to Barry Humphries,' she wrote in her diary after the show. 'He really is brilliant – almost impossible to realize one's talking to a man!' Humphries gave her a huge koala bear as a present – one of her most treasured souvenirs of her time down under, alongside the tam-o'-shanter which had been lovingly crocheted for her in the course of a public appearance and presented at the end of a meeting by 'a young man who said he was a homosexual'.

It's the shadow of such potential affinity that makes the sudden glare of Whitehouse's true feelings seem particularly harsh.

Turning back to her correspondence with the BBC, the jolts come thick and fast.

The 1979 broadcast of a *Play for Today* with the self-explanatory title of *Coming Out* was the cause of a characteristically choleric series of exchanges with BBC executives. First comes Whitehouse's angry anticipatory letter to the BBC governor George Howard (soon to be chairman Lord Howard), which receives an appropriately crisp response.

Letter to BBC governor

5th April, 1979

Dear Mr. Howard,

  It has been widely reported that the 'Play for Today' series is very shortly to submit a play about homosexuals called 'Coming Out'.

  Reports claim that the play includes homosexual 'love scenes' and that it will be preceded by a warning announcement.

  I am writing, on behalf of this Association, to ask if the Governors have previewed this play and, if not, if they will consider doing so since only full knowledge of what is to be transmitted will enable them to fulfill their duty as defenders of the public interest.

  I would only add that it must surely be clear that any such play could only give great offence, not least because even the warning would have the effect of drawing the attention of young people in particular to it.

  Yours sincerely,

  (Dictated by Mrs. Whitehouse and signed in her absence)

Reply from George Howard

17 April, 1979

Dear Mrs. Whitehouse,

  Thank you for your letter of 5 April, and the copy of

your letter to Sir Michael Swann of 12 April. You will
not, I am sure, expect an individual reply from me since
you will no doubt be hearing from the Chairman on behalf
of the Board.

  I should, however, say that the last paragraph of your
letter of 5th April demonstrates a clearly prejudiced
opinion in the sense that you have pre-judged the play
without seeing it, by saying 'it must surely be clear
that any such play could only give great offence'. This
plainly shows that you do not believe that any play
about male homosexuals should be transmitted.

  Yours sincerely,
  George Howard

Once she had actually watched the programme in question,
Mary Whitehouse was – unsurprisingly – able to confirm that
it had caused her just as much displeasure as she expected. Sir
Michael Swann's typically patient and meticulous reply gave her
no significant ground at all, but concluded with his trademark
small tactical concession.

Letter to the chairman of the BBC

12th April, 1979

Dear Sir Michael,

  We are firmly of the opinion that the play 'Coming Out'
should never have been broadcast, not least because of
the part played by the young boy. To involve a child
in the homosexual scene, to litter his script with bad
language and engage him in blackmail is unforgiveable —
and hardly an enlightened contribution by the BBC to the
Year of the Child.

  Furthermore the BBC is well aware that a very large
number of children below the age of fourteen are still
watching long after 9.25, when this play began. To
involve such young viewers with a play dealing with

homosexual promiscuity and practice, and the foul language which went with it, is totally to abdicate the responsibility laid upon the Governors.

Furthermore it is difficult to believe that the play did anything to help homosexuals who are looking for genuine help and understanding — rather the reverse.

I wish to draw your attention also to the fact that this play was dealt with very sympathetically on 'Start the Week' last Monday and immediately 'Coming Out' finished it was discussed — again very sympathetically — with one of the actors, on 'Campaign 79'. It is difficult to understand what the play had to do with the Election, and one has certainly been left with the impression that the 'Gay' lobby has very powerful friends at the BBC.

Yours sincerely,

Mary Whitehouse

Reply from Sir Michael Swann

8th May, 1979

Dear Mrs. Whitehouse,

I am writing in reply both to your letter of 5th April, written before 'Coming Out' was broadcast, and to your later letter of 12th April, in which you express your reaction to that play.

In your first letter you asked that the Board of Governors should consider previewing the play if they had not already done so. In making this request I am afraid you show some misunderstanding of our proper role. It is to act as 'trustees of the public interest', in the time-honoured phrase. Of course, this means playing a leading part in the exercise of editorial control. But I should stress here that editorial control is exercised by the BBC at all sorts of levels, which vary according to the importance of the question at issue. Plays do not get broadcast on television by chance: they are transmitted as the result of a

succession of different decisions, some of which, if the
play is thought to be controversial, may have been taken
at a senior internal level.

It would clearly not be practicable for the Board of
Governors to view any but a few programmes in advance.
However, my own view, which has been shared by many
Chairmen before me, is that it is not desirable for us
to preview any at all. The way we exercise editorial
control is by retrospective review. We make our views of
programmes known after transmission and where necessary
we make them known strongly. We are, after all, the final
court of appeal as it were. If a television play arouses
controversy it is for us to decide whether we think
the decision to broadcast it was right or wrong and in
reaching our decision we try to do so on behalf of the
whole audience, not just one section of it, which may
have been offended for rather special reasons. Clearly,
if we ourselves had seen the play in advance and had
approved the decision to put it out, our judgement after
the event could not be expected to carry much weight. We
should then be failing in our role as 'trustees of the
public interest'.

To turn now to the play itself, I note your view
that it should not have been broadcast. As you know,
'Play for Today' is recognised to be a general title
under which fictional works sometimes deal with difficult
social and moral themes. I must put it to you that,
if homosexuality is not a proper subject for such
treatment, then neither are wife-beating, drug-taking,
homelessness, alcoholism and all the other ills and
problems of society that have been dealt with in widely-
acclaimed works in this series in the past — along,
of course, with many other much-praised plays on
uncontroversial subjects.

As to the part played by the boy, I should point out
that the plot did not involve the character he portrayed
in any homosexual activity. On his likely knowledge of
the subject matter of the play, I can only think that

you misjudge the extent of information possessed by
adolescents. I understand that the boy's parents were
entirely conversant with the nature and content of the
play and had no reservations about his taking part. I am
sorry that you were offended by some of the language.
The BBC is, as you know, opposed to the gratuitous use
of offensive terms but takes the view that there are
times when these are justified by the dramatic situation.

You assert that the play did nothing to help
homosexuals in search of understanding. A different view
was taken by the homosexuals who have written to us on
the subject, who in general expressed warm appreciation
of the play.

Finally, may I say that public reaction to this play
— by heterosexuals as well as admitted homosexuals —
has on the whole been favourable. We have inevitably
received complaints, but these have been outnumbered by
appreciations. In this, the favourable comments on the
two programmes you mention were not unrepresentative. We
do acknowledge, however, that the item on the play in
'Campaign '79', as the 'Tonight' programme was called
during the pre-election period, may have appeared
incongruous to those not realising that the programme
did not deal exclusively with electoral issues.

Yours Sincerely,
Michael Swann

Tracking back through the Whitehouse archive, there are
numerous similar exchanges. In a protracted epistolary bout
with the BBC head of religious affairs John Lang about a 1975
edition of the Christian magazine show *Anno Domini* which
had dared to show sympathy with an (in Mary's estimation)
'obviously homosexual' Anglican priest, who (Whitehouse felt)
was 'losing his faith', she complained that the resulting programme 'would please no-one but the advocates of "Gay Lib"'.
When questioned as to the disapproving implication she seemed

to be giving to that final phrase, she insisted – very much against the evidence of her previous letter – that she 'did not, in fact, use such a term'.

Mary Whitehouse's devotion to her own truth was absolute, so on the – not infrequent – occasions when this pristine and well-ordered body of opinions came up against that far messier and less coherent entity, *the* truth, there was only ever going to be one winner. Her default strategy in complaining about programmes that made any reference to homosexuality was first to say a version of what she really thought – which was that the subject matter was in some way or other 'unsuitable' – and then to vehemently deny that she had said it, citing as evidence for her fair-mindedness in this area her earlier praise for *The Naked Civil Servant* (the groundbreaking ITV film of Quentin Crisp's life story, to which numerous NVALA members had expressed vehement opposition), and the fact that she had once 'happily been on a programme' with Crisp.

Considered en masse in a determined attempt to locate a unifying subtext, the one thing that really stands out from Whitehouse's huge reams of what can with hindsight be resolutely classified as anti-gay correspondence is how much of it – either directly or indirectly – involved the Church of England. In so far as these connections reflected her frustration that (to quote her response to the Archbishop of Canterbury's refusal to support the *Gay News* blasphemy prosecution) 'the church allowed itself to be so overwhelmed with what you might call the general gay lobby', they are not news. A more eye-catching underlying concern is with a specific yet still shadowy adversary.

The third corner of what was not so much a love triangle as a Dairylea of hate (Mary Whitehouse's evangelical constituency at one end and the Gay Lib movement at the other being the two opposing ends so far identified) was the liberalising tendency within the Church of England; most particularly those practitioners in the orbit of her old South Bank theologian adversary Mervyn Stockwood who were willing to countenance the blessing of homosexual relationships and even the ordination of openly gay priests. Of all the many personal animosities which Whitehouse fostered over the years, none came closer to outright war than her dealings with Stockwood.

Letter to the Bishop of Southwark

STRICTLY IN CONFIDENCE
22nd June, 1979

My Dear Lord Bishop,
   Since your Diocesan letter dealing with, amongst other things, love between men and men published yesterday has already been interpreted by the 'Gay' movement as an endorsement of its view that 'love should be fully expressed in personal sexual relationships' will you state publicly and quite specifically whether you are endorsing the practices of mutual masturbation and buggery common among some homosexuals, and whether you expect the Church to do the same and whether you see such practices as the will of God?
   This would do much to clarify the confusion and, hopefully, ease the concern caused by the publication of your letter.
   With best wishes,
   Mary Whitehouse

Presumably feeling that she had not made her point strongly enough in the above letter, Mary Whitehouse seems to have made a hot-tempered follow-up phone call. The details of this were revealed not by Mary herself, but at second hand, in a NVALA supporter's shocked account of Mervyn Stockwood's reciprocal outburst.

Letter from NVALA supporter

23rd July, 1979

Dear Mrs Whitehouse,

During a two day 'visitation' to this Parish, Bishop
Mervyn Stockwood answered questions put to him last
night in the Village Hall.

In answering one of the questions put to him, he took
up five minutes or more in what came over to me as an
attack on you.

Mervyn Stockwood stated that he had submitted a draft
of his diocesan letter to the Arch Bishop of Canterbury
who had given it full approval and it was therefore
printed. You had, apparently, telephoned him (he did not
know where on earth you had found his number) and had
made some sort of tirade against 'sodomy' etc. and that
he was supporting all this. His Secretary (who answered
your call) asked you if you had read the Bishop's letter
and you admitted you had not done so and had 'just seen
the headlines in the papers', but you were going to write
to the papers about the Bishop's attitude on the subject.

Listeners were given to understand that you would be
better occupied devoting your time to more important
matters such as drug abuse instead of being 'so obsessed
with sex.'

I wonder if you would be kind enough to telephone me
as soon as possible.

Whitehouse's correspondent registered his misgivings about
what actually sounds like an unusually lively episcopal visitation
with Stockwood's chaplain. A couple of weeks later, he received
a stern point by point rebuttal, questioning on what authority
Mrs Whitehouse had come by the bishop's ex-directory private
phone number, and culminating in the ominous news that
copies of the whole correspondence were being forwarded to
the diocesan solicitor.

In 1994, at the age of eighty-one, the by then retired Mervyn Stockwood was one of a group of ten Anglican bishops 'outed' by Peter Tatchell's guerrilla gay rights group OutRage!. Some will no doubt consider this action – as Tatchell presumably did – a legitimate response to the hypocrisy inherent in a man in Stockwood's position having chosen to keep his sexual orientation to himself. Others will find it a somewhat shoddy and disreputable move to pull on someone who had done so much to advance the cause OutRage! was theoretically created to espouse.

Either way, Stockwood died a few months later, and there was little doubt that this painful and embarrassing coda to his outspoken career would have given Mary Whitehouse a certain macabre satisfaction. In theory, she and Peter Tatchell (who once described her as 'God's Rottweiler') made the unlikeliest of bedfellows, but in practice, perhaps their respective zealotries ensured that this odd couple of fanatical campaigners shared more common ground than either of them would have been keen to admit.

The Most Topical FRINGE Of All!

COME AND SEE
[Short Extracts Only!]
HOW BAD ARE EVEN <u>LEGAL</u>

`VIDEO NASTIES'

MARY WHITEHOUSE
ON
HOW BEST TO CONTROL THEM
- Will Mr Graham Bright's Bill Do The Trick?

'FRINGE MEETINGS'
in
The Prince William Suite, Clifton Hotel, Talbot Square, Blackpool.

11th, 12th, 13th, October   12.45 p.m. and 5.45 p.m.

Lunch/Sandwiches Available At The Hotel

Turn left out of the WINTER GARDENS and the
CLIFTON HOTEL is 5 minutes walk

MOREAU PRINTING SERVICES -
Tel. Colchester (0206) 231040.

Flyer for 1983 Tory Party conference fringe event

15. Mary in the Eighties

Fifteen years almost to the day after the Birmingham Town Hall meeting, Margaret Thatcher's election victory of May 1979 seemed to promise the fulfilment of all Mary Whitehouse's hopes for an evangelical conservative fightback.

Letter to Margaret Thatcher

9th May, 1979

Dear Mrs Thatcher
  I am sure you must be inundated with congratulations and well wishes. May I just, very briefly, add my own most heartfelt ones?
  In doing so, I am in no doubt that I echo the feelings of countless others who, perhaps, may not put pen to paper, but who have so hoped and prayed for your success and for you personally and will go on doing so in the very demanding days which lie ahead for you. And so will I.
  It was a wonderful thing to have a Prime Minister utter those marvelous words of St. Francis before the whole world — already one senses a lifting of the spirit!
  With all good wishes,
  Yours very sincerely,
  Mary Whitehouse

As the living embodiment of Little England's aspiration to moral rectitude, Mary Whitehouse had defined both the constituency and the carefully maintained public image – at once a bulwark against and an incitement to the ingrained sexism of the time – that brought Margaret Thatcher to power, and would keep her there for the next eleven years. The temptation to see Whitehouse – from a Victorian values perspective – as John the Baptist to Margaret Thatcher's Jesus should, however, probably be resisted.

In a speech given at the Cambridge Union in the year of Mrs Thatcher's first election victory, Mary Whitehouse expanded her ritualised denunciation of pornography to proclaim, to an audible intake of breath from an uncomprehending crowd, 'The new tyrants in our day are the libertarians'. This was to prove truer than even she had imagined, as Thatcherism's much-vaunted Christian component turned out to be a fig-leaf for naked greed and corporate (and individual) profiteering.

The gospel of market forces was the only one that mattered now. On the face of it, Mary Whitehouse's influence had never been greater. Mrs Thatcher gave her a CBE in 1980, government ministers received her deputations with exaggerated shows of respect, and the Prime Minister even stepped up to present a NVALA award (to her favourite TV show, *Yes Minister*). Yet it was perhaps the concluding irony of the many in Mary Whitehouse's career that the political decisions made by the Thatcher government – from setting up Channel 4 and paving the way for satellite TV, to the relaxation of retail rules restricting the sale of porn – did more to hasten Britain's divergence from what Mary regarded as the proper Christian course than any decision Marcia Falkender ever persuaded Harold Wilson to make.

The process of disillusionment was slow, but steady. Its single most powerful activator was the advent of Channel 4 in the spring of 1982. The long-awaited second ITV channel was Mary Whitehouse's most prurient cheese-dream made uncensored flesh: Sir Hugh Greene's BBC, with knobs on.

Letter from shocked Channel 4 viewer

6th August, 1985

Dear Mrs. Whitehouse,
   I refer to a film on Channel 4 Television last night
(5th August) entitled Godard's Cinema Numero Deux. This
film was in French with English subtitles and contained
scenes such as the following;-
   A woman masturbating a man.
   A man having sexual intercourse (either real or
simulated, the woman bending over and the man behind her
(either real or simulated intercourse).
   A woman performing oral sex on a man.
   There were also four letter words spoken and subtitled
in English for the following:-
   A vagina. A penis, testicles.
   Sexual intercourse. (f---)
   There were probably others but I cannot remember. If
this isn't pornography, I would like to know what is.
   I had thought of writing to the IBA complaints office,
but on reflection thought it might be more effective
writing to you as you are experienced in pursuing this
kind of thing.
   Yours faithfully,

For someone who liked to present herself as the voice of the
moral majority, the idea of a station created specifically to cater
to the tastes of previously overlooked minorities was the opposite of catnip. It wasn't just Channel 4's willingness to push
back the frontiers of what could be shown on TV that was
calculated to get up Mary Whitehouse's nose. The new channel's partial public service remit placed it in a dangerous middle
ground between the BBC's (at least nominal) state supervision
and ITV's more malleable commercial mindset. The patrician
disdain with which chief executive Jeremy Isaacs swatted away
Mary's increasingly dyspeptic jeremiads drove her to a level of

impotent fury not seen since the bad old days of the pre-Lord
Hill BBC.

Reply from Channel 4

5th September, 1985

Dear Mrs Whitehouse,
  Thank you very much for writing. It is good to hear
from you.
  As usual, I take careful note of your views, balancing
them against those of others who enjoy the programmes of
which your members complain.
  I hope you still continue to find something you enjoy
on Channel Four.
  All good wishes,
  Yours sincerely,
  Jeremy Isaacs

Further reply from Channel 4

8th September, 1986

Dear Mrs Whitehouse,
  Thank you for writing. I am glad to see the Home
Secretary's unexceptional reply to your unnecessary
letter.
  Channel Four operates under the Broadcasting Act, and
is content to do so. The new warning symbol is intended
to offer sensitive viewers further protection — not
to absolve us from any of our responsibilities. It is
irresponsible of you to suggest otherwise.
  Yours sincerely,
  Jeremy Isaacs

  Small wonder that Mary Whitehouse found correspondence
with Jeremy Isaacs 'not particularly fruitful' (as she put it with
untypical understatement in a letter to another Channel 4 exec-

utive). With the tabloids in full cry behind her, she wrote to the
chairman of the IBA insisting that he had 'no alternative but to
sack Mr. Isaacs and hand over Channel 4 to someone with a
greater sense of responsibility'. Needless to say, the Rt. Hon. the
Lord Thomson of Monifieth saw things differently.

In the meantime, the Channel 4 virus seemed to be spreading.
As if the Liverpudlian rough and tumble of *Brookside* – 'without doubt, quite the worst programme ever seen on television
during what the IBA euphemistically describe as family viewing
time' (NB the expression 'family viewing time' was one largely
of Mary's own creation) – wasn't bad enough, there was also
EastEnders to contend with.

NVALA monitoring report on EastEnders, autumn 1985

A typical 'East Enders' story line is that of Nick Cotton, who
has a criminal record.

He steals the keys of the Doctor's surgery, makes a wax
impression, with new keys enters surgery, rifles medical records,
takes duplicates of Kathy Beale's which shows she had an abortion
at 14. He blackmails her in most menacing fashion, she steals
from and lies to her husband, and when confronted by Cotton on
bonfire night with the fire filling the screen after long, bitter
pause she viciously hisses 'Go <u>burn</u>'. (End of prog).

16 year old schoolgirl, Michelle becomes pregnant by the
publican Den — father of her 15 year old friend. Den is married,
and also has a mistress. This story line has been defended because
the girl refuses to have an abortion. Surely an extraordinary
justification.

<u>Sept. 17th</u>
Finding his 15 years old daughter Sharon attempting to seduce
Lofty the barman, Den hits her viciously across the head.
When her mother comes to her defence, Den hits her across the
head also.

The central relationship in the serial is that between Den
and his wife Angie. This relationship is one of undiluted and
continuous bitterness, lying, deceit and verbal abuse.

Story line in which Angie sets up 'hen night' in the pub in
which they had a male stripper — appeared most appreciated by
everyone including even 'Grandma'.
  Language used — 'bleeding' this and that. 'Bloody hell',
'bastard' 'kick in the crutch'.

10th Nov.
Kathy Beale described in detail how she felt when she was
raped as a 14 year old.
  Pete Beale takes out carving knife from kitchen drawer to
attack Nick Cotton.
  'Bastard', 'For Christ's sake' and 'Jesus'.

12th Nov.
Stripper to Mary 'You've got to know the market — they like
schoolgirls' they also 'like whippers'.

14th Nov.
Lofty finds 10p on floor of pub, gives it to Angie and she says
'is this some kind of early morning proposition? If it were
later in the day when I've had a couple of gins it might be
different'.
  Mary to coloured stripper 'Took me ages to get my bra off'.
Stripper replies — 'let one of them take it off for you'.
Suggested Mary might take as many as 'three a night'. 'You daft
pillock'— one of the expletives in the programme.

No doubt the prominence of a prostitute called Mary in early
EastEnders storylines was the most innocent of coincidences,
but Whitehouse could certainly be forgiven a measure of para-
noia in dealing with the network that brought her *Swizzlewick*.
The promissory note of legislative influence which Margaret
Thatcher's election had seemed to hold out was going to have
to be redeemed, or who knew what dangers the nation's morals
might be subject to?
   The Iron Lady had already proved herself no pushover in earlier dealings with Mary Whitehouse. As a minister in Edward
Heath's government she had steadfastly refused to accept

Mary's proposal that parents should be allowed to demand an opt-out clause from sex education classes if they wished to protect their children from the horrors that must inevitably come with knowledge. Once safely ensconced in number 10 Downing Street, she was not going to take orders from anyone.

In a letter written to Margaret Thatcher as early as 1981, Mary Whitehouse was talking of 'a reaction not only of profound disappointment and dismay but of disillusion and incredulity' at the Home Office's 'thoroughly hypocritical' refusal to formally disown the Williams Report on Obscenity and Film Censorship. Whitehouse's concerns over the ensuing proliferation of sex shops – 'Since the Williams Committee reported fourteen months ago pornographers have been buying up small retail shops as they have become empty all over the country' – fell on deaf ears.

Five years later, a draft NVALA proposal for tightening up the obscenity laws in the aftermath of a 1983 election promise to 'introduce specific legislation to deal with this problem' met with a devastating response from David Mellor, a Home Office minister so brazenly liberal he might as well have been in the SDP.

Extract from David Mellor's response to proposed revision of the obscenity law

i. 'Depicts by sounds'
If, however, the term 'depicts by sounds' is intended to be confined to non-verbal depictions, it is difficult to see what would be caught other than the sorts of 'grunts and groans' which at worst are perhaps offensive rather than obscene and which may not even be that if used light-heartedly in a comedy programme or in a ritualized manner on a pop record.
ii. 'Indecent exposure'
The reference to 'any sexual act which is contrary to the common law or statute law' might catch the sort of scene quite often included in comedy programmes, and shown in the opening sequence of 'Cagney and Lacey'.

iv. 'Explicit acts of human urination or excretion'

Although there would probably be little argument that acts of
human urination or excretion in a sexual context were obscene,
it is not clear that all depictions of human urination (or
perhaps of human excretion) should be so regarded. The provision
would seem to catch. eg, a picture of a baby urinating in
a nappy advertisement; or a photograph of the mannequin in
Brussels which serves as a fountain.

v. 'Mutilation, flagellation or torture'

Other examples which have occurred to us include:

mutilation:	King Lear, bull fighting, hunting;
flagellation:	certain religious paintings, films of Tom Brown's School Days, or Nicholas Nickelby;
torture:	war films, Madam Tussauds.

Mary Whitehouse had not so much backed the wrong horse
– Michael Foot's Labour opposition were hardly likely to take a
sympathetic view of proposals for the public flogging of 'Nasty
Nick' Cotton – as been sold a pup. She expressed her anger in
the following tightly controlled terms (look out for the textbook
Freudian slip which renames Douglas Hurd 'Mr Hard').

Letter to the Prime Minister

21st July, 1986

Dear Mrs Thatcher,

  We have always been most grateful for and encouraged
by the interest you have shown in our work over the
years and I have endeavoured to keep you fully informed
about what our association has been trying to do ever
since you became leader of the Conservative Party.

  I sent to you a copy of the paper 'Recommendations on
an Amendment to the Obscene Publications Act, 1959 and
to the Broadcasting Complaints Commission' we presented
to the Home Secretary in preparation for our meeting
with him at the Home Office on July 7th. Since then I

have been much exercised in my mind as to whether or
not I should write to you about what transpired on that
occasion. But encouraged by the kindness you have shown
on previous occasions I have now decided to do so.

We were grateful to Mr. Hurd and Mr. Mellor for
giving us so much of their time but the truth is that
I have never been more disappointed in any meeting with
any Minister throughout the years of our campaigning,
not least perhaps, because as a Conservative Home
Secretary I and my colleagues had hoped for some kind of
positive encouragement from Mr. Hard. Instead of which
we received a categorical 'No' to our question as to
whether the Government would introduce a new obscenity
law in the next session of Parliament and the impression
was given that there was little prospect that any such
legislation would appear in the next Conservative
election manifesto.

What I personally found so bitterly disappointing was
that this was precisely the kind of 'permissive society'
Home Office response which we have come to recognise over
the years and which we had hoped so much would have
changed under your leadership.

Yours sincerely,

Mary Whitehouse

President

There were fleeting moments of success, like the passage of
Luton MP Graham Bright's 'video nasties' bill, which her campaigning had done a great deal to shape, in 1983. However, Mary
Whitehouse's overriding fear – that the new age of cable and satellite TV was about to be ushered in by the same (as she saw
it) criminally lax regulatory framework that had allowed Jeremy
Isaacs's subversive instincts free rein at Channel 4 – proved very
well founded.

'No-one can doubt the genuineness of the Prime Minister's
concern for the family and for moral values, and we can sym-

pathise and understand her pre-occupation with industrial and economic affairs,' Whitehouse wrote pleadingly in an apprehensive NVALA briefing on 1982's Hunt Report on Cable Expansion and Broadcasting Policy.

'What is decided in the weeks immediately ahead as far as cable TV is concerned', she continued, 'will vitally and on the whole irredeemably affect the quality of television in the foreseeable future. And by so affecting television will profoundly influence the whole quality of the nation's life.' Her dire warnings were ignored, Hunt's recommendations for gossamer-light regulation of new cable TV and satellite channels passed into law, and within a few years' time, millions of households in Britain woke up to find that – wittingly or otherwise – they now had porn channels on tap.

Alongside the long-hoped-for landmark of Margaret Thatcher's election, another event that had qualified 1979 as a red-letter year for Mary Whitehouse had been the publication of Michael Tracey and David Morrison's book *Whitehouse*. Although its academic brief ensured it did not get all the attention it might've done at the time, this meticulously researched and scrupulously fair account of her methods and motives – based on lengthy interviews which Whitehouse was allowed to query and correct at suitably inordinate length – would be an invaluable reference point for all subsequent attempts at analytical assessment (including this one).

Whitehouse's last chapter – entitled 'Towards a New Theocracy' – outlined the kind of piously minded state power which Mary's campaigning utterances seemed to imply would constitute her ideal form of government. It can be retrospectively noted that such a regime did actually come into being in 1979, but its leader was not – as Whitehouse might have hoped – Margaret Thatcher. It was Ayatollah Khomeini.

In the absence of a grass-roots religious upsurge such as the one that had taken place in Iran, Mary Whitehouse valiantly carried on the struggle throughout the eighties (which were her seventies) – fighting it out for column inches with Boy George and other still less like-minded rivals.

Letter from the features editor of the Daily Mail

```
30th November, 1982

Dear Mrs Whitehouse
  I was very disappointed not to be able to use your
excellent feature on your meeting with the Home
Secretary. Up until 6 o'clock last night, it looked
highly likely that it was going to be a leader page
article or on page 7.
  But then the Gary Gilmore story came in from America,
which was highly favoured by the Editor and I was not
able to use both.
  My sincere apologies.
  Yours sincerely,
  Features Editor
```

Sometimes – for example when forwarding to the BBC a NVALA member's impassioned request for the return of the 'clean, wholesome and entertaining' *Black and White Minstrel Show* (a programme which she herself had earlier described as 'delightful') – there's an almost overwhelming sense of her shutting the stable door after the horse has not only bolted but been hit by a lorry at a roundabout on the bypass. Alongside one of her innumerable rants about Barry and Colin in *EastEnders*, she also passed the following critical note on to the BBC, which fans of the *French and Saunders* sketch in question will consider a real collector's item.

Note from NVALA sympathiser

```
Has anyone told you about the 'French and Saunders'
programme (BBC 2 Friday 11 March 9.00 pm)?
```

I had never seen this series before and I left the TV
on after 'Gardeners' World' just to see what it was like.

The second sketch consisted of two fat, dirty, middle-
aged, beer-swilling lesbians watching a beauty contest
on TV and virtually masturbating, one against their
'television screen' and the other to one side of the
'room' as well as in their armchairs. There seemed to be
no other content to the sketch.

I don't think I have ever seen anything so lewd and
revolting and degrading on TV in my life, but perhaps
that is because I only watch the programmes I have
selected.

Reply from the Secretary of the BBC

20th April, 1988

Dear Mrs. Whitehouse,

Thank you for your letters of 16th March to the
Chairman, enclosing a copy of a note from one of your
members, and of 23rd March, enclosing a copy of a letter
to Mr. John Birt. I am replying on both the Chairman's
and Mr. Birt's behalf.

In the episode of 'EastEnders' shown on Tuesday, 15th
March, it is quite true that Barry tried to bribe Colin
by offering sexual favours in return for the £200 he
needed to set up a new venture. What your letter did
not mention was that Colin vociferously refused saying
that he was not to be bought, a highly moral scene,
surely, which would have quite the opposite effect from
the one you feared. The episode was, in fact, referred
to Jonathan Powell Controller of BBC-1, who gave it his
approval.

Your member's note referred to a sketch in the 'French
and Saunders' comedy programme shown on Friday 11th
March. Dawn French and Jennifer Saunders are two female
comediennes whose brand of humour is often directed
against stereotypical attitudes held against women.

Although they themselves played the two characters in the sketch, they were unmistakably portrayed as <u>men</u>, not lesbians as your member has said. The sketch was intended as a comment on the frame of mind which many women feel is engendered in men by the showing of beauty contests on television. Much of the humour in 'French and Saunders' is adult in character, which is why the series is shown after the 9 pm watershed. This sketch was typical of the kind of anarchic, iconoclastic humour for which French and Saunders have become well known.

  Yours sincerely,

  (John McCormick)

Mary Whitehouse's physical powers were, inevitably, on the wane. This process accelerated after she sustained a serious spinal fracture in the garden of the house in rural Essex ('Constable country', as she called it, lovingly) which she had moved to way back in 1975. The cause of this accident was an object lesson in the dangers that can lurk within even the most tranquil of domestic environments – she was carrying clumps of dock by hand when she should have used a wheelbarrow.

However, Whitehouse retained the capacity to deliver that unique blend of alarm and reassurance that was her Unique Selling Point as a public figure (the cautious viewer's equivalent of Colonel Sanders's secret recipe) until well into the nineties. Gamely trundling round the country with a caseful of pornographic videos, she was a travelling saleswoman of religious reawakening.

Letter from NVALA supporter

15th October, 1983

Dear Mrs. Whitehouse,

  I would have spoken to you at your meeting in the New Clifton Hotel, Blackpool last Thursday lunch-time but, regretfully, I had to leave before the end.

Having seated myself at the back of the room, I
did not have a clear view of the screen for which,
I confess, I was quite grateful as I really did not
want to watch whatever was to come and had attended
the meeting out of respect for the courageous stand
you have taken against the obsenity, pornography, etc.
thrust down our throats by the media in Britain today.
However, I eventually decided I was being cowardly in
not watching what was being shown and stood up at the
back in time to see the whole of the third part of the
film. If I say that I don't think I will ever again watch
horses in a stable without remembering with disgust that
particular video and that I quite understand why you
could only bear to watch it once, then you will realise
the total revulsion that filled me, a middle-aged widow,
as I watched. The most horrifying thing of all was the
fact that you told us that the excerpt shown was by no
means the worst of the material available for viewing by
our young people — and all in the name of entertainment.
    I am sending £2. as a subscription to National VALA. I
do not know if there is a branch near here but if so, I
would be interested to have details. I have indicated on
the application form my willingness to help along with a
query as to what would be involved in public speaking.
(I do not drive a car and have very limited financial
resources.)
    With my hopes and prayers for the success of the work
of VALA,
    I am,
    Yours sincerely,
    P.S. I hope your voice has recovered.

   The extent to which many people with strong religious convictions found Mary Whitehouse's voice comforting rather than
strident can be clearly discerned in this appreciative letter from
a German nun.

Letter from a German nun

September 14, 1988

Dear Mary,

A group of us here from Britain and Germany meet regularly to pray for the situation in Britain, and we have been remembering you very especially. We were so moved to hear that you plan to go to court to get 'The Last Temptation of Christ' banned. We do thank the Lord for raising you up and giving you the courage to stand up for Him and His commandments.

Since we have heard that you are laid up because of a fracture in your spine, we have been especially upholding you in prayer. In what pain you must be in! I couldn't help thinking that the Lord has allowed this suffering for a special purpose. In Colossians 1:24 Paul says, for instance, 'Now I rejoice in my sufferings for your sake, and in my flesh I complete what is lacking in Christ's afflictions for the sake of his body, that is, the church.' All your life you have worked for the good of young people, and the Lord has let you share in the Fellowship of His sufferings.

We are really praying for the stand you are taking against 'The Last Temptation of Christ', because it grieves us so deeply that Jesus' heart is being pierced anew through this film. We can only guess how much this stand is going to cost you, and we ask the Lord to touch you and strengthen you in every way for this effort. We shall never forget all you did to get the Thorsen film banned in Britain and your court case against the blasphemous poem.

May our Lord increase your time and protect you. Our loving thoughts and prayers are with you.

Yours in Jesus' love,

Sister Eulalia

For those less inclined to see things Mary's way, I have saved up this final triptych of Whitehousian tableaux, in the hope that they might speak for her with the matchless eloquence of Geoffrey Robertson or even John Mortimer.

Order of ceremony for NVALA annual award presentation, 20 January 1984

The Waldegrave Hall, All Soul's Church, Langham Place, London, W.1.

<u>PROGRAMME</u>
Guests arrive at 12.00 noon
Prime Minister arrives 12.15pm with Press Officer and
   Private Secretary.
Mrs. Whitehouse and Mr. Hughes to meet Prime Minister at
   entrance to All Soul's.
Party to proceed down right hand staircase to Waldegrave
   Hall.
Peter Moore, Town Crier of London, to announce arrival
   of Prime Minister.
Mrs. Whitehouse shows the Prime Minister to left of
   centre on platform.
Mr. Stuart Young shown to right of centre seat. Mr.
   Howard-Davies to second left hand seat.
Mrs. Whitehouse to second right hand seat, Mr. Hughes to
   centre seat.
Mr. Hughes, Chairman of National VALA, to welcome Prime
   Minister, stage party and all present.
Mr. Hughes to call upon Mrs. Whitehouse to speak and
   Mrs. Whitehouse then calls upon the Prime Minister to
   present the Award.
Mr. Paul Eddington, Mr. Nigel Hawthorne, Mr. Anthony Jay
   and Mr. Jonathan Lynn to accept Award and say a few
   words if they wish.
Miss K. and Miss E. Whitehouse present the Prime
   Minister with a posy.
Mr. Hughes calls upon Mr. Stuart Young to reply for BBC.
Mr. Hughes to announce that the buffet is in the
   refectory and to give directions.

For anyone not yet sufficiently struck by this occasion's subliminal resemblance to a lavish wedding, perhaps a glimpse of the seating plan will do the trick.

Seating Plan for NVALA awards ceremony

by
gangway

FRONT ROW LEFT
Paul Eddington
Nigel Hawthorne
Jonathan Lynn
Antony Jay
Peter Whitmore
Gareth Gwenlan

SECOND ROW LEFT
" Col. Booth-Tucker
Sir John Biggs-Davison
Michael Bunce
Mrs. A. Hughes
Mrs. Whitmarsh
Mrs. Kilpin

THIRD ROW LEFT
" Romula Christopherson
+ one

Peter Kruger
Norman Fairfax
Rt. Rev Mark Hodson
Mr. F. Whitmarsh.

FOURTH ROW LEFT
Mr. R. Sykes
Mrs. Sykes
Mr. J. Smytt
Mrs. Smytt
+ 2 from Standrings party

by
gangway

FRONT ROW RIGHT
Richard Whitehouse
Kathy Whitehouse
Elizabeth Whitehouse
+ 3 Press

SECOND ROW RIGHT
6 Press

THIRD ROW RIGHT
3 Press
E. R. Whitehouse
Nicola Whitehouse
Fiona Whitehouse

FOURTH ROW RIGHT
Lord Longford
Guest
Rt. Rev. John Gray
Mrs. Gray
D. Atkinson
Lord Somers

FIFTH ROW RIGHT
Mr. R. Standring and
Party (6)

So who or what were the two entities being joined here that no man should put asunder? Some would consider the union of Thatcher and Whitehouse to be a marriage made in hell at the best of times, but the connection being made here was not of such a directly personal nature, nor was it as reductively abstract as 'Mary and Power' or 'Mary and Prestige'. The goal this ceremony seemed designed – consciously or otherwise – to achieve was to locate Whitehouse at the centre of a narrative: brokering an exchange between culture and political power that is somehow conducted in the currency of her own family life.

Everyone – the cast and crew of *Yes Minister*, the PM herself – was getting something they wanted out of the ensuing transaction, but there's very little doubt as to the identity of its ultimate beneficiary. Mary Whitehouse's grandchildren presenting Margaret Thatcher with a posy was an especially inspired touch in that context (what was this, *The Godfather*?).

The headlines in the next morning's papers were all about the specially written *Yes Minister* skit which gave Margaret Thatcher the opportunity to showcase the lack of a sense of humour for which she was globally renowned (a comic foray almost as painful – albeit for different reasons – as Tony Blair's superficially more successful appropriation of Catherine Tate's 'Am I bovvered?' catchphrase on *Comic Relief* two decades later). Mary Whitehouse wouldn't have minded playing second fiddle in the press, though, as she was playing a longer game.

Mindful of the symbolic significance of the location she had chosen – just a stale bread roll's throw across Portland Place from the BBC's home – Mary Whitehouse wasn't going to let a chance such as this pass her by. Accustomed as she was to public speaking, she took the opportunity to say a few words about the day's place in history. Here are some of them in draft form.

Draft of Mary Whitehouse's speech

Must say first how very greatly honoured and delighted we are
to have the Prime Minister with us today and very grateful to
her for giving so generously of her very precious time.

I would like to mention too, and this is something which
only dawned on me a few days ago that this very day January
20th is the 20th anniversary of the launching of what was
known then as the Clean-Up T.V. Campaign!

There were just four of us then — Basil and Norah Buckland,
Ernest and myself — and if anyone had suggested to us then
that twenty years on we would all be here today in these most
auspicious circumstances, in the presence of the Prime Minister
and perhaps even more incredible if possible, the presence of
the Chairman of the BBC I suspect we would have thought he was
hallucinating. Say how very pleased to welcome him.

Now to Award itself. We try to give it to different type
of broadcasting each year and we have ranged from Sir Adrian
Boult for his contribution to music. ITN as — dare I say it!
— the best news programme 'Tomorrows World' — expertise and
presentation. Granada TV for its drama. Songs of Praise — best
religious — Archbishop of Canterbury attended. Jim'll fix it
— best childrens. To both BBC and ITN for their early radio
courage of the Falklands crisis — Major General Sir Jeremy
Moore presented the award.

This time to Light entertainment. One of the unique aspects
of public re-action to this programme is that there have been
no 'buts' in people's re-actions to it! So often, one hears
in relation to popular programmes — yes, I did enjoy it but
. . . some sort of qualification. But with 'Yes Minister' that
just has not happened — this has been comedy which has relied
on the brilliance of writing and acting and production and not
on the double entendre — to say the least!

For one moment, towards the end of the event – as Mary
moved to join the Prime Minister for 'a little quiet chat' on the
platform – tragedy beckoned. 'Trying to negotiate the steps onto
the platform', Whitehouse recalled in *Quite Contrary*, 'I slipped
and caught my shin across the edge of one of the steps, sending
my plate of sandwiches . . . flying across the floor with a crash.'

Happily, help was at hand. 'But what amazed me – and still does –', she gushed, 'was the speed with which the PM put herself between my agony and the hovering press.'

At the first defining event of Whitehouse's eighties, disaster had not been so successfully averted. Of all the public spectacles she created in her career (and there were so many of them, one might have suspected some godless prankster of sneaking Guy Debord's situationist text *The Society of the Spectacle* onto an early MRA reading list), Whitehouse's private prosecution of Michael Bogdanov, director of the 'controversial' National Theatre play *The Romans in Britain*, was perhaps the most plainly farcical.

Howard Brenton's play itself was a simple-minded piece of leftist agitprop (and I say that as someone who normally likes that sort of thing) drawing a rather crass parallel between the Roman occupation and British policy in Northern Ireland two thousand years later. However, the eighteen-month-long drama Mary Whitehouse improvised on this somewhat creaky stage was little short of a masterpiece.

Having tipped off a contact at Scotland Yard about the possibility of a homosexual rape scene graphic enough to warrant an obscenity prosecution, she was initially disappointed by the DPP's refusal to proceed, until her legal team had the brainwave of prosecuting the director; not under Roy Jenkins's famously (or notoriously, depending on your point of view) lax Theatres Act of 1968, but for the sexual offence of 'procuring persons for an act of gross indecency in a public place'. The media circus that ensued incorporated daily live readings of the Old Bailey court transcripts at a theatre in Oxford, a crisis of conscience on the part of Whitehouse's QC, and the ultimate collapse of the case in a welter of anguish and recrimination.

Throughout the unfolding drama, Whitehouse stood firm on her determination not to see the play ('What was the point? . . . The important thing about it was not what I thought about it, but whether it broke the law'). The case ultimately turned on how far away from the action her loyal solicitor Graham Ross-Cornes was when he saw something which he thought was an actor's penis, but which actually turned out to be the resourceful thespian's thumb. When Ross-Cornes was confronted with a seating plan and asked to confirm his viewing position, he marked his X in the very back row and the defence more or less rested.

Sadly, the quest for further elucidation draws a blank in the archive. Far be it from me to suggest that Mary Whitehouse might have buried that particular box file in the garden, but it is interesting to note that although there is a long (if tremendously selective) account of this utterly mortifying courtroom farrago in Mary Whitehouse's penultimate volume of memoirs, *The Romans in Britain* doesn't even get a mention in *Quite Contrary*. By the early nineties, she had obviously decided that discretion was the better part of NVALA.

In his forensically detailed 2005 account of the *Romans in Britain* case in the *Guardian* Mark Lawson observed that the National Theatre chief Sir Peter Hall 'regarded the lack of plays about Ireland as one of the failures of late 20th-century British theatre'. Yet an accusation that might hold up rather better in court would be that the massed ranks of UK dramatists failed to create more – if indeed they created any – characters as resonant and compelling as Mary Whitehouse.

As a closing piece of evidence for the above proposition, I would like to present one last episode of courtroom drama. (Besides, as someone who never missed an opportunity to have the last word, it seems only fair that Whitehouse should be allowed to sign off with a more felicitous legal entanglement.)

On 14 August 1983, the *Observer* published an extract from a new biography of Sir Hugh Greene written by the co-author of *Whitehouse* Michael Tracey. Four days later, they received the following writ:

Writ issued from Mary Whitehouse to the Observer

IN THE HIGH COURT OF JUSTICE
QUEEN'S BENCH DIVISION
Writ issued the 18th August 1983
BETWEEN:
MARY WHITEHOUSE   Plaintiff
-and-
THE OBSERVER LIMITED   Defendants

Draft/STATEMENT OF CLAIM
1. The Plaintiff is the Chairman of the National Viewers and
Listeners Association.
2. The Defendants company is the proprietor of The Observer,
a National Sunday newspaper with an enormous circulation
throughout the jurisdiction.
3. On the 14th August 1983 on the front page of the Observer
Review section the Defendants published the following words
which are defamatory of the Plaintiff:-

'Greene saw Whitehouse as dangerous to freedom, tolerance
and adventures.

   I thought that Mrs. Whitehouse was the sort of person
who would have been at home in Nazi Germany or at home
in Communist Russia. And that is the sort of thing which
through all my early experience I have learnt to hate. I saw
Mrs. Whitehouse as a sign of an unattractive degree of filthy
madness in this country as shown later in such things as the
National Front. Even though I am sure that Mrs. Whitehouse
herself would disown the National Front, they would tend to
approve of her.

   To Roy Shaw, who had written suggesting that they do a
counter-assault on what he described as "dark forces", Hugh
Greene replied:

   "One has the feeling that people who would be the potential
supporters of a Nazi regime in this country have found a focus
in Mrs. Whitehouse, even if she is not as bad as all that."'

4. In their natural and ordinary meaning the said words
meant and were understood to mean that the Plaintiff is
dangerous to freedom and tolerance, a supporter of and
sympathiser with totalitarian regimes including Nazi and

Communist dictatorships, a sign of an unattractive degree
of filthy madness as exemplified by the National Front, the
leader of dark forces, and the focus of potential supporters
of a Nazi regime in this country.
5. In consequence the Plaintiff's reputation has been
seriously injured and she has been grossly libelled.

And the Plaintiff claims:-
Damages
Served

The *Observer*'s deputy editor, Anthony Howard wrote a personal letter to Mary – optimistically marked 'without prejudice' – in which he pronounced himself 'more than a little surprised, after what I had hoped was a pleasant association between us, to receive a writ from your solicitor a week ago'. 'So far as I remember,' Whitehouse's reply shot back a few days later, 'we have met only once – in a corridor when we exchanged "Good mornings" and passed on. If you want to elevate that to a pleasant association I have no objection, but it does not give the "Observer" the right to publish to the world the appalling picture of me painted by Sir Hugh Greene.'

She then received something she had been awaiting for fully twenty years (and perhaps we might allow ourselves a restrainedly Reithian drum roll at this point) – a letter from Sir Hugh Greene.

Letter from Sir Hugh Greene

23rd August, 1983

Dear Mrs. Whitehouse,
  I understand that you have deeply resented certain
phrases of mine which have been quoted in the 'Observer'
of the 14th August, 1983.
  I should like to make it absolutely plain to you
that it was never my intent in those words, or indeed

anything else I have said or written concerning you,
to suggest that you have ever identified yourself
with totalitarianism, and in particular those forms
associated with Nazi Germany or Communist Russia.

All I was intending to convey was that in my view your
attitude and activities in regard to censorship were
in some ways more consistent with the approach of a
totalitarian regime than that of a democratic and free
society.

What I did not intend to say or imply was that you
have in any way identified yourself with any totalitarian
regime or that you could be expected to sympathise with
the policies and conduct of that type of regime and
particularly in relation to the appalling persecutions
that those sort of regimes have been, and are still,
responsible for. It is true, as I say in the quotation
in question, that unfortunately a number of totalitarian-
minded groups (such as the National Front) have seen fit
to support some of your views relating to censorship
but, as made clear in the quotation published by the
'Observer', I know that you would disown and have disowned
any kind of approbation of movements of that character.

I do recognise that some of the phraseology of the
extract, if wrenched out of its context, might appear
to be going rather beyond the narrow confines to which I
intended it to apply. There is, of course, a fundamental
difference of opinion between us as to the manner in
which a democratic state should approach moral issues
(such as pornography) and the role the state should
play in matters of censorship. On the other hand I
am confident that there is no disagreement between us
(and there never has been) as to the desirability of
preserving a democratic and free form of society. Our
difference is as to the extent to which the enforcement
of moral attitudes is compatible with such a society. In
so far as my remarks went beyond legitimate criticism of
your views on moral issues and censorship, I sincerely
regret it.

Please feel free to use this letter in any way you
like. Should you wish to have it printed in 'The
Observer' I shall, of course, do my utmost to arrange
for its publication this coming Sunday.
    Yours sincerely,
    Sir Hugh Greene

The following is her draft reply. While there is no way of
knowing if these were the exact words Greene finally read,
Mary did ultimately settle the libel suit for a sum of money
which –while not made public – was certainly enough to buy
her a tennis court.

Draft letter from Mary Whitehouse to Sir Hugh Greene

It was good of you to write to me on the 23rd August,
but publication of your letter in the 'Observer', with
its grudging and conditional expression of regret would
do more harm than good.
    I do not suppose that you or I will ever persuade the
other to admit error but I had hoped that our arguments
would remain on a civilised plane. Since you are, I
believe, the Chairman of Bodley Head you will certainly
have seen a copy of the letter which my Solicitor wrote
to the 'Observer'. That letter sets out my complaint.
Your letter does nothing to remedy it.
    Still, it was something of an achievement to get
a letter from you after all these years. I wish the
circumstances had been more pleasant, and less painful.

£34
FOR
THIS !

Published by:

THE NATIONAL VIEWERS' & LISTENERS' ASSOCIATION

Ardleigh, Colchester, Essex, CO7 7RH.

Tel. Colchester 230123

Front cover of NVALA brochure

Epilogue:
Mary in the Afterlife

Mary and Ernest Whitehouse made it into the twenty-first century, but only just. Ernest died in July of 2000, Mary in November of 2001. This time he led and she followed. For the last year or so of their married life together, ill health had driven them from 'Blackernae', their much-loved last family home at Ardleigh, near Colchester – from whence she'd arranged the transfer of her archive to nearby Essex University, whose students had once picketed her front garden – to a nearby care home.

Let's not remember them that way.

Letter to the producer of Bergerac

29th January, 1990

Dear Sir,
  As someone who used to watch and enjoy 'Bergerac' may I say how disappointed I am with its new style.
  Last nights episode (28.1.90) was almost impossible to watch and indeed we turned it off — not least because of the close-up, rapidly changing camera work. Its mood and style was quite unsuitable for family viewing time and one suspects that many adults went to bed with a headache and many children had nightmares!
  Can we hope that in future it will be considerably less intense and more watchable.
  Yours sincerely,
  Mary Whitehouse
  President
  copy to: Duke Hussey
  Lord Rees-Mogg

I prefer to think of them at ease in their own bespoke Valhalla: a place where the dream of a future in which the adventures of the Channel Island-based detective Bergerac might be 'considerably less intense and more watchable' has somehow been realised. Everyone – believer or unbeliever, from John Milton to Ricky Gervais – has their own conception of the afterlife, even if that conception is nothing grander than a great void (which, come to think of it, is pretty much the grandest thing there is).

The one incarnation of the hereafter whose existence can be scientifically verified – although its workings would have seemed no less miraculous to the rationalists of yesteryear than the idea of heaven and hell – is the internet. As at once a kind of oceanic Channel 4, and a limitless incitement to the kind of self-censorship Dennis Potter aimed for, but couldn't always achieve, the digital cloud makes an eminently suitable last resting place for Mary Whitehouse.

It's fun to imagine some celestial post-Assange cyber-Mary hacking into one of those personal messages from 'Wikipedia founder Jimmy Wales' and replacing it with her own words: 'Let us remember that freedom dies when moral anarchy takes over, and that it lives when citizens accept limitations upon themselves for the greater good of the community as a whole.' LOL that, Facebook troll.

Unexpected echoes of Mary Whitehouse's methodology can be discerned in some of the internet's most self-satisfied enclaves. Was her oft-derided practice of counting the bloodys really any more absurd than the notion that aggregative websites (or Pitchfork's decimal-point-based albums review system, come to that) have become the ultimate repository of all human wisdom?

As the great Jimmie Hendriks might so easily have put it, 'The Web Cries Mary'. In the same way that the Egyptian pharaohs had their golden amulets buried with them in the pyramids, Whitehouse's online mausoleum is a glittering treasure trove.

There are songs you (or at least I) never knew existed, like Deep Purple's 'Mary Long' (the 'composite character' of Whitehouse and Lord Longford was put in her place by Ian Gillan with the following not so withering put-down: 'Mary Long you're not alone, but you're a long way behind our times'), or the Sensational Alex Harvey Band's similarly unsubtle 'Mrs Blackhouse' (do you see what he did there?). I should say at this point that Alex Harvey's chorus – 'Can you hear us Mrs Blackhouse? Do you listen? / Are you gonna put a ban on people kissin'?' – actually works much better when he sings it than it does on the page, thanks to his Scottish lilt.

The classic episode of *The Goodies* in which Bill Oddie, Graeme Garden and Tim Brooke-Taylor fall foul of Beryl Reid's 'Desiree Carthorse' while trying to make an educational film on the subject of 'how to make babies while doing dirty things' is out there on YouTube to be enjoyed in full. Monty Python's 'Tory Housewives Clean-Up Campaign' can be watched with Chinese subtitles, and it's fascinating to see what an unusually direct (and accurate, given the success of her long-term policy of keeping her blatantly obvious party political affiliations hidden in plain sight) satirical approach Mary drew out of them (Monty Python that is, not the Chinese subtitlers).

A 2012 enquiry about Mary Whitehouse to the online catalogue of the British Library did admittedly meet with the slightly unhelpful response 'Do you mean Amy Winehouse?' But that doesn't mean Mary has vanished from our cultural horizon – in fact, far from it. In recent years, Whitehouse's reputation has undergone the kind of low-level cultural rehabilitation that is generally commensurate with being played by Julie Walters in a TV biopic.

In the autumn of 2011 – just as the deal to facilitate the publication of this book was being struck with NVALA's inheritors at Mediawatch – there were three Whitehouse sightings on TV in the space of a week. Alice Cooper turned up on *Top Gear* to trot out that well-rehearsed 'sending her flowers for helping "School's Out" get to number one' anecdote. Then the similarly charming Tom Baker reiterated an equally familiar tale on Laurie Taylor's Sky interview show *In Confidence*. In the very unlikely event that you haven't heard it, it involves stopping off at a stranger's house in the midst of a Saturday-night car journey to watch an episode of *Doctor Who* which Whitehouse had complained about.

As so often, it was left to *Antiques Roadshow* to show us something we had never seen before. In a brief but remarkable appearance by Mary's oldest son Richard on an episode filmed in Colchester, viewers were treated to a Rolf Harris-style portrait of his mother (actually done by the distinguished artist John Bratby, and valued at a handsome £5,000). There was also an exclusive glimpse of the kitchen table on which she wrote so many of the letters in this book, and an admission that her three sons 'didn't believe in what she stood for' when they were growing up, because – being the teenage boys that they were – 'sex and violence were all we were really interested in'.

As an erudite evangelical blog-site called 'Bartholomew's Notes on Religion' pointed out, the significance of Mary Whitehouse's virtual *Antiques Roadshow* manifestation lay not only in its content, but also in its context. 'The programme was broadcast from 8pm to 9pm – viewers could then switch over to Channel 4, where there was a satirical drama in which the Prime Minister of the UK is obliged to have sex with a pig on live television in order to save the life of a kidnapped princess.'

The twenty-first-century consensus on Mary Whitehouse which seemed to be emerging through these three posthumous TV appearances was that as much as we might have complained about her when she was alive, we sort of miss her now she's gone – like a wobbly tooth, or Fabio Capello. Yet as even the most cursory perusal of the preceding chapters will have made clear, to picture Mary Whitehouse as simply someone who mystifyingly objected to things we now regard as harmless is to fall at least two dimensions short of the reality.

In formulating a more nuanced response, distinguished commentators from Richard Hoggart to Dominic Sandbrook have tended to grant that Mary Whitehouse expressed a legitimate grievance in some areas, while insisting that if only she had placed greater emphasis on issues which chimed more easily with subsequent liberal assumptions, rather than those which made people feel awkward (i.e. prioritised violence over sex, or the racial epithets of Alf Garnett over strangulation by obscene vegetable matter), she might have been more effective. This Whig interpretation of Whitehouse overlooks one of the fundamental truths of her career, which is that the whole point of Mary Whitehouse's existence was to make the intellectual elite feel uncomfortable.

As Michael Tracey and David Morrison's *Whitehouse* pointed out, 'Mary Whitehouse is in fact offering a total philosophical package – you take the lot or you take nothing.' This doesn't mean that if one thing she says strikes a chord with you, you have to be in harmony with her complete belief system, but rather that if you accept the validity of a particular critique, you have to accept that this validity was generated from within her world-view, rather than yours.

The great thing about Mary Whitehouse was that you didn't have to agree with her. If something she said struck you as absurd or overstated, all you had to do – Britain being a (broadly) free country – was state a contrary opinion, like this witheringly sarcastic letter-writer to *The Listener*, who had been struck by the implications of Whitehouse's observation to David Dimbleby that she 'felt sorry' for those who were 'driven' to have oral sex.

Extract from a reader's letter to The Listener

sir: Mrs. Whitehouse is of course right in sympathising
with people who are 'driven to oral sex' because
'normal sexual experience' has been unsatisfactory ('The
Listener', 5 July). I feel a similar pity for people who
eat Chinese and Indian food, their 'normal' food must be
awful. As for people who listen to more than one kind of
music or read more than one author . . . !

Her capacity to inspire dissent was one of Mary Whitehouse's
great contributions to the gaiety (in both senses of the word) of
the nation. From the affectionate ribbing of Sir Michael Swann,
to the Gay Liberation Front activists who dressed as nuns in
order to infiltrate the inaugural Festival of Light meeting at
Westminster City Hall – kissing and sounding horns and releasing mice in the aisles (an incredibly effective disruptive strategy,
albeit one with a slight question mark over it from an animal
rights perspective) – she somehow managed to be a figure of fun
and a figure of not-fun at the same time.

As far as satire went, Whitehouse was the gift that kept on
giving. She brought the worst – misogyny, snobbery, ageism –
out of some people, but the best out of many more, from the
Goodies with their Pye camera turned into a machine gun, to
Monty Python with their £500 donation to the *Gay News* campaign fund. Michael Palin's diary records a live performance at
the Birmingham Hippodrome on his thirtieth birthday where
Eric Idle's mother came onstage as Mary, and the urge to imper-
sonate Mary Whitehouse seems to have been quite widespread.

Although not present at the birth of Barry Humphries's
Dame Edna, Mary's career certainly helped inspire that character's long-term development. Whitehouse's 1987 appearance
on LWT's excellent *The Dame Edna Experience* incorporates
a deafening clash of artificial fibres. It's also funny to see how

much more at ease she is with Dame Edna's remorseless innuen-
dos than her fellow guest – the celebrity brothel-keeper Cynthia
Payne – who just seems really stiff and awkward.

Mary Whitehouse was also a big influence on another acid-
tongued chat-show host – Caroline Aherne's mid-nineties alter
ego Mrs Merton – whose on-screen meeting with the woman
who inspired her was one of Whitehouse's most memorable TV
appearances. 'Oh Mary, it's *horrible*,' Merton insisted of some
notional salacious viewing option or other, 'you should watch it.'

Such was the calibre of public responses that Whitehouse
inspired, but some of the personal ones were no less instructive.
The following heartfelt missive was sent by one of many viewers
to have their mind changed about Mary by David Dimbleby's
radically fair-minded BBC profile *Person to Person* in 1979 (that
year again!).

The restrictions of typesetting will inevitably shave off a good
20 per cent of this letter's scruffily handwritten charm, but hopefully it will set the right mood if I say that it comes with a note in
a speech bubble at the top proclaiming 'Here we go! Yet another
letter, and this one's a long one too. All in a day's work for Mrs
Whitehouse. Or her secretary? Or both? I hope you've got a
sense of humour whoever you are . . .'

Letter from a teenage admirer

5th July, 1979

Dear Mary Whitehouse,
 I am one of the scores of people I know who use you
as a dirty word. Mary Whitehouse this, Mary Whitehouse,
the other. I remember your name from along time ago as a
kind of mythical witch with a big whip who went around
telling every-body what they ought to be doing. Tonight
I have watched David Dimbleby's interview with you and
discover that you are a very intelligent woman. You

have got a lot of valid things to say and I'm pleased I
wasn't too biased to realise this. I'm fairly certain
that I disagree with you on most personal and moral
issues, but these didn't seem to be the important ones
you were talking about.

What I have felt most strongly against you recently
has been the fact that you consider yourself responsible
for dictating to us, the viewers, our moral standards. I
am now a little confused; you say that your aim is not
to dictate to anybody but to make sure that nobody is
subjected to anything they find offensive or that they
don't wish to see. This seems to be your role as a voice
and censor for the people.

You also, however, seem to feel that the moral state
of the world today is terrible and that something ought
to be done about it.

My confusion is that I agree to an extent with
your role as a censor, but disagree [here the word
'completely' is crossed out, with an arrow to a
parenthetical comment proclaiming 'Notice the way I
crossed out "completely"' followed by a smiley face and
an exclamation mark] with your aims for religious and
moral reform in this country (or in this world). Perhaps
you could enlighten me further on how you feel about
·your role in society.

I would also like to discuss my own personal views and
opinion and see what you think:

I agree that people should take a responsibility about
television issues of concern etc by voicing their views
and this is partly the reason I'm writing this letter
to you, right now (because I talk too much and act too
little). This is also why I admire you.

On the subject of censorship I believe for instance
that woman should not have to be affronted by the
blatant sexual displays as they walk through Soho. I
believe that people should not be subjected to violence
and sex that they find offensive. On the other hand
I strongly believe that people should be allowed to

carry out whatever practices they want if they are not offending or hurting anybody else (ie in the privacy of their own home).

An example where I think you have drawn the line between these two things in the wrong place is in the fact that you got the editor of 'Gay News' sent to prison. The argument was that the poem in question was blasphemous and offensive to Christians and to a large number of people in this country. However, I think that you were probably one of a very small minority of people who read 'Gay News' who would have read the poem and found it offensive, and I've no doubt the only reason you read 'Gay News' is because there are things to complain about in it. And in this sense this poem was being published within the Gays 'own home' as no-one of your nature would dream of reading 'Gay News'.

However, this is only a specific example, and my ideas about censorship of sex and violence in a general sense are what matters.

My attitude toward violence is fairly straightforward, there is too much of it in the media and it is dealt with too lightly and not with its realistic consequences taken into account (e.g. people don't worry about what happens to a guy's wife when he gets blown up or shot in a 'Starsky and Hutch' programme).

My attitudes towards sex are more complex. I am one of the 'adolescents' you like to talk about so much, indeed who adults in general like to talk about so much. I personally rejoice in my own sexual freedom, lack of inhibitions and understanding of sex. You probably think it's disgusting that I have made love at 15 and enjoyed oral sex but I happen to think its wonderful and my understanding and sensitivity towards every-one around me is greatly increased because of it. I doubt very much that I would have been so unrepressed and uninhibited if I had grown up 20 years ago without the permissiveness and open sexuality of our society today. (And I'm certain I wouldn't have been able to talk to my mother

about it so openly and consequently get to know her as
well as I do now).

  Perhaps I have gained at the expense of everyone else?
What do you think?

  I have really far too much to say than can be said in
a letter and I'd love to talk to you but if that's not
possible or if you have no interest in meeting me then
I'd be glad of a letter from <u>you</u>, that is assuming this
ever gets to you through the red tape.

  Yours sincerely,

  ps I thought about typing this out but what you can't
read is probably not worth reading
  pps I am the person who rang on Friday the 5th

  After the underlined 'you' a few lines above, this precocious
correspondent (who identified himself after his signature as
being '15 years of age') added another parenthetical comment –
'(as opposed to your secretary)' – with another smiley face and
two exclamation marks at the end of it. His 'Yours sincerely'
was originally followed by a further three words, which he'd
obviously thought better of – perhaps they were a little cheeky
– as they are determinedly scrubbed out, with an arrow pointing to the resulting inky mess proclaiming 'You try reading it
now'.

  One of the many valuable life lessons the above letter-writer
seemed to have learned at an early age was the capacity to be
enriched by someone you disagree with. Somewhat against her
worst instincts, Mary Whitehouse also managed to absorb this
fundamental principle of democracy (at least, she did on her
better days). This enabled her both to make Geoffrey Robertson
and his girlfriend a friendly cup of tea when she met them by
chance blackberry-picking in the lane outside her home, and –
on a more strategic level – to absorb vital lessons in media strategy from the American radical Jerry Rubin.

The following quotes from Rubin – a man whose appearance at the ICA once led Whitehouse to try and get that notoriously permissive institution's Arts Council funding cut off – were initially typed out and preserved in her archive as evidence for MRA conspiracy theories about subversion in the media. Yet judged, as she should be, by her actions, Mary ultimately used them as a tactical primer.

Quotes from American 'yippie' radical Jerry Rubin

```
The Media does not report 'news', it creates it . . .
The presence of a camera transforms a demonstration,
turning us into heroes . . . TV time goes to those
with most guts and imagination . . . You can't be a
revolutionary today without a television set - it's
as important as a gun . . . Every guerrilla must know
how to use the terrain of the culture he is trying to
destroy.
```

Alongside the capacity to apply the single-minded ruthlessness of a great revolutionary leader to protest campaigns about TV comedy shows, one of Mary Whitehouse's most overlooked qualities was her (admittedly intermittent) acuity as a critic. It wasn't just that the furores she orchestrated around 'The Love That Dares to Speak Its Name' or *The Romans in Britain* were based on valid criticisms of the works concerned, they were also demonstrably (as the great rock journalist Lester Bangs once insisted of a scabrously eloquent review of an especially mediocre Lou Reed album) 'better art'.

No wonder a good slagging from Mary Whitehouse became a kind of avant-garde badge of honour. The resulting flesh wounds were a mark of status, just as having your red carpet outfit torn to pieces by Joan Rivers is a rite of passage for today's Hollywood star.

The best of the boundary-pushing cultural phenomena she

complained about – from *Cathy Come Home* to Andy Warhol
to *Doctor Who* to Dennis Potter's *The Singing Detective* – had
a funny way of surviving her strictures unscathed. The Beatles'
'I Am the Walrus' even survived being sung by Russell Brand
at the 2012 Olympics closing ceremony, an event which – cli-
maxing as it did with Eric Idle reprising 'Always Look on the
Bright Side of Life', the crucifixion singalong that concludes *The
Life of Brian* – could almost be portrayed as a subliminal Mary
Whitehouse tribute. This might have been why it felt so much
more conservative than Danny Boyle's audacious opening pro-
jection of a colonial guilt (and '66 World Cup)-free Britain – a
vision in which, needless to say, the shadow of Mary made no
appearance.

As pithily as she could dish it out, Mary Whitehouse certainly
had to be able to take it. The mockery to which she had always
been subject found one of its clearest expressions in the late 1980s
– just as her powers were on the wane – when a group of four
Cambridge University comedians made a radio show (subsequently transferred to TV) called *The Mary Whitehouse Experience*.

The intention behind this backhanded tribute was presumably
to express their iconoclastic disdain for Whitehouse's outmoded
value system, but what it actually crystallised was a sense of
continuity. Far from being in any way new and daring, the disdain felt by a privileged Oxbridge elite for a woman who steadfastly refused to acknowledge the inevitable triumph of a set of
ideas that she – and millions like her – simply didn't agree with
had been a constant presence in Mary Whitehouse's life from
the moment she first entered the public sphere.

The dignity with which she bore the slights and the stink-
bombs, the death threats and the *Spitting Image* puppets, was,
in its own quiet way, a credit to Christianity. Even the most
resolute atheist might feel a twinge of envy at the effectiveness of
the coping strategy she outlined in *A Most Dangerous Woman?*:

'If I allowed the personal attacks to pierce my being, they would destroy me,' she wrote. 'Since – however inadequately – I was doing what I believed God wanted me to do, when the attacks came, I must deflect them upwards for him to absorb . . . He would carry the burden, not me.'

When interviewed by David Dimbleby for *Person to Person*, Mary's husband Ernest spoke of her in the same breath as the suffragettes and the great anti-slavery campaigner Lord Wilberforce. Yet look around twenty-first-century Britain for traces of Whitehouse's imposing ideological edifice, and it's easy to get sidetracked by the more conventionally signposted ruins.

Of course, neither the 2005 campaign against *Jerry Springer: The Opera* mounted by Stephen Green's right-wing evangelical pressure group Christian Voice, nor the *Daily Mail*'s orchestration of the Sachsgate furore five years later would have existed in the forms that they did without Mary Whitehouse's prior example. Yet these tightly focused and somewhat petty initiatives bear the same slavish 'Mini-Me'-type relationship to her inspiration as *Geordie Shore* does to *Jersey Shore*, or the films of Christian Slater do to those of Jack Nicholson.

More significant traces of Whitehouse's fallen empire are to be found in a broader cultural field. While the gruesome activities of the Taliban provide daily evidence of the consequences of repressive religious attitudes to sexuality, the Mumsnet campaigners trying to encourage 'girls to be girls' march to the beat of Mary's drum in a slightly different direction.

Where would the frontier anti-tax-avoidance campaigners of UK Uncut be without Whitehouse's core strategy of making people at the helm of large private or public corporations personally accountable for their decisions? And, while one can't draw generalised conclusions from an ideological contrast between the activities of particular children and those of their parents, there was a real sense of 'what goes around comes around' in the 2009 publication of *Living Dolls*. Not only was this book's feminist critique of the commercialised sexualisation of childhood a thesis with which Mary would have found much to agree, it had also been written by Natasha Walter, daughter of Whitehouse's arch-rationalist nemesis and occasional circulator of obscene poems, Nicholas Walter.

One of the most intriguing subtexts of the Whitehouse archive relates to the apparently closed character of the British establishment. As the years passed and the Dimblebys and Attenboroughs of this world moved seamlessly upwards and sideways through overlapping networks of power and privilege, Mary Whitehouse had to keep finding new ways of making her presence felt. She once told an editor of the Radio 4 morning news, 'It's almost as though anyone who lives as far away from London as I do can't exist as a real person.' After all, she was – in the argot of J.Lo – just Mary from the Wold (To her it was like breathing).

How can someone who comes from outside those structures hope to have any lasting influence on them? In carving out a place for herself at the highest level of Britain's cultural and political life for almost forty years, Mary found a way. Two of the many pub quiz questions to which 'Mary Whitehouse' is the answer are 'Name a fifty-nine-year-old ex-teacher who got invited to David Frost's New Year's Eve party' and 'Who is the one close personal friend of Cliff Richard who knows what it is like to be blandished by both Sir Lew Grade and Archbishop Robert Runcie?'

There is some particularly engaging evidence of the subterranean workings of the British media and political establishment in the polite letter she received from a Cambridge undergraduate in the autumn of 1971. Mary had asked for a copy of his college magazine account of her riotous Union debate with *Oz*'s Richard Neville so it could be reprinted in *The Viewer and Listener*.

The well-mannered student journalist (whose name was Jeremy Paxman) responded in the most courteous terms that he would have no objection to her reprinting his article, provided the identity of the author was clearly acknowledged, and a copy of the relevant issue of *The Viewer and Listener* could be sent to 'my usual address' – St Catherine's College, Cambridge. This decorous missive represented a historic first – someone actually requesting a copy of *The Viewer and Listener*.

Paxman's actual account – written with all the authority of the ambitious undergraduate – was quoted at length in *Quite Contrary*. So delightfully grandiloquent is his warm response to Mary's attack on the double standards of the counterculture that it merits another outing. 'The commercialization of sex', wrote *Newsnight*'s grand inquisitor in waiting, 'is a manifestation of senescent capitalism and there is really little difference between the exploitation of people in the pre-Factory Act world, and the exploitation of their personal identities and bodies in blue movies.'

If Jeremy Paxman liked her style, and Margaret Thatcher stole her clothes, what was the substance of Mary Whitehouse's legacy? Looked at in narrow focus, she might be said to have won the battle but lost the war. The initial goal of first the Clean Up TV Campaign and then NVALA was to stop the more conservative segments of the British viewing public being excluded from decision-making processes which were supposedly being conducted on their behalf. With the advent of the Broadcasting Standards Commission in 1996 – now part of Ofcom – this dream of statutory regulation was finally realised (albeit in a considerably less draconian fashion than she would have liked).

And yet, by the time of Mary Whitehouse's death – shortly after the landmark victory of the gay Irish air steward Brian Dowling in *Big Brother* 2 (perhaps it was for the best that she didn't live long enough to see Jade Goody light up series 3) – the landscape of British TV (at least as seen through her eyes) owed less to John Constable than it did to Hieronymus Bosch. Let's not even talk about what was happening on the internet.

Viewed from an anguished liberal perspective, the truly frightening thing about Mrs Whitehouse is not the nature of her opinions, but how many things she got right. Whether prophesying the career of the chef Gordon Ramsay – 'Unless something is done and done quickly, we'll have four-letter words littering our programmes in future, just as "bloody" does now' – or issuing a critique of the age of the 'kidult', whose precision is all the more impressive for having originated several decades before that term was even invented – '"Let's all be kids together" cry the adults, as if only child's play helps them to come to terms with what they have made of the world' – the most apocalyptic predictions of this Nuneaton Nostradamus had a troubling tendency to come true.

Yet to talk simply in terms of CUTV or NVALA's success or failure is to misunderstand the nature of the leader of those two organisations' achievement. Her grandest and most improbable mission – that of being Mary Whitehouse – was resoundingly accomplished.

Permissions

The publishers gratefully acknowledge permission granted to reproduce material copyrighted to the following individuals and institutions:

Acknowledgements

Thanks to Hannah Griffiths for achieving the perfect balance of enthusiasm and acuity; to Jonny Trunk and Jo Wheeler for letting me bring up their baby; to Andy Miller for finding a new vocation as a super-agent; to Nigel Cochrane at the Albert Sloman Library for being there to let me in; to Ian Rawes of the British Library Listening Service for helping me find exactly which of the 101 tracks on Sore Throat's classic album *Disgrace to the Corpse of Sid* was 'Mary Whitehouse Raving Mad', and then not minding when it didn't turn out to be of any interest; to John Grindrod, Alex Holroyd, Paddy Fox and all at Faber for technical help and professional encouragement; to Luke Bird for the lovely cover; to Kate Ward and Anne Owen for design expertise and not stressing about the schedule; to Ruth Atkins for industriously hunting down permissions and marshalling a crack team of interns – Sarah Stoll, Sophie Scan, Rebecca Horsley and Ruby Lott-Lavigna – to scan huge piles of letters; to RefineCatch Ltd for retyping them so accurately, even the handwritten ones; to my copy-editor Merlin Cox for (among other accomplishments) knowing that Terry-Thomas should have a hyphen; and last – and most – to Nicola Barker, for buying me a copy of Michael Tracey and David Morrison's *Whitehouse* in 1988, and then not complaining when the spare room filled up with Mary's box files twenty-four years later . . . in the words of Asher Senator (one of Mary Whitehouse's favourite reggae MCs), 'To whom respect is due, respect it must go through.'